Cliff Mallett and Sergio L: rview of sport
and sports coaching in thei   *nning Coaches:*
Caring Determination. Long term success is what every sporting coach is seeking
and this latest instalment by Cliff and Sergio provide strategies used by long term
successful coaches. In the immortal words of Winston Churchill, "The farther
backward you can look, the farther forward you can see".

—**Michael Bohl OAM,** *A serial winning coach to multiple medallists in 5*
OG from 1992, 2008–2020 and coach to 8 Olympic and 1 Paralympic
medallists, who won 14 individual medals, including 5 gold

"While the athlete or team make excellence happen, the coach makes excellence
possible. But how do you create possibility repeatedly and consistently? The
why? What? And how? Of that are brilliantly set out in these pages".

—**Frank Dick OBE,** *Multiple Olympic medal winning coach in Athletics, Head*
Coach UK Athletics in their "golden era" and
global leader in coach development

"With this magnificent research, Cliff Mallett and Sergio Lara-Bercial provide
answers to one of the biggest questions in sport: what do serial winning coaches
do? What has allowed them to be successful repeatedly and stay at the top for so
long? An outstanding piece of work".

—**Marti Perarnau,** *Former Olympian and Author of best-selling*
Pep Guardiola: The Evolution and Pep Confidential

"The powerful insights provided by serial winning coaches and the authors of
this book provide rich material for both practicing coaches and those responsible
for the identification and development of coaches in elite sporting settings".

—**Barry Dancer,** *Australian Men's Olympic Hockey Gold (Athens, 2004)*
and Bronze Medal (Beijing, 2008) winning coach

"This research outlines the ingredients required to be a successful coach based on
outstanding individual coaches' journeys and pathways across different sports. It
creates an excellent reference point for football coaches who aspire to greatness.
A road map to self-evaluate and continue to grow as a coach. Unmissable".

—**Frank Ludolph,** *UEFA Head of Technical Development*

"The authors reveal the key attributes of superstar sports coaches. This unique study explains how great coaches develop into world leading coaches. It should be on the bookshelf of every ambitious coach".

—**Malcolm Brown,** *former National Coach at British Athletics and British Triathlon and Coach to Olympic, World, European and Commonwealth Champions*

"Successful coaches are open-minded and relentless learners who take the time to grow in different areas of leadership. This research provides you with a very practical framework to reflect on your leadership approach and be more specific in your own personal and professional development".

—**Barry Pauwels,** *Senior Director Technical Development US Soccer*

"This book offers a unique perspective on the journey of successful coaches, exploring their developmental milestones and leadership practices. Discover how the balance of care and determination can lead to both high-performance coaching and athlete well-being. A must-read for any aspiring coach".

—**Pyry Lukkarila,** *Head of Coach Development Finnish Ice Hockey Association*

"This book is a great tool to inspire coaches to become the best version of themselves and to be successful. It's a great example of how research can support sports, coaching, and coach education. It provides practical tools to critically think about yourselves and to be led on your personal journey as a coach by these serial winning coaches".

—**Kris van der Haegen,** *Head of Coach Education, Royal Belgian Football Association, and Assistant Manager Belgium Women's Football team*

LEARNING FROM SERIAL WINNING COACHES

Learning from Serial Winning Coaches provides performance coaches and directors, coach developers, and researchers with the knowledge and tools to affirm and challenge policy and practice and conduct further research to inform future policy and practice in the identification, recruitment, and development of performance coaches.

Leading an athlete or team to an Olympic or world championship gold medal or professional league title is a great achievement for a coach; a dream that comes true for a small group of privileged coaches. This outstanding accomplishment can become the defining moment of their careers. Winning multiple golds and championships with different athletes or teams, and across multiple major events spanning decades, is the prerogative of an exclusive club of coaches.

This book reveals the secrets, experiences, and practices of 17 of these coaches across 10 sports and 10 different countries. Through a combination of in-depth interviews with the coaches and their athletes and a detailed analysis of their personality and motivational profiles, Mallett and Lara-Bercial offer a unique portrait of the day-to-day workings of these coaches: who they are, how they operate, their leadership style, and their inimitable and often serendipitous journeys to the top of the sporting world.

Learning from Serial Winning Coaches goes beyond the description of isolated coaching behaviours provided by previous research to explore the personal realities of these exceptional men and women, coaches, and athletes. The emerging multi-dimensional picture sheds light on the unique conditions and practices that lead to the unparalleled success of these true outliers.

This book is key reading for researchers, coaching and coaching psychology students, performance coaches and directors, and coach developers, providing a novel evidence-based theoretical framework to conduct further research, shape and reshape coach development, and facilitate the identification and recruitment of the next generation of serial winners.

Cliff Mallett is a Professor of Sport Psychology and Coaching at the University of Queensland (Australia) and has enjoyed distinguished careers in high-performance sport and academia. He is an Olympic and world championship podium coach in athletics and also an internationally renowned researcher and coach developer who has been honoured with prestigious professorial fellowships at the Technical University of Munich and the National Institute of Education at NTU in Singapore. Cliff consults to many national and international sport (World Athletics) and corporate organisations and has published more than 150 peer-reviewed papers and presented 29 invited international keynote addresses in more than 12 countries.

Sergio Lara-Bercial is a Professor of Sport Coaching at Leeds Beckett University in the UK and Vice President for Strategy and Development at the International Council for Coaching Excellence. He has published widely on many sport-related topics including youth sport and coach development. Sergio consults to many high-level organisations, including Nike, IOC, UEFA, and FIBA. He is a former international basketball coach for Great Britain and has coached in the National League for over 25 years and won 19 national titles with both male and female teams.

LEARNING FROM SERIAL WINNING COACHES

Caring Determination

Cliff Mallett and Sergio Lara-Bercial

Routledge
Taylor & Francis Group

NEW YORK AND LONDON

Designed cover image: Getty Images

First published 2024
by Routledge
605 Third Avenue, New York, NY 10158

and by Routledge
4 Park Square, Milton Park, Abingdon, Oxon, OX14 4RN

Routledge is an imprint of the Taylor & Francis Group, an informa business

© 2024 Taylor & Francis

ISBN: 978-0-367-34721-5 (hbk)
ISBN: 978-0-367-34718-5 (pbk)
ISBN: 978-1-003-42729-2 (ebk)

DOI: 10.4324/9781003427292

Typeset in Bembo
by MPS Limited, Dehradun

CONTENTS

List of figures   *ix*

List of tables   *x*

SECTION A
Introduction   **1**

1 Serial Winning Coaches (SWC): Why, Who, What, and How   3

2 Coming to Know the Person Behind the Coach: Personalities of Serial Winning Coaches   14

SECTION B
Pathways   **33**

3 The Learning Journeys of Serial Winning Coaches   35

4 The Career Pathways of Serial Winning Coaches   57

SECTION C
Caring Determination 79

5 Caring Determination – Serial Winning Coaches
as Leaders 81

6 Expressions of Caring 91

7 Expressions of Determination 103

8 Drivers, Enablers, and Benefits of Caring Determination 121

SECTION D
Striving, Surviving, and Thriving in Elite Sport 139

9 Striving and Becoming a SWC 141

10 Surviving in the Highly Performative Environment
of Elite Sport 153

11 From Surviving to Thriving: Holistic Development 170

12 Learning from SWC to Inform HP Coach Development 188

Index *200*

FIGURES

2.1   Understanding behaviour: Person, context, and culture.
      (Adapted from Sheldon et al., 2011)   21
10.1 A challenge-support matrix (cited in Fletcher & Sarkar,
      2016, p. 142 and adapted from Daloz, 1986; Sanford, 1967)   158

TABLES

2.1   Serial winning coaches' descriptive data   22
3.1   Summary of learning opportunities of SWC and their
        nature and impact   50
4.1   Pre-conditions for success in SWC   66
4.2   Differentiated career journeys of SWC based on their
        athletic career   71
6.1   The manifestations of caring   92
7.1   The manifestations of determination   104
8.1   The drivers of caring   122
8.2   The drivers of determination   123
8.3   The enablers of caring determination   125
8.4   Caring determination benefits for athletes   129

SECTION A

Introduction

1

SERIAL WINNING COACHES (SWC)

Why, Who, What, and How

International and major professional league success in sports is highly contested. Winning is the only game and consequently, at the highest performance level, most athletes fail. Indeed, relatively, very few athletes make it to the podium at the Olympics, World Championships, or win professional league titles in major sports. Even fewer athletes are consistently successful over an extended period, say two Olympic games. So, when an athlete or team regularly makes it to the podium, unsurprisingly, they are revered and celebrated and, in some cases, become national icons. A consistent factor in elite athlete and team success is the (potentially) significant contribution of the coach.

Coaches are responsible for guiding athletes' and teams' performances in the international sporting arena and usually held liable in producing medallists and trophy winners (Mallett & Côté, 2006). In this evolving vocation of coaching, teasing out the specific contributions of the coach to athlete podium success is highly problematic and obfuscated. Nevertheless, the coach is central to athlete success and although it is impossible to specify their exact contributions, this should not deter scholars from investigating what we can do from these consistently successful people to inform policy and practice in sport including the development of future generations of coaches and athletes. However, coaching work is varied, complex, and not well understood by others (e.g., media and administration).

High-performance (HP) sports coaching is complex, chaotic, largely uncertain, and unpredictable (Potrac & Jones, 2009). In this highly contested, turbulent, and uncertain context, coaches are expected to deliver winning outcomes. Furthermore, these coaches of elite athletes and teams face increasing challenges to succeed in an environment that has limited coaching jobs, increased

DOI: 10.4324/9781003427292-2

international competition, unpredictable and unstable employment, and often a lack of status within the sporting organisation (Mallett & Lara-Bercial, 2016). The work of coaches of elite athletes has become increasingly more difficult and accountable due to often extensive resourcing (e.g., teams of support personnel; funding for competitions) to produce successful outcomes (winning), which reflect contemporary societal transformations (Mallett, 2010). *Can we predict who is likely to perform well in these complex and chaotic conditions?*

Identifying and recruiting coaches of elite athletes and teams is typically a serendipitous and organic process (Lara-Bercial & Peña-Garces, under review; Mallett & Lara-Bercial, 2016). We typically appoint coaches, who were good elite players (Blackett et al., 2018; Gilbert et al., 2006; Trudel & Gilbert, 2006), but know little about them. These athletes-cum-coaches are sometimes poorly prepared for coaching and undergo limited and differential coach development once in the job (Mallett et al., 2016). Moreover, many coaches are appointed because of who knows who (accrued social capital), which is not dissimilar to other workplaces. There is limited information about what makes a coach consistently successful; therefore, a key challenge is identifying, recruiting, and developing high-performing coaches. What (if anything) makes them so special?

Sport coaches of successful athletes and teams are performers in their own right. Coaches' performances directly and indirectly impact athletes' performances (Gould et al., 2002; Lara-Bercial & Mallett, 2016; Mallett & Lara-Bercial, 2016; Parkes, 2018). Positioning coaches as performers is important to foster research that examines what helps and hinders their performance. Therefore, a key question is what can we learn from coaches of athletes who are perennially on the podium?

International Council for Coaching Excellence (ICCE) and Innovation Group of Lead Agencies (IGLA)

The ICCE (www.icce.ws) established the IGLA in 2011, bringing together a number of leading national coaching organisations with the aim of advancing coach education and development, including coaches of elite athletes. Led by ICCE President Mr John Bales (Canada), the IGLA members initiated this research project entitled "Serial Winning Coaches" (SWC). The aims of SWC project were to study those coaches who have, repeatedly and over a sustained period, coached teams and athletes to gold medals or trophies at the highest level of competition, such as the Olympic Games, World Championships, and major professional leagues. The IGLA members wanted to explore what we can learn from SWC to improve the identification, recruitment, and development of the next generation of coaches working in the elite performance context as well as those already coaching at that level. Therefore, a comprehensive examination of a unique group of extreme outliers was undertaken. Specifically, we sought to investigate a multi-layered understanding of the personality of these SWC from a whole-person perspective using different ways of knowing that reflect each of McAdams' three personality layers – social actor, motivated agent, and autobiographical author. This novel approach to learning about this unique cohort of coaches enabled us to learn more about how these SWC typically behave, why they behave the way they do, and how they make sense of their life experiences that inform their unique identities. Overall, our goal was to create a meta-story or meta-stories that capture the essence of who these coaches are, their goals, values, and how these understandings shape their narrative identities.

What do we know and not know that is important to know?

Over the past few decades, researchers have provided some insights about successful HP coaches. Based on this extant research, what can we say with some confidence? Several researchers have examined the developmental experiences of successful coaches (e.g., Erickson, Côté, & Fraser-Thomas, 2007; Gilbert et al., 2006; Lefebvre et al., 2021; Nash & Sproule, 2009; Rynne & Mallett, 2012;); their key qualities and characteristics (e.g., Filho & Rettig, 2018; Ruiz-Tendero & Salinero-Martin, 2011); their motivations (e.g., McLean & Mallett, 2012) and perceived psychological needs (e.g., Allen & Shaw, 2009); how sports scientists help to shape their coaching knowledge and practices (Reade, Rodgers, & Spriggs, 2008); and their psychological disposition, skills, and coping strategies (e.g., Allain et al., 2018; Heelis et al., 2020; Olusoga, Maynard, Hays & Butt, 2012). Importantly, insights from athletes and their interpretations of their coaches' practices have emerged (e.g., Purdy & Jones, 2011). With respect to the empirical accounts of coaches' personalities, researchers have focused on broad dispositions or traits (e.g., Becker, 2009; Lee, Kim, & Kang, 2013; Nash & Sproule, 2009; Olusoga et al., 2012) and some trends have emerged from these investigations (e.g., high work ethic and resilience). However, whilst these insights are somewhat helpful to understanding successful coaches, they lack deeper insights and richer accounts into who is the person behind the successful coach. Broad dispositions or traits are insufficient to provide a more complete portrait of successful coaches. Another limitation of the research (published in the English language) is that it has been confined to a few countries, typically, the United States, Canada, the UK, and Australia. Furthermore, much of this research has concentrated on the "what" of coaching practice (e.g., behaviours and traits) and unfortunately, it (unintentionally) marginalises the importance of the person in context. There is a dearth of research that has investigated: (a) the most successful coaches in the world; (b) the perspectives of coach-athlete dyads; and (c) a deep insight into who these coaches are (e.g., meaning making) beyond what they do (attributes and behaviours) that reflects a person's full experience in the world using a multi-layered and integrated approach.

What did we want to know that is important to know?

The primary aim of this project was to advance coach learning and development, especially HP coaching. Indeed, there was strong intent to contribute to the professionalisation of the emerging vocation of sports coaching.

The overarching research question that informed this project was: *What can we learn from serial winning coaches to inform the identification, recruitment, and development of the next generation of high-performing coaches?* This begs the question: *Who is considered a serial winning coach?* For the members of the ICCE's IGLA group, there was complete agreement: "a coach who had won Olympic and World Championship gold medals and/or major professional league titles over a prolonged period with different athlete/teams and/or contexts". These are indeed outliers amongst the outliers, whose achievements are rare. We recognise the limitations of equating "winning" with good or effective coaching. However, we believe these limitations are outweighed by the benefits of a uniquely selective and diverse sample. To be consistently successful on the world stage in different circumstances over an extended time suggests something "special" about these SWC and/or what they do. Hence, we were enthusiastic to examine this unique cohort of SWC to inform policy and practice related to HP coach learning and development.

The book is structured into three broad sections with relevant chapters. In the next section, we provide some insights of the chapters that follow.

Caring determination: learning from serial winning coaches

Section A. Introduction

Chapter 1, *Serial Winning Coaches (SWC): Why, Who, What, and How*

There is something special about HP coaches who consistently produce athletes and teams to win at the "big event". Very few coaches and athletes win Olympic gold and professional league titles. These outliers amongst the outliers are indeed special. This sustained success is rare in HP contexts across, sport, business, and government. Coaches, as architects and sculptors of athlete performance, are responsible for delivering winning outcomes. However, these coaches perform in a highly contested, chaotic, complex, uncertain, unpredictable, and ambiguous environment. Understanding the contribution of the coach to successful athlete performances is not well understood. Nevertheless, sustained excellence is not accidental. There is something special about these SWC. Who are they? Why are they so successful? What are their impactful behaviours? How do they coach? We wanted to know what can we learn from SWC to inform HP coach identification, recruitment, and development?

Chapter 2, *Coming to Know the Person Behind the Coach: Personalities of SWC.*

Coming to know these SWC requires a comprehensive approach. So, we adopted a unique and multi-layered framework for knowing and understanding these SWC. McAdams' three-layered understanding of a person has been adopted. This novel theoretical and conceptual approach in sport psychology and coaching has its genesis in clinical psychology. This lens provides a deeper understanding of people and their behaviours, which makes the contribution to the field of coaching and coach development important, unique, and subsequently insightful. The first layer explores these SWC's behavioural signatures or personality traits (i.e., SWC as *social actor*). The second layer of personality is concerned with SWC broadly strive to achieve deals in everyday behaviours (i.e., SWC as *motivated agent*). Finally, the third layer of McAdams' integrative framework provides insights into their identities and specifically how the SWC make sense of their life journey to date and in the future (i.e., SWC as an *autobiographical author*).

Section B. Pathways

Chapter 3, *The Learning Journeys of SWC*

There is often curiosity in how people become so successful. To satisfy this curiosity, we explore the learning journeys of these SWC and how these idiosyncratic pathways shaped the development of their coaching craft. In their developmental pathways, we examine pivotal incidents and varied sources of learning. Learning to become a highly successful coach is understandably complex and contingent upon many factors. Life histories in sport as athletes, children, and young people, where you live, what opportunities present and when, who and what learning sources influence you, and of course, the athletes and teams you work with. We provide an analysis of their key developmental milestones and influences, coupled with the examination of the different forms of learning they engaged with, and how these different forms shaped and re-shaped their coaching practices that, in turn, help to inform coach development.

Chapter 4, *The Career Pathways of SWC.*

Building on the learning journeys of SWC, we continue to explore the developmental journeys of these SWC – this time from a career pathway perspective. Although the idea of a preferred or best pathway might be seductive for coaches and coach developers, there is no one pathway to becoming a SWC. Becoming a SWC is a consequence of building upon and complementing your prior experiences. Unfortunately, some people who employ HP coaches have beliefs and cognitive biases towards some pathways over others that should be challenged. The idiosyncratic pathways to becoming a SWC supports the importance of understanding the person in context. The SWC steps into and through coaching, the personal characteristics and circumstances that affected their progression, and their career-making decisions are examined. In addition, how these features vary according to their athletic histories is considered. These insights can support the recruitment and career planning of future HP coaches.

Section C. Caring determination

In the next four chapters, we provide clarity on how these SWC led themselves, other staff, and athletes/teams. The concept of *caring determination* is introduced and over the four chapters elaborated upon with extensive examples of that approach in action.

Chapter 5, *Caring Determination – Serial Winning Coaches as Leaders*

Conceptualising *coaches as leaders* is not common language in coaching or coach development. In this chapter, the practices of SWC are analysed through the lens of leadership. The novel but defining concept of Caring Determination is hereby introduced – the careful interplay between the SWC's genuine desire to support athletes, staff, and themselves in a considerate and compassionate way (care) and their relentless pursuit and need to win (determination). This topic on leadership and the obsessive pursuit of winning at any cost is most relevant in light of ongoing reviews about toxic cultures in sport in many countries. In this chapter, the scene is set for the following chapters in providing rich examples of what caring determination looks like in action.

Chapter 6, *Expressions of Caring*

Care is foundational to developing healthy relationships between coaches, staff, and athletes. It is assumed that most coaches and coach developers talk about the importance of care in coaching. However, moving from the rhetoric of care to actioning care is less well understood and rarely expressed and elaborated upon in HP coach development. In this chapter, there are several rich examples of embodying care in the HP sport context.

Providing depth to the notion of *caring determination*, this chapter specifically communicates an elaboration of how "caring" is embodied in the practices of SWC through their athlete-centredness, the provision of a stable and dependable environment, the use of highly responsive and adaptive coaching behaviours, and the implementation of a shared leadership model.

Chapter 7, *Expressions of Determination*

These SWC are unapologetic about their obsessive desire to win. This clarity of purpose gives direction and impetus for what they do in everyday practice. What does this obsessive pursuit of being the best and continuing to improve look like in everyday practice and at the major international championships? How is this pursuit understood within the frame of leading with caring determination? Complementing the previous chapter on expressions of caring, in this chapter the expressions of "determination" central to the practices of SWC are examined, including a clear focus and the need for *simplexity*, total commitment with some risk-taking, standards setting and accountability, behaviour modelling, and individual resilience.

Chapter 8, *Drivers, Enablers, and Benefits of Caring Determination*

The final chapter in this section identifies the drivers and enablers of this leadership approach – *caring determination*. Genuine care reflects an authentic interest in people and passion for helping others. This burning desire to succeed is shaped by many factors, including some insecurity. These SWC also report an overwhelming sense of duty towards others. Cognitive and emotional flexibility enable them to, not only survive, but thrive in this complex and highly charged context. The ability and consistent demonstration to be responsive to a dynamic environment with adaptive impact was foundational to behavioural flexibility and showing caring determination. In this chapter, we also explore the benefits of this approach to the athletes.

Section D. Striving, surviving, and thriving in elite sport

In the next three chapters, we consider three core concepts related to the pursuit and achievement of high performance and wellbeing – striving, surviving, and thriving. Importantly, these three concepts should be considered as inter-dependent, and we suggest likely somewhat sequential and iterative. There is some empirical support for those interdependencies, which we discuss in the following chapters.

Chapter 9, *Striving and Becoming a Serial Winning Coaches*

People are typically goal driven. These personally meaningful goals shape peoples' behaviours in a particular context. A basic psychological need of people is the perception they are competent (Deci & Ryan, 1985) and in the context of elite sport, coaches want to be perceived as competent by self and others but likely in differential ways. In pursuing this sense of competence, we experience a range of challenges and opportunities that might influence these perceptions. Society also influences how competence is conceptualised. So, in this chapter, the personally meaningful goals of these SWC are explored. Why are they meaningful and important? In this chapter, we explore the personally meaningful strivings (goal pursuits) of these SWC that lay the foundations for the following two chapters – surviving and thriving in becoming who we want to be. To begin, an analysis of these SWC personal strivings (e.g., *personal growth*) is presented to frame the remainder of the chapter. Passion, identity, optimism, and authentic care contribute to their ability to get along to get ahead and also to *get ahead and stay ahead*.

Chapter 10, *Surviving in the Highly Performative Environment of Elite Sport*

HP coaching is challenging work and inconsistent with the weekly routines of most jobs. As coaches engage in their HP coaching journeys, they experience many opportunities and challenges that reflect the complexity, chaos, ambiguity, and pathos associated with that work. In this highly contested landscape, how might coaches and coaching teams navigate myriad opportunities and challenges that present daily and require fluidity, adaptability, resilience, and fortitude? A successful navigation requires some adaptive personal qualities from these SWC. In this chapter, a deeper conceptualisation of resilience is presented and supported with powerful insights from the SWC. We explore some of the challenges and opportunities identified and how these SWC navigated this turbulent context in learning their craft and becoming a SWC.

Chapter 11, *From Surviving to Thriving: Holistic Development*

Few people consistently thrive in elite sport due to the turbulence of challenge, support, and unpredictability of performance outcomes. Thriving is aspirational for most HP coaches but probably few HP coaches experience this transformational growth. Many experience exhaustion and burnout. In this chapter, we recognise the pressures HP coaches operate under, review existing literature, and provide the Serial Winner's perceptions of the stresses of the job, as well as their coping strategies to endure for so long in this demanding and volatile vocation. A contemporary conceptualisation of this psychological construct is presented and distinguished from like constructs such as flourishing and resilience. We identify that thriving (holistic functioning) is key to achieving and sustaining success in this highly contested environment. Indeed, learning is central to thriving. In the chapter, we highlight how these SWC transition from surviving long enough to thrive both themselves and how they create an environment for others to thrive.

Chapter 12, *Learning from SWC to Inform HP Coach Development*

This chapter serves as a corollary for the book and in doing so addresses the question "So what?" We highlight seven key findings. It is proposed that HP coach development is a *wicked* problem. In defining this wicked problem, which is considered in relation to the central tenet of this book *caring determination*. How might HP coach development programs embrace this concept of *caring determination* in formal, informal, and non-formal learning? Then the challenges for progressing HP coach development are considered, especially in terms of formal, informal, and non-formal learning opportunities. In the final section, some thoughts on how to proceed going forward to continue to increase the evidence base around the development, recruitment, and practices of HP coaches are proposed.

Prior to publishing this book, we published three related papers (see Lara-Bercial & Mallett, 2016; Mallett & Coulter, 2016; and Mallett & Lara-Bercial, 2016) and have presented the findings to numerous sporting agencies across the world. In these forums, we have enjoyed the opportunities to discuss these data with HP coaches who have, in turn, shaped and re-shaped our thinking as well as highlighting the importance of sharing the additional data because of the high-quality engagement from HP coaches across the world. Therefore, the primary reason for writing this book was that we believed there was so much richness in the data that was not represented in the three publications that we felt compelled to share these additional findings.

Acknowledgements

Firstly, we thank the participants in this study – both coaches and athletes. They were generous with their time and sharing their wisdom. Second, we acknowledge and thank the Innovation Group of Leading Agencies (IGLA), who commissioned the research project. Members of the IGLA were coach developers representing 12 of the more advanced national sports systems. This group financially contributed to the project and supported access to some of the world's most successful coaches in Olympic and professional sports. These twelve national bodies represented North America (Canada), Europe (UK, Netherlands, Germany, France, Switzerland, Norway), Africa (South Africa), Asia (Israel), and Oceania (Australia, New Zealand). Next, we acknowledge the contributions of several colleagues who supported us through this journey – *it takes a village to raise a child* and we could not have completed this study and book without their direct and indirect support along the journey. Our sincere thanks to Dr Jarred Parkes (The University of Queensland; UQ), Dr Vanessa Wergin (UQ; Technical University of Munich), Mr Michael O'Keefe (UQ), Associate Professor Steven Rynne (UQ), Dr Tristan Coulter (Emeritus Professor Richard Tinning (UQ), The University of Queensland & Queensland University of Technology, Australia), Professor Dan McAdams (Northwestern University, USA), Professor Jefferson Singer (Connecticut College, USA), Dr Kath O'Brien (Queensland University of Technology, Australia), the late Professor Pat Duffy (ICCE), John Bales (ICCE), Professor Jim McKenna, Professor Julian North and Dr Andy Abraham (Leeds Beckett, UK) for their counsel at various stages of the project and expertise in shaping the project in direct and indirect ways. These research outputs are contingent upon a team of high-quality people supporting the intent of research and we are most grateful for their insights. Furthermore, we were most grateful for the collegial advice and reviews from Routledge's editorial team in shaping this book.

Cliff – To Jill, Luke, and Tom, who have been my constant inspiration. I am most grateful for your continual support and amazing patience.

Sergio – To Susana, Luca and Dario. My greatest win.

References

Allain, J., Bloom, G. A., & Gilbert, W. D. (2018). Successful high-performance ice hockey coaches' intermission routines and situational factors that guide implementation. *The Sport Psychologist, 32*(3), 210–219.

Allen, J. B., & Shaw, S. (2009). Women coaches' perceptions of their sport organizations' social environment: Supporting coaches' psychological needs? *The Sport Psychologist, 23*, 346–366.

Becker, A. J. (2009). It's not what they do, it's how they do it: Athlete experiences of great coaching. *International Journal of Sports Science & Coaching, 4*, 93–119. 10.1260/1 747-9541.4.1.93

Blackett, A. D., Evans, A. B., & Piggott, D. (2018). "Active" and "passive" coach pathways: Elite athletes' entry routes into high-performance coaching roles. *International Sport Coaching Journal, 5*(3), 213–226.

Deci, E. L., & Ryan, R. M. (1985). *Intrinsic motivation and self-determination in human behavior.* Plenum.

Erickson, K., Côté, J., & Fraser-Thomas, J. (2007). Sport experiences, milestones, and educational activities associated with high-performacne coaches' development. *The Sport Psychologist, 21*, 302–316. 10.1123/tsp.21.3.302

Filho, E., & Rettig, J. (2018). The road to victory in the UEFA Women's Champions League: A multi-level analysis of successful coaches, teams, and countries. *Psychology of Sport and Exercise, 39*, 132–146.

Gilbert, W., Côté, J., & Mallett, C. (2006). Developmental paths and activities of successful sport coaches. *International Journal of Sport Science & Coaching, 1*(1), 69–76.

Gould, D., Greenleaf, C., Guinan, D., & Chung, Y. (2002). A survey of US Olympic coaches: Variables perceived to have influenced athlete performances and coach effectiveness. *The Sport Psychologist, 16*(3), 229–250.

Heelis, W. J., Caron, J. G., & Bloom, G. A. (2020). The experiences of high-performance coaches in the management of difficult athletes. *Psychology of Sport and Exercise, 51*, 101751.

Lara-Bercial, S., & Mallett, C. J. (2016). The practices and developmental pathways of professional and Olympic serial winning coaches. *International Sport Coaching Journal, 3*, 221–239. doi:10.1123/iscj.2016-0083

Lara-Bercial, S., & Peña-Garces, M. (under review). Coach development in a basketball context: Identification and development of youth performance coaches in Spain. *The Routledge handbook of coach development in sport.* In S. B. Rynne & C. J. Mallett (Eds). Routledge.

Lee, Y., Kim, S., & Kang, J. (2013). Coach leadership effect on elite handball players' psychological empowerment and organisational citizenship behavior. *International Journal of Sports Science & Coaching, 8*, 327–342. 10.1260/1747-9541.8.2.327

Lefebvre, J. S., Bloom, G. A., & Duncan, L. R. (2021). A qualitative examination of the developmental networks of elite sport coaches. *Sport, Exercise, and Performance Psychology, 10*(2), 310–326.

Mallett, C. J. (2010). High performance coaches' careers and communities. In J. Lyle & C. Cushion (Eds.), *Sports coaching: Professionalism and practice* (pp. 119–133). Elsevier.

Mallett, C. J., & Côté, J. (2006). Beyond winning and losing: Guidelines for evaluating high performance coaches. *The Sport Psychologist, 20*, 213–221.

Mallett, C., & Coulter, T. (2016). The anatomy of a successful Olympic coach: Actor, agent, and author. *International Sport Coaching Journal, 3*, 113–127.

Mallett, C. J., & Lara-Bercial, S. (2016). Serial winning coaches: People, vision and environment. In M. Raab, P. Wylleman, R. Seiler, A-M. Elbe, & A. Hatzigeorgiadis (Eds.), *Sport and exercise psychology research: Theory to practice* (pp. 289–322): Elsevier.

Mallett, C. J., Rossi, T., Rynne, S., & Tinning, R. (2016). In pursuit of becoming a senior coach: The learning culture for Australian Football League coaches. *Physical Education and Sport Pedagogy, 21*(1), 24–39.

McLean, K. N., & Mallett, C. J. (2012). What motivates the motivators? An examination of sports coaches. *Physical Education & Sport Pedagogy, 17*, 21–35. 10.1080/17408989. 2010.535201

Nash, C. S., & Sproule, J. (2009). Career development of expert coaches. *International Journal of Sports Science & Coaching*, *4*, 121–138. 10.1260/1747-9541.4.1.121

Olusoga, P., Maynard, I., Hays, K., & Butt, J. (2012). Coaching under pressure: A study of Olympic coaches. *Journal of Sports Sciences*, *30*, 229–239. 10.1080/02640414.2011.639384

Parkes, J. (2018). *Coach as performer: Coach emotion, coping, and the coach-athlete performance relationship.* Doctoral thesis. The University of Queensland.

Potrac, P., & Jones, R. (2009). Micro-political workings in semi-professional football coaching. *Sociology of Sport Journal*, *26*, 557–577.

Purdy, L. G., & Jones, R. L. (2011). Choppy waters: Elite rowers' perceptions of coaching. *Sociology of Sport Journal*, *28*, 329–346. 10.1123/ssj.28.3.329

Reade, I., Rodgers, W., & Spriggs, K. (2008). New Ideas for High Performance Coaches: A Case Study of Knowledge Transfer in Sport Science. *International Journal of Sports Science & Coaching*, *3*, 335–354. 10.1260/174795408786238533

Ruiz-Tendoro, G., & Salinero-Martín, J. J. (2011). El entrenador de alto nivel en triatlón: entorno próximo y cualidades fundamentales para el rendimiento. (High level triathlon coach: Close environment and basic performance qualities). *RICYDE. Revista Internacional de Ciencias del Deporte*, *7*, 113–125. 10.5232/ricyde2011.02304

Rynne, S. B., & Mallett, C. J. (2012). Understanding the work and learning of high performance coaches. *Physical Education & Sport Pedagogy*, *17*, 507–523. 10.1080/ 17408989.2011.621119

Trudel, P., & Gilbert, W. (2006). Coaching and coach education. In D. Kirk, D. Macdonald, & M. O'Sullivan (Eds.), *The handbook of physical education* (pp. 516–539). Sage.

2

COMING TO KNOW THE PERSON BEHIND THE COACH

Personalities of Serial Winning Coaches

In 1995, Dan McAdams (Northwestern University, Chicago) penned a paper titled, *"What do we know when we know a person?"*. We think it is worth pondering this question for a few minutes and perhaps conversing with another coach. This is an important matter for coaches because we are in the people business – understanding self and others is necessary to forge functioning and healthy partnerships. Making sense of people is typically the domain of personality psychologists or "personologists", a term first coined by Murray in the 1930s, albeit the idea of individual differences dates back to at least the Ancient Greeks. Typically, personality psychologists focus on individuality and consider the interaction between the person and environment. However, getting to know people in a deeper way is complex and requires extended time as well as quality questioning and active listening. Of course, we need to be conscious of premature judgements of people (which seems to be part of being human) and then succumbing to potential unconscious biases (e.g., confirmation, affinity, and halo effect). Of course, these (often uniformed and premature) judgements are problematic and, in our view, unfair, and can potentially impact coaches' careers. Unfortunately, the same regularly happens in how we make sense of coaches, how we recruit and develop them and evaluate their performances. More important than judging people is to collect information over time to better understand people. In our pursuit of knowing these SWC, we were guided by many questions that explored the *what*, *why*, and *how* of these extreme outliers.

DOI: 10.4324/9781003427292-3

Who is the person behind the coach or athlete? Why is this important to know? How are successful coaches similar but different?

There are many approaches to making sense of the psychology of an individual person, which speaks to the complexity of individuals (e.g., Coulter et al., 2016). This complexity is reflected to some degree in the famous quote that "every man is in certain respects (a) like all other men; (b) like some other men; and (c) like no other men" (Kluckhohn & Murray, 1953). However, this complexity in understanding people, their similarities, and individual differences is not a new concept. Plato (350 BC) was reported as saying "No two personas are born exactly alike, but each differs from the other in natural endowments, one being suited for one occupation and the other for another". Typically, personality psychologists have focused either on individual differences (e.g., traits) or motivation (e.g., intrinsic/extrinsic); however, there is a third tradition, which is focused on the whole person or holism – (McAdams & Pals, 2006) that has often been (unintentionally) marginalised in the literature (Coulter et al., 2016).

Holism is based on the concept that component parts (e.g., traits) cannot explain the whole system (e.g., personality). Indeed, holism derives comes from the Greek word *holos*, which means whole or entire, and is consistent with the famous quote that "the whole is more than the sum of its parts". Holism was associated with the humanistic movement (3rd wave) in psychology in the mid-20th century.

In recent years, there has been a return to an integrated approach to understanding people, rather than single (and narrow) views of personality. Early and mid-20th century intellectuals, such as Allport, Murray, and Eysenk, argued for complementary views for understanding people. For example, Gordon Allport, who progressed empirical examination of human personality, challenged the pervasive psychoanalysis and behaviourism movements of the time and argued for a more eclectic and humanistic approach to personality psychology. Allport underscored the saliency of the person and the present context and Eysenk (1960) also considered the interaction between the person and the environment in explaining human personality. Indeed, knowing self and others requires an understanding beyond some partially inherited psychological traits and includes how people make sense of their lived experiences and in context (subjective identities). A deep understanding of self and others seems necessary to understand the *what* and *why* of behaviour. Importantly, this understanding is not about judging one's behaviour but to make sense of *why we do what we do*. Furthermore, a deeper understanding of a person has the potential to help coaches and athletes to have greater awareness and clarity of who they are (McAdams & Cox, 2010; Tabano & Portenga, 2018) so that they can form healthy and adaptive relationships to enhance both performance and wellbeing.

To know a person requires a comprehensive, holistic, and multi-layered understanding of the individual (McAdams, 1995, 2013; McAdams & Pals,

2006; Mischel & Shoda, 2008). Nevertheless, understanding the person should also be considered in relation to their context. Indeed, context matters; therefore, an appreciation of the interdependencies between a multi-layered understanding of the person within a broader socio-cultural context (McAdams, 1995) is essential in developing a coherent and holistic framework for person-based psychology (Mayer, 2005; McAdams & Pals, 2006; Mischel & Shoda, 2008).

In recent times, McAdams' integrative framework for understanding the person has been used in examining personality in sport (e.g., Coulter et al., 2016, 2017, 2020; Mallett & Coulter, 2016). This multi-layered approach to understanding a person considers personality across three different aspects of who we are: (i) dispositional traits (broad consistencies in thought, affect, and behaviour); (ii) characteristic adaptations (personal goals and values displayed at particular time points, places, and in light of social role); and (iii) narrative identity (personal narratives that define meaning, unity, and purpose in life). Independently, these three layers offer some insights into understanding a coach's personality but in and of themselves they are limited. The strength of McAdams integrated approach is the complementary information that can be considered to understand a person.

Knowing and understanding people (e.g., coaches and athletes) should embrace several layers of a person including, traits/dispositions (e.g., conscientiousness), personal goals (e.g., being a successful coach), and one's sense of self (e.g., identities) (Taylor, 2018). Importantly, McAdams developed his integrated personality framework with the understanding that there are different and emerging layers of the psychological development of people (McAdams & Manczak, 2011) that over time are uniquely situated in specific socio-cultural contexts (McAdams & Pals, 2006).

McAdams' integrated framework of personality

In recent times, McAdams' integrative framework for understanding the person has been used in examining personality in sport (e.g., Coulter et al., 2016, Coulter, Mallett & Singer, 2017; Coulter, Mallett & McAdams, 2020; Mallett & Coulter, 2016). This multi-layered approach to understanding a person considers personality across three different aspects of who we are: (i) dispositional traits (broad consistencies in thought, affect, and behaviour); (ii) characteristic adaptations (personal goals and values displayed at particular time points, places, and in light of social role); and (iii) narrative identity (personal narratives that define meaning, unity, and purpose in life). Independently, these three layers offer some insights into understanding a coach's personality but in and of themselves they are limited. The strength of McAdams' integrated approach is the complementary information they provide to understand a person.

McAdams and Pals (2006) described personality as a person's "unique variation of the general evolutionary design for humans, expressed as a developing pattern of dispositional traits, characteristic adaptations, and integrative life stories complexly and differentially situated in culture" (p. 212). Five key symbiotic interdependent concepts were considered in developing this integrated conceptual model of personality psychology: evolution, traits, adaptation, life narratives, and culture (McAdams & Pals, 2006). Based on the evolutionary and general design of people to survive as a species and adapt to a dynamic environment, McAdams and Cox (2010) created three metaphors to capture the evolving and increasingly complex interplay of three complementary layers or perspectives of knowing a person: *social actor*, *motivated agent*, and *autobiographical author*. In the next section, we elaborate on who we are as actors (behaving), agents (striving), and authors (narrating meaning) (McAdams & Olson, 2010).

Social actor

The Ancient Greeks recognised psychological individuality and how these dispositional qualities differentially shaped people's behaviours in social contexts. Since then, there has been an evolving understanding of these key dispositional traits, which are broad, internal, and comparative aspects of psychological individuality (McAdams & Olson, 2010). There seems to be consistency in what scholars think those Big Five traits are: extraversion, neuroticism, conscientiousness, agreeableness, and openness to experience[1]. Both genetics and environmental influences shape these broad traits that reflect some consistency in behaviours (McAdams & Olson, 2010) that were described by McAdams (2013), as one's *behavioural signature*. This social reputation emerges as one interacts with others across time, context, and role (e.g., coach) (McAdams, 1995). In performative contexts, such as elite sport, human behaviour is regularly on display and coaches are typically judged and labelled accordingly. Unfortunately, observations of one or two episodes of a coach in action can result in an inappropriate social judgement (e.g., neurotic) that over time can lead to potential confirmation bias of a perceived social reputation. It is noteworthy that these judgements of a coach's social performance are relative to others (i.e., comparative). The strengths of dispositional traits and their measurement are that they are normative and de-contextualised; however, these two strengths are also considered their weaknesses (McAdams, 2013). For example, context does matter, and we might consider if we always behave the same way in different social contexts, or do we behave consistent with the norms and values of a particular social group (e.g., family, work, and sport)? How we behave depends on who we are with (Haslam, Reicher & Platow, 2011), which is a key tenet of Social Identity Theory (Tajfel & Turner, 1979), and used extensively to examine prejudice, stereotypes, and spectator behaviour in sport. While dispositional traits offer some important insights into the uniqueness of people, a reliance on traits does little to help us understand people more fully. An over-reliance on trait profiles is problematic and limited in how we understand people. Dispositional traits provide a skeletal outline for knowing self and others. What these traits do not tell us is how their traits are expressed in a coaching context; nor does it help us to understand what the coach values, wants to achieve and why that is important, and how they make sense of self and indeed others.

Motivated agent

Despite a focus on dispositional traits, it is noteworthy that many of the most renowned personality theorists (e.g., Freud, Adler, Erikson, Rogers, Maslow, and Bandura) foregrounded motivational and social-cognitive constructs (McAdams & Olson, 2010) rather than dispositional traits. This shift in focus recognised the increasing influence of socio-cultural forces shaping individual personality development, which McAdams and Pals (2006) refer to as *characteristic adaptations*. These motivational forces represent, for example, one's values, goals, and strivings that reflect what a person wants, what one values, and how one copes with everyday challenges (McAdams, 2015; Singer, 2005). As autonomous, purposeful, and motivated agents, people plan their lives and make choices – "life is about choice, goals, and hope" (McAdams & Olson, 2010, p. 524).

This agentic self, which is the second layer of personality development, emerges in the psycho-socio-emotional transition from early- to mid-childhood, around the ages of 5–7 years (White, 1965). Children at this stage of personality development become goal-directed agents whose motivational agenda is expressed in how and where they invest their time and effort (Bandura, 1989; Erikson, 1963; Harter, 2006; 2013; McAdams, 2013; Piaget, 1970). As goal-directed agents, how do coaches think about their goals and everyday strivings in pursuit of what they value and want? It seems plausible that highly successful coaches are ambitious goal-directed agents who might even be somewhat obsessive; but what drives these ambitions? Understandably, this layer of personality development, which is more fluid, and dynamic compared to traits, provides important and complementary insights into people. Indeed, why coaches invest so much time in their coaching, sometimes at the expense of their own family and wellbeing, warrants examination beyond a reliance on broad and de-contextualised traits.

This second layer provides deeper insights into people and their values, goals, strivings, and cognitive style and therefore complements an understanding of their dispositional traits. Nevertheless, there remains an important aspect of humans that contributes meaningfully to an integrated and holistic portrayal of people – a coach's narrative identity – what gives meaning is to make sense of one's identity (*Who am I?*).

Autobiographical author

About 40 years ago, there was another shift in personality psychology that re-cognised people as storytellers (e.g., McAdams, 1985; Singer & Salovey, 1993; Tomkins, 1987) and how their stories revealed deep insights into their person-ality. Of course, storytelling has a long history pre-dating written language. As storytellers, we try to convey an internalised and evolving story that provides some sense of coherence, meaning, and purpose, which begins to take shape in late adolescence and early adulthood (McAdams & Olson, 2010). In late ado-lescence, young people have usually developed cognitive skills for self-authorship that over time continues to evolve into early adulthood. This evolving story is also differentially shaped by what society suggests is a "typical life". As people age into mid-life, adults are likely to construct increasingly more complex and coherent stories (Baddeley & Singer, 2007); for example, how critical events might be connected enabling the creation of potential thematic and causal coherence (Habermas & Bluck, 2000). Importantly, these first-person accounts represent our evolving identity (Erikson, 1963) and how we tell these stories moves beyond content to weave a meaningful self-defining narrative of how one comes to be and who one is becoming (McAdams & Pals, 2006). This often cohesive and purposeful life narrative and identity complement the data from the two previous layers (social actor and motivated agent). It is noteworthy that coherence in storytelling across all three layers should not be assumed (McAdams, 2015). This integration of data from all three layers is about confirming our stories rather than challenging them; that is, making sense of them. Sometimes there might not be coherence, which might be linked to some ill-being.

This storied autobiographical self captures our past, present, and imagined future. One's "narrative identity gives individual lives their unique and culturally anchored meanings" (McAdams, 2008, p. 248) that underscores the significant role of culture in how we make sense of who we are across our lives. Culture has differential influence on all three layers of personality (McAdams, 2008). There is a modest influence of culture on traits (e.g., display rules), a stronger effect on characteristic adaptations (e.g., timing and content of goals and strivings), and its strongest influence is on the stories we tell about ourselves (meaning-making; what does society tell us is a good story to tell?) (McAdams & Pals, 2006). In telling their story, people reflect upon "why the actor does what it does, why the agent wants what it wants, and who the self was, is, and will be as a developing person in time" (McAdams, 2013, p. 273). What are the stories that successful coaches tell about their (coaching) lives? What gives these coaches meaning and purpose in their lives, including their coaching work?

Holistic understanding of self and others

Knowing and understanding people is central to getting the best from oneself and those with whom we work and live, which is most relevant to coaches who work with elite athletes and often a team of support personnel. Sport coaching is concerned with multiple relational interdependencies (e.g., coach–athlete; athlete–athlete), the goal of which is to hopefully work collaboratively to enhance the performance and wellbeing of all actors. Indeed, coaching is a complex social endeavour (Cassidy et al., 2004; Jones, 2007) and central to working in adaptive ways with others is contingent upon a deep understanding of both self and others. So, returning to our opening statement *"What do we know when we know a person"* is a critical question that requires consideration beyond a narrow and reductionistic knowledge and understanding of self and others. Knowing self and others requires myriad questions related to, for example, behaviours, values, goals, identity, and in context, that enables one to examine who we are in depth. Integrating information that captures these three inter-related layers of a person (*actor, agent,* and *author*) enables a deeper and more comprehensive understanding of these highly successful coaches.

Coming to know

In learning about these SWC, we sought to report some unique stories and accounts of their experiences in coaching and in their personal lives. It is not uncommon for national sporting agencies, boards, and coaches themselves to be in search of the "holy grail" … what is the success profile of coaches? What predicts a highly successful coach? The search for these "great man" (Carlyle, 1841) qualities or traits of successful elite coaches is as futile as the pursuit in predicting successful leaders. Research that has examined variables that are likely to predict who will become a great leader has identified few factors that, at best, are weak predictors (see Haslam, Reicher & Platow, 2011). Indeed, the best predictor, intelligence, only predicted 5% of the variance in leadership. Professor Alex Haslam, a world expert in the social identity approach to leadership, reported that it is not if you are intelligent but whether followers (athletes and staff) consider you (coach) to be intelligent. Another key question is how intelligent do you need to be to be successful in your social role? Again, what was missing from the empirical investigations was an understanding of the social context (i.e., sport setting). The empirical challenges in explaining the success of coaches in elite sport based on broad personality traits – fixed qualities or attributes – are highly problematic and insurmountable because the role of the environment and context is usually marginalised or ignored (Haslam et al., 2011). Behaviour and one's personality should be understood within a social context (Turner et al., 2006; see Sheldon and colleagues' 2011 Multilevel Personality In Context [MPIC] model) – *how we behave depends on who we are with* (McAdams, 1995) (see Figure 2.1). Understanding people in context is necessary to fully understand a successful coach. To access some insights into that social context (coach–athlete setting), we sought these SWC athletes' perceptions of their coach's personality.

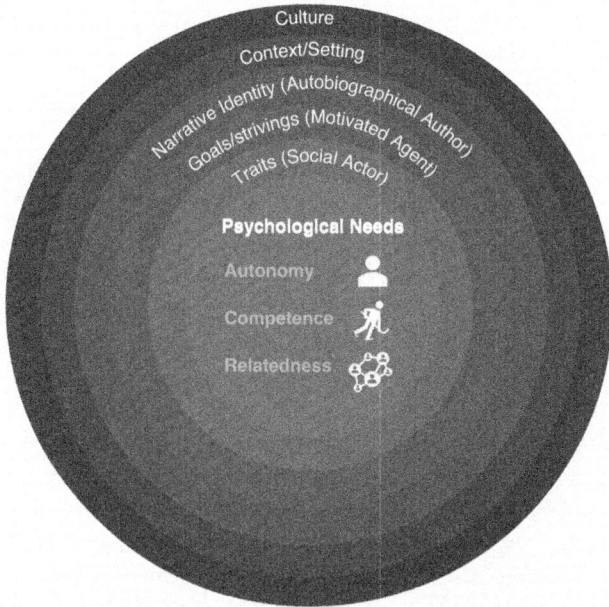

FIGURE 2.1   Understanding behaviour: Person, context, and culture. (Adapted from Sheldon et al., 2011).

Hence, our quest was not for an "ideal success profile" (holy grail) but to empirically examine these SWC to inform policy and practice in coach identification, recruitment, and development.

Methodology

The genesis of the idea of distinguishing between idiographic and nomothetic approaches in studying the person is attributed to the German philosopher, Wilhelm Windelband (Thomae, 1999). This distinction is important because it recognises both the individual's unique phenomenological experience as well as normative comparisons in understanding a person. Both approaches can provide complementary information in studying the person. In pursuing this study of SWC, we considered the complementarity of idiographic and nomothetic approaches to understanding serial winning coaches. Recently, Coulter and colleagues (2016) encouraged researchers to embrace integrative approaches in studying the person in sport.

We incorporated several research paradigms in this study of SWC, including a diverse mix of positivist, critical realist, and phenomenological paradigms that correlated with the McAdams and Pals (2006) three-layered conception of personality (McAdams & Pals, 2006). Furthermore, the specific methods to collect data included the use of both structured and unstructured questionnaires (traits and strivings, respectively) and a semi-structured interview enabled an integration of data from each of three layers of a person providing a deeper insight into who these SWC are.

Participants

A purposive sample of several of the world's most successful coaches was deliberately recruited for this project (Patton, 2002). These SWC met clear criteria that considered them as experts, including repeated success in multiple contexts (different countries, leagues, athletes, teams, and gender) over a sustained period of time, to purposefully elicit rich information about these *outliers amongst the outliers*.

In the past few years, we have collected multiple data sets from 17 SWC, who collectively had coached athletes and teams to over 160 gold medals and major professional league trophies. It is noteworthy that the SWC from professional leagues can only win one trophy annually. What makes these SWC so special is that they were repeatedly successful over an extended period and in different contexts. These "outliers among outliers" had won major international championships with many athletes/teams and in multiple contexts. These participant SWC came from ten different countries and represented ten sports, including five teams and five individual sports. Furthermore, we collected data from 19 of their successful athletes to complement the coach data. The interviewed athletes met the following criteria: (i) that s/he won a gold medal or title with the coach; and (ii) worked with that coach in the last five years and for a minimum of two years.

The 17 SWC were on average 55.7 years old when we collected their data (Range = 44–75) and had coached for a mean of 29.2 years (Range = 7–45) (see Table 2.1). It was unfortunate but despite several attempts by several people to

TABLE 2.1 Serial winning coaches' descriptive data

Number of Coaches	17 (2 female) including 1 Paralympic coach
Sports	Field Hockey (2), Ice Hockey (2), Basketball (2), Speed Skating (2), Sailing, Windsurfing, Rowing (4), Swimming, Judo, and Athletics
Countries	Australia, Canada, China, France, Germany, Israel, Italy, Netherlands, Serbia, UK
Gender coached	Male (4), Female (1); Male and Female (12)
Number of combined Gold Medals/Major Championships/ Professional League titles	160 (at time of publication)
Age	44–75 years (M = 55.7 years)
Coaching	8–45 years (M = 29.2 years; Elite M = 25.2 years)
Experience as an athlete	International (10, National/Regional (6), None (1)

recruit many serial-winning female coaches, only two agreed to participate in this study. We respected the decision of those female coaches not to participate. We hope that in the future we will "hear their voices" in a similar study. All but one of the coaches were married (one had re-married) and 15 had children. Except for one coach, all were university educated. The non-university-educated coach at the time could not afford the cost of higher education but reported attending lectures but obviously did not sit any exams. Ten SWC were ex-internationals and six competed at the regional or national level. One did not have any high-level athletic experience. The majority of SWC with an athletic career transitioned from playing to coaching in a relatively short period of time (within a few years).

Procedure

Prior to data collection, institutional ethics was obtained. The participant coaches consented to contribute to this study of their own volition and not all invitees participated. The SWC completed both the self-report NEO-FFI-3 (traits) and Personal Strivings (Emmons, 1989) measures. Then, SWC participated in an interview that lasted between 60 and 180 minutes. The athlete participants completed the NEO-FFI-3 (observer report) and an interview. Interview data were transcribed verbatim, which produced over 1,000 pages of double-spaced text. We were fortunate that many of the members of the participating orga-nisations (IGLA) provided us with an extensive network of contacts, which enabled us to access a unique and exclusive sample of SWC.

Measures

There were two primary aims of this research: (i) to elicit a deep understanding of the person behind the SWC; and (ii) investigate the daily practices of SWC, their education and development journeys, and their insights into key challenges facing high-performance coaches in the future. To achieve the above aims the following tools were used.

Biographic and demographic data

These data were collected prior to the interview and included sport and disci-pline, family background and occupations, coaching settings, experience, and achievements.

NEO-FFI-3

The NEO Five-Factor inventories (self and observer reports) are the most popular measures of traits within contemporary psychology research (McAdams & Pals, 2006); they are the gold standard for measuring traits. The 60-item

NEO-FFI-3 (Costa & McCrae, 2010) is a self-report measure that collects data specific to the first layer of personality – self as social actor (McAdams & Pals, 2006). There is also an observer report that the athletes completed. The NEO-FFI-3 assesses the well-established five-factor model of personality – openness, conscientiousness, extraversion, agreeableness, and neuroticism (Costa & McCrae, 1992; McAdams & Pals, 2006).

For each item, respondents are asked to rate the degree to which they agree that the description is true of them (1 = strongly disagree to 5 = strongly agree). Several studies have shown psychometric support for the NEO-FFI-3 as well as convergent validity with the longer 240-item NEO-Personality Inventory (NEO-PI-3; McCrae & Costa, 2007). Earlier versions of the NEO-FFI have received satisfactory support for its validity, including convergence with other measures of personality (Costa & McCrae, 1992). The 240-item NEO-PI-3 has occasionally been used in sport contexts (e.g., Allen et al., 2011; Hughes et al., 2003) but we used the shorter version of the NEO due to the focus on collecting data on multiple layers of the person. Firstly, we were cognisant of the expected duration of the data collection process, and secondly, a deeper insight into traits was not the focus of the research but an integration of data from each of the three layers of a person.

Personal strivings

Emmons' (1989) strivings measure provides insight into people as motivated agents. SWC were asked to consider what they typically are trying to do in everyday behaviour and responded to the stem: "*On a daily basis I typically try to … .*"; for example, "help my athletes", "care for my family", or "avoid looking incompetent". These strivings represent what you typically want and value. They also give insight into the underlying organisation of how individuals think about how they plan and integrate their goals. Participants listed 12–14 strivings that formed a personal *striving assessment* matrix. They were asked to reflect on each striving and rate them along a continuum from 1 (not very) to 5 (very) on the following questions: How committed are you to this behaviour?; How important is this striving to you?; How likely is it that you will be successful in doing it?; How challenging is this striving for you?; How much satisfaction or joy does it bring to you when you achieve it? From this matrix, striving content is coded followed by the abstraction of content themes (agency or communion and approach or avoid), and motivational themes (e.g., affiliation, achievement, intimacy, power, personal growth and health, generativity, spirituality, and self-defeating).

Semi-structured interview (including life story and defining moments)

The purpose of the interview was to (i) identify and make sense of critical life incidents and how they have shaped the personal narrative of who they are, how and why they do what they do (coach), and the meaning and purpose of coaching in their lives; that is, to understand the SWC as an *autobiographical author* (Life chapters, key scenes/events, future script, challenges, personal ideology, life themes, and reflection) (see McAdams (2008) for the interview schedule); and (ii) elicit complementary information about their coaching journeys, including insights about what it takes to win, key qualities and developmental experiences that helped them become successful coaches, and what the future might look like for coaching and coaches in elite contexts.

Some key questions for the second part of the interview schedule included: *What does it take to coach an athlete/team to a Gold Medal at a major event? What is it that you do that has allowed you to become a Serial Winner (SW)? How have you developed into the coach that you are today? What do you think is the future of high-performance coaching?*

Athlete interviews

Each athlete interview included two parts: (i) NEO-FFI-3 (Observer Report); and (ii) semi-structured interview (60–90 min), which consisted of the following questions: *In your experience, what are the key reasons why your coach has been so successful at the top level over the years? What are the skills, attitudes and behaviours that allow your coach to be successful? How has your coach evolved since you started working with him/her? What have been the most noticeable changes in his/her way of doing things? What are the main differences between this coach and other coaches you have worked with/ known that perhaps are not as successful consistently? What is the key role your coach plays in managing you, your progress, and your performance? Is there anything you would want your coach to do more of or change in his/her coaching that would enhance your experience?*

Making sense of the data

Making sense of these data was a challenging and laborious process, which required both of us to repeatedly challenge each other and our sense-making. It was important and necessary to mitigate against potential subjective biases (from both our coaching and researcher backgrounds), such as confirmation bias. Indeed, we were sensitive to the importance of reflexivity and sincerity (Tracy, 2010), and creative dialogue (Mason, 2006) necessary in collaborative mixed-method research to produce appropriate accounts in making sense of the data (Coulter et al., 2016). Firstly, we made sense of the data for each SWC and then co-created themes across the sample of SWC.

Indeed, we were focused on describing and understanding psychological individuality in preference to searching for potential (mal)adaptive functioning (Mallett & Lara-Bercial, 2016). A "logic of person perception" approach to data analysis was used to make sense of the multiple data sets (surveys and interviews) representing multiple layers of a person's psychology (McAdams & Manczak, 2011; p. 41). This three-phase sequence integrated findings across the three 'levels' of understanding the participants – from macro (broad and de-contextualised traits) to micro (personalised life story). This logic suggests that we can scaffold and deepen our understanding of people as we move from traits to motives to narrative identity that give a life its meaning and purpose. Initial analysis was conducted on personality trait data (NEO), which was followed by analysis of the personal strivings (content and motivational themes); then we integrated the findings for the first two layers (*social actor* and *motivated agent*). This was followed by an analysis of the life story data, (third layer; *autobiographical author*), which was subsequently integrated with the first two layers to produce an assimilated and comprehensive story about the SWC (Singer, 2005). Although we reported these findings in an earlier publication (Mallett & Lara-Bercial, 2016) we highlight these key outcomes in several chapters in this book. To assist the analysis and data integration phase, clinical guidelines developed by Levak and colleagues (2013) were followed to integrate different data sets to generate a more complete understanding of these SWC. Levak et al. suggest several practical steps for managing and integrating multiple data sets that were relevant to this study, including: (i) generation and refinement of anchor hypotheses; (ii) ex-panding and refining anchor hypotheses by incorporating supplementary data; (iii) blending of potentially conflicting data; (iv) integration of life history data; and (v) providing feedback about preliminary analyses.

In making sense of the life story data, it was important and necessary to consider both the content (i.e., *what* was said) and *how* stories are told. McAdams' (1988) life story model of narrative identity provided guidance in making sense of the life story data. There are four key aspects of this model including, *ideological setting* (values or belief systems people use to suggest how the world around them operates), *imagoes* (archetypal characters that express idealised aspects of the self), *nuclear episodes* (significant self-defining memories that shape people's lives), and *generativity scripts* (expectations about how one's story will end). Furthermore, to identify key themes, plots, and narratives, two key elements of theme and structure were considered (McAdams, 1988): *thematic lines* (the motivational themes within a narrative) and *narrative complexity* (the degree of nuance, con-tradiction, and ambiguity within the narrative).

For the second part of the coach interview and the athlete interview data, we used thematic analysis to make sense of the data and identify patterns. We fol-lowed the six-step approach proposed by Braun and Clarke (2006; 2021) which included a period of familiarisation with the data through repeated readings of the data; a phase of initial generation of codes; categorising the general codes into themes; reviewing the themes; defining and refining the themes. The coaches' and athletes' interview data were coded separately after which key themes from both data sets were compared.

What did we learn?

So, what did we learn about the multi-layered understanding of these SWC personalities? We briefly present an overview of these analyses. A more detailed analysis is presented in Mallett and Lara-Bercial's (2016) paper, *Serial winning coaches: People, vision, and environment.*

In terms of psychological traits (*social actor*), we can say with some confidence that as a group, these coaches presented themselves as conscientious, extraverted, and emotionally stable. These findings are consistent with the literature (e.g., Olusoga et al., 2012; Thelwell et al., 2008). The trait profiles of these SWC were also generally consistent with their athletes' observer reports, which suggests that these SWC possessed healthy self-awareness. The overall picture we see is that these SWC are proactive, have clarity of vision and purpose, and are passionate about their personally meaningful goals and the need to work hard to achieve them. They present themselves as emotionally regulated performers who lead and mobilise others. Indeed, they and their athletes described them as confident and socially competent.

As *motivated agents*, the personal strivings of these SWC were clearly approach-rather than avoidance-oriented. Their strivings were described as optimistic and solution-focused, which are consistent with their traits as upbeat optimists (low N, high E) and self-starters and doers (high E, high C). Most of SWC strivings were agentic (e.g., insatiable thirst for knowledge; self-improvement, learning); however, some of these agentic strivings were also related to helping others; for example, "I need to learn as much as I can so my athletes benefit from my knowledge". In summary, these meaningful and personal strivings were helpful in identifying the why behind their high work ethic and need to achieve. We found that these SWC are highly motivated to be successful and fuelling this need for accomplishment were the following preoccupations:

1 personal growth and development for self and others; that is, *getting along* (McAdams, 2015);
2 to be highly successful and achieve through thorough planning and contingency plans that internally fuelled their desire to challenge themselves; and
3 lead through the positive influence over others (i.e., power); that is, *getting ahead* (McAdams, 2015; Mallett & Lara-Bercial, 2016; p. 302)

The need to become the best they could be became obvious; however, what we did not know was why that was so important to them and why that meant so much to them in the context of their lives? Data from the third layer (autobiographical author) of a person generated useful information to address the above questions. Two main narratives underpinned these SWC and their thirst for success. Firstly, several SWC were on a personal crusade for atonement (aka, the *Righteous Avenger*), which is categorised under the broad term, redemptive stories. Many SWC did not perceive their success as an athlete as fulfilling their ambitions and expectations. This self-perception of athletic failure provided the fuel for several SWC to be relentless in their pursuit of success as a coach. We described this passion as "serial insecurity" (Mallett & Lara-Bercial, 2016; p. 313). Every time these SWC's athletes succeeded, these morally driven SWC were consistently and subconsciously reminded of their own failures as an athlete, which partly explains the ongoing pursuit to atone for their previous failures. They were described in Lara-Bercial and Mallett (2016) as *righteous avengers,* however, for them, there will never be full reparation. Second, a few SWC were described as *higher-purpose altruists*. Indeed, the drive to be successful was fuelled by higher meaning and purpose in what they did and pursued. This higher duty and responsibility for others (e.g., country) often came at some cost to the SWC, although, their pride in representing this higher purpose reinforced their strong moral position, which was to benefit others (*altruism*).

Although there might have been a more dominant narrative for each SWC, overall, there seemed to be aspects of multiple narratives in action – one was foregrounded, and others backgrounded. For example, all SWC seemed to be *grounded realists* (aka, *Homer Simpson*), who were able to remain grounded, humble, and keep things in perspective despite the significant challenges in working in this highly performative and contested context, which is often uncontrollable. These findings are expanded upon in Chapter 8 and also elaborated upon in previous publications from this study (Mallett & Lara-Bercial, 2016).

We take this opportunity to bring this chapter to a close but before we do, we add another layer of the person that we did not focus on in our previous papers. Foundational to all three layers of a person and part of human evolution (biological determinism) are the basic psychological needs of humans. Although there might be some contestation as to what these psychological needs are, there seems consensus amongst psychologists and researchers that we have evolved to satisfy psychological needs that require nourishment in the development of one's personality. The three basic psychological needs we adopt were acknowledged by Ed Deci and Richard Ryan (1985), in a seminal text, *Intrinsic Motivation and Self-Determination in Human Behavior,* which reports a popular theory of motivation to explain *why we do what we do*. These three psychological needs, which have been researched by hundreds of scholars and produced hundreds of peer-reviewed papers, are autonomy (self-determination), competence (mastery, effectiveness), and relatedness (belonging). When we re-analysed our data, we can say with confidence that there was significant empirical support for the nourishment of these three needs in the coaches, the athletes they coached, and the support staff. For example, in the pilot study of the SWC (Mallett & Coulter, 2016), the highly successful Olympic coach sought to prove himself to his father (providing some nourishment to all three needs: competence, autonomy, and relatedness). The atonement for perceived previous failings as an athlete was the fuel for striving to feel worthy through "passion, mastery, and ultimately success" as a coach (Mallett & Coulter, p. 123), which is reflective of a commitment script (Tomkins, 1987).

Coming to know the personalities of these SWC provides insightful information to understand their behaviours in context, which will be presented in subsequent chapters. In the next section, we focus on the journeys of these coaches in becoming a SWC.

Note

1 Extraversion is a measure of engagement with the outside world and is related to sociability, excitement, stimulation, and social interactions. Neuroticism is associated with degree of emotional stability and un/pleasant experiences. Conscientious people tend to be organised, goal-oriented, purposeful, and determined. Agreeableness is associated with interpersonal tendencies or style (e.g., sympathetic/altruistic, egocentric, competitive versus co-operative). Openness to experience is concerned with broad interests, curiosity, open-minded versus practical, down-to earth, conventional. Adapted from Costa and McCrae (2010).

References

Allen, M. S., Greenlees, I., & Jones, M. V. (2011). An investigation of the five-factor model of personality and coping behaviour in sport. *Journal of Sports Sciences, 29*, 841–850.

Baddeley, J., & Singer, J. A. (2007). Charting the life story's path: Narrative identity across the life span. In J. Clandinan (Ed.), *Handbook of narrative research methods* (pp. 177–202). Sage.

Bandura, A. (1989). Human agency in social-cognitive theory. *The American Psychologist, 44*, 1175–1184. PubMed doi:10.1037/0003-066X.44.9.1175.

Braun, V., & Clarke, V. (2006). Using thematic analysis in psychology. *Qualitative Research in Psychology, 3*(2), 77–101. 10.1191/1478088706qp063oa.

Braun, V., & Clarke, V. (2021). *Thematic analysis: A practical guide.* Sage.

Carlyle, T. (1841). *On heroes, hero-worship, & the heroic in history.* Fraser.

Cassidy, T., Jones, R. L., & Potrac, P. (2004). *Understanding sports coaching: The pedagogical, social and cultural foundations of coaching practice.* Routledge.

Costa, P. T. Jr., & McCrae, R. R. (1992). *Revised NEO Personality Inventory (NEO-PI-R) and NEO Five-Factor Inventory (NEO-FFI) Manual.* Psychological Assessment Resources.

Costa, P. T., & McCrae, R. R. (2010). *NEO inventories: Professional manual.* Psychological Assessment Resources.

Coulter, T., Mallett, C. J., & McAdams, D. (2020). Personality assessment I: An integrative approach. In D. Hackfort, & R. Schinke (Eds.), *The Routledge international encyclopaedia of sport psychology: Volume 1: Theoretical and methodological concepts* (pp. 439–454). Routledge.

Coulter, T. J., Mallett, C. J., & Singer, J. (2017). A three-domain personality analysis of a mentally tough athlete. *European Journal of Personality, 32*(1), 6–29. doi:10.1002/per.2129

Coulter, T., Mallett, C. J., Singer, J., & Gucciardi, D. F. (2016). Personality in sport and exercise psychology: Integrating a whole person perspective. *International Journal of Sport and Exercise Psychology, 14*(1), 23–41.

Deci, E. L., & Ryan, R. M. (1985). *Intrinsic motivation and self-determination in human behaviour.* Plenum. doi:10.1007/978-1-4899-2271-7

Emmons, R. A. (1989). The personal striving approach to personality. In L. A. Pervin (Ed.), *Goal concepts in personality and social psychology* 87–126. Erlbaum.

Erikson, E. H. (1963). *Childhood and society (2nd ed.).* New York, NY: Norton.

Eysenk, H. J. (1960). *Personality and behaviour therapy.* Sage.

Hughes, S. L., Case, H. S., Stumemple, K. J., & Evans, D. S. (2003). Personality profiles of Iditasport ultra-marathon participants. *Journal of Applied Sport Psychology, 15,* 256–261.

Habermas, T., & Bluck, S. (2000). Getting a life: The emergence of the life story in adolescence. *Psychological Bulletin, 126,* 748–769. 10.1037/0033-2909.126.5.748

Harter, S. (2006). The self. In N. Eisenberg, W. Damon, & R. M. Lerner (Eds.), *Handbook of child psychology, Vol. 3: Social, emotional, and personality development* (pp. 505–570). Wiley.

Haslam, S. A., Reicher, S. D., & Platow, M. J. (2011). *The new psychology of leadership: Identity, influence and power.* Psychology Press.

Jones, R. (2007). Coaching re-defined: An everyday pedagogical endeavour. *Sport, Education, and Society, 12,* 159–173.

Kluckhohn, C., & Murray, H. A. (1953). Personality formation: The determinants. In C. Kluckhohn, H. A. Murray, & D. M. Schneider (Eds.), *Personality in nature, society, and culture* (2nd ed., pp. 53–69). Alfred A. Knopf.

Levak, R. W., Hogan, R. S., Beutler, L. E., & Song, X. (2013). Applying assessment information: Decision making, patient feedback and consultation. In T. M. Harwood, L. E. Beutler, & G. Groth-Marnat (Eds.), *Integrative assessment of adult personality: 3rd edition* (pp. 373–412). The Guildford Press.

Mallett, C., & Coulter, T. (2016). The anatomy of a successful Olympic coach: Actor, agent, and author. *International Sport Coaching Journal, 3,* 113–127.

Mallett, C. J., & Lara-Bercial, S. (2016). Serial winning coaches: People, vision and environment. In M. Raab, P. Wylleman, R. Seiler, A-M. Elbe, & A. Hatzigeorgiadis (Eds.), *Sport and exercise psychology research: Theory to practice* (pp. 289–322). Elsevier.

Mason, J. (2006). Mixing methods in a qualitatively driven way. *Qualitative Research, 6,* 9–25.10.1177/1468794106058866.

Mayer, J. D. (2005). A tale of two visions: Can a new view of personality help integrate psychology? *American Psychologist, 60,* 294–307. doi:10.1037/0003-066X.60.4.294

McAdams, D. P. (1985). *Power, intimacy, and the life story: Personological inquiries into identity.* Guilford.

McAdams, D. P. (1988). Biography, narrative, and lives: An introduction. *Journal of Personality, 56,* 1–1810.1111/j.1467-6494.1988.tb00460.x.

McAdams, D. P. (1995). What do we know when we know a person? *Journal of Personality, 63,* 365–396.

McAdams, D. P. (2008). Personal narratives and the life story. In O. P. John, R. W. Robins, & L. A. Pervin (Eds.), *Handbook of personality: Theory and research* (3rd Ed.), (pp. 242-262). Guilford.

McAdams, D. P. (2013). The psychological self as actor, agent, and author. *Perspectives of Psychological Science, 8,* 272–295.

McAdams, D. P. (2015). *The art and science of personality development.* Guilford.

McAdams, D. P., & Cox, K. S. (2010). Self and identity across the life span. In R. Lerner, A. Freud, & M. Lamb (Eds.), *Handbook of life span development* (Vol. 2, pp. 158–207). Wiley.

McAdams, D. P., & Manczak, E. (2011). What is a "level" of personality? *Psychological Inquiry, 22,* 40–44. doi:10.1080/1047840X.2011.544026

McAdams, D. P., & Olson (2010). Personality development: Continuity and change over the life course. *Annual Review of Psychology, 61,* 517–542.

McAdams, D. P., & Pals, J. L. (2006). A new big five: Fundamental principles for an integrative science of personality. *American Psychologist, 61,* 204–2017.

McCrae, R. R., & Costa, P. T. Jr. (2007). Brief versions of the NEO-PI-3. *Journal of Individual Differences, 28*(3), 116–128. 10.1027/1614-0001.28.3.116

Mischel, W., & Shoda, Y. (2008). Toward a unified theory of personality: Integrating dispositions and processing dynamics within the Cognitive-Affective Processing System (CAPS). In O. P. John, R. W. Robins, & L. A. Pervin (Eds.), *Handbook of Personality* (3rd Ed., pp. 208–241). Guilford.

Olusoga, P., Maynard, I., Hays, K., & Butt, J. (2012). Coaching under pressure: A study of Olympic coaches. *Journal of Sports Sciences, 30,* 229–239.

Piaget, J. (1970). Piaget's theory. In P. H. Mussen (Ed.), *Carmichael's manual of child psychology* (Vol. 1, 2nd ed., pp. 703–732). Wiley.

Patton, M. Q. (2002). Two decades of developments in qualitative inquiry: A personal, experiential perspective. *Qualitative Social Work, 1*(3), 261-283.

Sheldon, K. M., Cheng, C., & Hilpert, J. (2011). Understanding well-being and optimal functioning: Applying the Multilevel Personality in Context (MPIC) Model. *Psychological Inquiry, 22,* 1–16.

Singer, J. A. (2005). *Personality and psychotherapy: Treating the whole person.* Guildford.

Singer, J. A., & Salovey, P. (1993). *The remembered self.* Free Press.

Tajfel, H., & Turner, J. (1979). An integrative theory of inter-group conflict. In W. G. Austin, & S. Worchel (Eds.), *The Social Psychology of Intergroup Relations.* Brooks-Cole.

Tabano, J., & Portenga, S. (2018). Personality test: Understanding the athlete as a person. In J. Taylor (Ed.), *Assessment in applied sport psychology* (pp. 73–82). Human Kinetics.

Taylor, J. (2018). Importance of assessment in sport psychology consulting. In J. Taylor (Ed.), *Assessment in applied sport psychology* (pp. 73–82). Human Kinetics.

Thelwell, R. C., Weston, N. J. V., Greenlees, I. A., & Hutchings, N. (2008). Stressors in elite sport: A coach perspective. *Journal of Sports Sciences, 26,* 905–918.

Thomae, H. (1999). The nomothetic-idiographic issue: Some roots and recent trends. *International Journal of Group Tensions, 28*(1), 187–215.

Tomkins, S. S. (1987). Script theory. In J. Aronoff, A. I. Rabin, & R. A. Zucker (Eds.), *The emergence of personality* (pp. 147–216). Springer.

Tracy, S. J. (2010). Qualitative quality: Eight "Big-Tent" criteria for excellent qualitative research. *Qualitative Inquiry, 16,* 837–851. 10.1177/1077800410383121.

Turner, J. C., Reynolds, K. J., Haslam, S. A., & Veenstra, K. (2006). Re-conceptualizing personality: Producing individuality through defining the personal self. In T. Postmes, & J. Jetten (Eds.), *Individuality and the group: Advances in social identity* (pp. 11–36). Sage.

White S. H. (1965). Evidence for a hierarchical arrangement of learning processes. *Advances in Child Behaviour, 2,* 187-220.

SECTION B
Pathways

3
THE LEARNING JOURNEYS OF SERIAL WINNING COACHES

The study of "how coaches learn and develop their craft" has received increasing attention over the last two decades. The realisation of the sheer size of the coaching workforce, and its impact on millions of people across the participation spectrum, has led governments and governing bodies of sport to turn their attention to this issue (Council of the European Commission, 2020; Lara-Bercial & Bales, 2022; Lara-Bercial et al., 2022). In the context of high-performance sport, it has almost become a question of state (Mallett, 2010; Rynne, 2014). Given the high level of financial, emotional, and temporal investment, into Olympic, Paralympic, and professional sport, ensuring that high-performance coaches (HPC) are best prepared has been prioritised in many countries. National sport councils, national Olympic and Paralympic committees, and governing bodies of sport have thus started to invest in programmes that enhance and accelerate the development of HPC (Australian Institute of Sport, 2021; English Premier League, 2020). Increasingly, HPC are considered as performers themselves (Gould et al., 2002; Chan & Mallett, 2011; Parkes, 2018) and, therefore, their training and continuous development have become institutionalised, but also interrogated.

Researchers have approached this topic from multiple perspectives: i) types of learning opportunities; ii) coaches' learning preferences; iii) expertise development; iv) types of knowledge; v) coach career development pathways; vi) the nature of the learning process; and vii) the impact of Coach Education and Development (CED) programmes. A full review of this research is beyond the scope of this introduction (see Lara-Bercial & Bales, 2022; Lyle & Cushion, 2017; Trudel et al., 2020). Notwithstanding this, we provide an overview of the extant CED literature, especially in relation to the learning and development of serial winning coaches (SWC) in the following section.

DOI: 10.4324/9781003427292-5

How do high-performance coaches (HPC) learn?

Coaching researchers have tried to understand what types of learning opportunities coaches have access to and which ones they prefer. We can say with some confidence that many studies have shown that HPC typically:

- Acknowledged the impact of their own athletic career as a significant source of knowledge and influence in their coaching praxis (e.g., Currie & Oates-Wilding, 2012; Erickson, Côté & Fraser-Thomas, 2007; He, Trudel & Culver 2018; Lynch & Mallett, 2006; Rynne, 2014; Rynne & Mallett, 2012). Previous athletic experience, especially at the elite level, has also been described as a central factor in facilitating HPC's initial forays into a coaching career (e.g., Blackett, Evans & Piggott, 2017; 2018; Erickson, Côté & Fraser-Thomas, 2007).
- Completed high-level qualifications in their sport and, in a high proportion, have also undertaken higher education degrees. Significantly, many of these degrees were in sport-related subjects (e.g., Carter & Bloom, 2009; Erickson, Côté & Fraser-Thomas, 2007; Lynch & Mallett, 2006; Nash & Sproule, 2009; Olusoga et al., 2012; Sherwin, Campbell & Macintyre, 2017).
- Engaged in the development of support and knowledge-exchange networks with other coaches through personal friendships and/or interactions during competitions and coaching clinics (e.g., Cassidy, Potrac & Jones, 2015; Lynch & Mallett, 2006; Nash & Sproule, 2009; Occhino, Mallett & Rynne, 2013; Olusoga et al., 2012; Reade, Rodgers & Spriggs, 2008; Sherwin et al., 2017; Stoszkowski & Collins, 2016). To a lesser extent, research has found that HPC also learnt from the regular interaction with their own staff (Reade, Rodgers & Spriggs, 2008) and their athletes (Rynne & Mallett, 2012).
- Used mentor-like figures (knowledgeable others) as both support and challenge mechanisms to enhance their development and practice (e.g., Carter & Bloom, 2009; Fairhurst, Bloom & Harvey, 2017; He, Trudel & Culver, 2018; Occhino, Mallett & Rynne, 2013).
- Emphasised the central role of on-the-job learning in facilitating practical knowledge acquisition and accelerating their development (Allen & Shaw, 2009; Nash & Sproule, 2009; Olusoga et al., 2012; Rynne & Mallett, 2012; Sherwin, Campbell & Macintyre, 2017).
- Highlighted the importance of self-reflection as a way of making sense of their own practice (Cruz, 2014) and facilitate change and development over time (Galvan, Fyall & Culpan, 2012; Irwin, Hanton & Kerwin, 2004; Jiménez-Sáiz, Lorenzo-Calvo & Ibañez-Godoy, 2008; Sherwin, Campbell & Macintyre, 2017).
- Invested significant amounts of time in self-directed learning activities such as reading books or watching videos, taking non-sport-related qualifications, observing others coach, and watching and analysing their sport (Cruz, 2014;

Jiménez-Sáiz, Lorenzo-Calvo & Ibañez-Godoy, 2008; Occhino, Mallett & Rynne, 2013; Sherwin, Campbell & Macintyre, 2017). This agentic process appears to be driven equally by an inherent thirst for knowledge and a constant need to plug knowledge gaps as demanded by their day-to-day practice Occhino, Mallett & Rynne, 2013; Olusoga et al., 2012).

The above findings support the view that HPC are consumers of a broad range of learning opportunities and sources spanning the spectrum of formal, non-formal, informal, mediated, non-mediated, and internal.[1] However, researchers have also reported that the extent to which HPC engage in these varied learning menus, and how much they take from them, depends on many factors. For instance, the stage of development of the coach influences their learning choices (e.g., He, Trudel & Culver, 2018; Mallett, Rynne & Billett, 2016; Trudel, Gilbert & Rodrigue, 2016). During the early part of their careers, HPC tend to rely on their athletic experiences, knowledge acquired through formal qualifications, and the use of selected mentors – all of this filtered and interpreted through their on-the-job experiences (e.g., Carter & Bloom, 2009; Erickson, Côté & Fraser-Thomas, 2007; Lynch & Mallett, 2006; Mallett, Rynne & Billet, 2016; Nash & Sproule, 2009). As coaches' careers progress, learning preferences may shift towards the development of what Occhino, Mallett and Rynne (2013) termed "dynamic social networks" – a set of relationships that change and evolve over time to reflect the changing needs of the coach. By contrast, mid-to-late career coaches appear to rely heavily on needs-led self-study and deliberate self-reflection supported by a small group of trusted critical friends or formal mentors/confidantes (Allen & Shaw, 2009; Erickson, Côté & Fraser-Thomas, 2007; Lynch & Mallett, 2006) and subject-matter experts (Reade, Rodgers & Spriggs, 2008). Indeed, Trudel, Gilbert and Rodrigue (2016) have suggested that, as their expertise increases, coaches move from relying on mediated learning opportunities towards more non-mediated and internal options exercising their growing agentic power (Occhino et al., 2013). Trudel and colleagues also argue that a constant stream of deliberate reflection is the greatest determinant of progress towards expertise.

Furthermore, the affordances in and through sport presented within their developmental ecologies have been reported as key influences of the learning journey of the HPC. Cultural and structural features of the specific context in which the coach works determine what learning opportunities are available, accepted, and promoted (e.g., He, Trudel & Culver, 2018; Nash & Sproule, 2009; Rossi, Rynne & Rabjohns, 2016). Finally, personal preference and agentic power, influenced by personal traits and previous learning experiences, have also been proposed as a determinant of the developmental repertoire of HPC (e.g., Mallett, Rynne & Billet, 2016; Rossi, Rynne & Rabjohns, 2016; Trudel, Gilbert & Rodrigue, 2016; Werthner & Trudel, 2006).

In summary, it is not surprising that the dynamic and personalised developmental process of the learning journeys of HPC have been reported as being highly idiosyncratic and difficult to compare (e.g., Carter & Bloom, 2009; He, Trudel & Culver, 2018).

Current limitations of HPC education and development

Despite the unique developmental journeys of individual coaches, largely shaped by their personal needs, HPC have vocalised their desire for additional, more coordinated, purposeful, and customised support in developing their craft (Allen & Shaw, 2009; Nelson, Cushion & Potrac, 2006; Sherwin, Campbell & Macintyre, 2017). The need to move beyond the existing CED "mass market" and "one-size-fits-all" model has been emphasised by many coach developers and researchers (e.g., sportscoachUK, 2012).

As part of this drive for customised support, HPC have indicated topics of preference, including learning theory (i.e., pedagogy/andragogy), psychology, sociology, talent identification, team management, media training, pastoral care, and reflective practice (e.g., Galvan, Fyall & Culpan, 2012; He, Trudel & Culver, 2018; Olusoga et al., 2012; Rynne & Mallett, 2012). HPC have also pointed out that improvements to mediated opportunities can be made not only in relation to the topics of choice, but especially to their applicability to real-life problems (Nash & Sproule, 2009; Sherwin, Campbell & Macintyre, 2017) and the specific context in which the coach works (Olusoga et al., 2012). In other words, HPC want to know and learn things that they need and will use in the present – and they want coach developers to support them in applying this new knowledge and skills immediately through reality/problem-based methodologies (sportscoachUK, 2012). HPC therefore prefer to learn "just in time" over "just in case".

So, what did we want to learn more about?

Indeed, the HPC's learning journeys are characterised by varied learning sources that are contingent upon the individual coach, their context, and their stage of development. Furthermore, HPC have expressed a desire for more bespoke, authentic learning that meets their specific needs in time and in context. Consequently, a key aim of the SWC project was to investigate the learning and development footprints of these repeatedly successful coaches and, specifically, compare and contrast them with what we know so far to inform future policy and practice in CED. Specifically, we wished to answer two broad research questions: a) How did SWC learn to coach?; and b) What learning opportunities were prominent and valued at key stages of their development?

What did we learn from SWC?

Serial winning coaches ranking of accessed and preferred learning opportunities

As part of the demographic questions, coaches were asked to rank both their most commonly accessed and preferred learning opportunities from 1 to 4 in descending order (Lara-Bercial & Mallett, 2016). SWC ranked coaching qualifications, coaching clinics, on-the-job learning, and self-study as the most commonly accessed learning opportunities. On the other hand, peer learning was consistently rated as the preferred learning opportunity followed by coaching qualifications, self-study, self-reflection, and on-the-job learning

The above data provided some initial insights into these SWC's learning. What we also wanted to know was a more nuanced understanding of each specific learning source, the individualised nature of how each coach may have interacted with that source, and the significance and frequency of each learning opportunity at different stages of the developmental journey of the coach. What were these deeper insights? We theme our findings into five categories. First, we discuss the impact of pre-coaching experiences. Using Eshach's classification (2007), we then explore in sequence the access to and impact of formal, non-formal, and informal learning opportunities before concluding with an examination of the role of internal learning (Moon, 2004) in facilitating coach development.

Pre-coaching experiences

SWC recognised the important contribution that pre-coaching experiences made to them learning to coach. Two types were identified, namely, experiences related to their early developmental environments (i.e., upbringing and close relationships), and the learning afforded by their own athletic careers.

Early developmental environment

Some SWC identified their parents and/or close relatives, and the environments they grew up in, as a key influence in their learning (Lara-Bercial & Mallett, 2016). For instance, Coach 14 said: *"I believe I learned to work hard from my Dad and I learned to talk to people from my Mum. Did University and other things along the way help that and affect that? Yes, but without those two foundational things I wouldn't be where I am"*. This sentiment was echoed by Coach 3 who recalled how he *"had the teaching gene in him from his parents"* who were both teachers, and how he did not see himself doing anything else than coaching or teaching. In other cases, the impact of their proximal environment in their early development was felt more at the level of the unconscious acquisition of certain traits through repeated exposure (e.g., a rural upbringing or being born into the sport).

Own athletic career

Out of the 17 SWC, 10 had been international and/or professional athletes, 6 had competed at national level, and only 1 had no experience of competitive sport. Of the ten former international athletes, five had won medals at major events, yet only two of them had won gold. All SWC with athletic experience emphasised differential contributions to their development as a coach. Specifically, three types of knowledge were identified: knowledge of the sport, knowledge about the coaching process, and knowledge about leadership.

With regards to learning about the sport, SWC acknowledged the benefits of having been trained by multiple expert coaches and how they picked up different things from each of them (Lara-Bercial & Mallett, 2016):

> So, I had six mentors—but I wasn't really thinking about it at the time—that influenced my approach to technique, and my approach to training. I just by chance—it's not like I was just in one club with one coach for 11 years and learned a lot from that coach, it just happened that there was six of them. (Coach 11)

Likewise, SWC appreciated the inherent opportunities to learn the intricacies of their sport from playing it at a high level. Coach 4, a former gold medallist and team captain with his national team, put it this way:

> It helped me for sure that I played the sport and it helped me that I played, with and against, the best players and it helped me that you know, in specific situations, I'm already ready, I have in my mind what to do [because I have lived through it].

In relation to their understanding of the coaching process, SWC highlighted that, even at a subconscious level, playing the sport had influenced the way they coach:

> You are partly moulded as a coach, even if you do not realise it, when you are a player yourself – you have worked with a number of coaches and in the way they work you notice things of which you say: hey, that works for me or that is bullshit. (Coach 5)

This ability to extract key cues and information from their athletic experiences while they were still competing, and for years after, denotes a significant level of agency and receptiveness to the processing and evaluating of these experiential learning affordances. In other words, not every elite athlete may have the disposition or capacity to capitalise on and bring their athletic experiences into their coaching practice.

The element most reported by SWC in relation to their athletic experience, however, was the impact it had on their leadership capabilities and management skills. One frequently cited component was the opportunity afforded by their own participation to play a leadership role before becoming a coach (Lara-Bercial & Mallett, 2016). Coach 1 reflected:

> I have also been a player-manager, a captain [...] I have always been in leading positions, I was class representative at school, too [...] I always did things like that, it's in me somehow. And on the pitch, I was a kind of a big-mouth, too, and somehow the others went along with it. It was all there.

Another element shared by SWC, who were former elite athletes, was the chance to experience firsthand a variety of leadership styles leading to an understanding of which one may suit you.

Notwithstanding the above, SWC regularly stressed that elite participation was not a pre-condition to becoming a successful coach. Coach 8 articulated this thinking clearly and extensively:

> The other side of the coin in my opinion is, do you, to be a good coach, do you have to yourself have been an Olympic gold medallist, or a world champion or a national champion or whatever? And the answer to that point in my opinion is no.

Formal learning as a springboard to becoming a better coach

Most SWC held high-level formal qualifications (Lara-Bercial & Mallett, 2016). Nine coaches had completed sports-related degrees (i.e., sport science, kinesiology, or physical education). One of them held an M.Sc. in Sport Science. Another four coaches had completed bachelor's degrees in unrelated subjects, and three coaches had not attended university. One coach did not answer this question. Fifteen coaches held the highest possible coaching qualification for their country. Two coaches did not respond to this item.

Overall, these SWC viewed formal coach education as a springboard during their early coaching careers, a fundamental first step that allowed them to start coaching with a baseline of knowledge they could build upon and an interpretive framework they used to make sense of their practice. Coach 3 explained:

> For me it was an excellent experience because it gave me a systematic idea of my sport, a global picture about the profession, about what the job is and then because it also gave me some specific knowledge about other topics, not too deep, but enough to be able to make sense of them.

Coach 15 reflected on how during his time in formal education:

There were things that seemed trivial initially. I told myself I'd never use them, and yet today I refer back to them a great deal [...] There's also things I did almost 30 years ago which are still useful for all sorts of reasons.

For Coach 9, the most important element of his formal education was the explicit links made between the acquired knowledge and actual coaching praxis:

I was already running a training group on my own with the supervision of the mentor coach. I had to write my own programme, [...] he was then watching, [...] or giving me some advice.

Whilst SWC valued their coaching accreditation awards, they appeared to be even more appreciative of their tertiary qualifications which they thought gave them an edge over other coaches and were far superior and contained broader knowledge than the courses delivered by the governing body.

In relation to the need for broader curricula in coach education, Coach 14 criticised the singular focus of coaching qualification on the sport to the detriment of other key elements of coaching: "The programme gives you knowledge which a coach needs, but not enough emphasis is placed on coaching skills - too much emphasis is placed on the certificate and not enough emphasis is placed on communication and other coaching skills".

Non-formal learning as a check and challenge process

Unsurprisingly, SWC reported high levels of engagement in non-formal education activities such as coaching clinics, continuous professional development opportunities, and self-study via books, DVDs, and generally just watching their own sport (Lara-Bercial & Mallett, 2016). These pursuits allowed them to regularly check and challenge their coaching practice and engage in a continuous process of fine-tuning and layering.

For instance, Coach 6 described the impact of attending coaching clinics: "There was so many of them [older coaches] here in the prime of their coaching careers or well established [...] running everyday community coaching seminars [that were so valuable]". She continued describing how these clinics led to the creation of coaching learning networks: "I can name off probably a dozen coaches that I grew up with through that system that I had daily and regular interaction with. So, I like to think we all made each other".

Coach 10 was able to articulate the benefits of non-formal, self-driven education:

The ones [learning opportunities] I've learned the most [from] are probably the ones I've gone and initiated [myself], but they have been based around what I can get out of it and how I can apply it practically to what I do day in day out.

It is important, however, to recognise that, in line with their personality and motivational profile described in Chapter 2, SWC were curious, thirsty for learning, and subsequently agentic in accessing formal and non-formal learning opportunities. Coach 7 explained that learning "is a constant process and so it should be, because, as the saying goes, standstill means decline". Coach 13 emphasised the agentic power of the coach to maximise learning: "I created my own [learning] opportunities and sought out and identified my winning points of difference. I am predatory in opportunity and in seizing the moment".

Notwithstanding this thirst for learning, there was also a recognition that HPC were cognisant of time constraints and therefore needed to find solutions to the challenge of "so much to know and so little time". For Coach 2, the key was to identify short reads: "I can't read more than 75 minutes, I want to get on the plane, read the darn thing, highlight, make notes on the side and go back later". Coach 7 solved the problem by tapping into those who had done all the reading already and could act as translators of knowledge: "I prefer to go to people who have read those 100 books and are able to summarize the core of it [...]".

Finally, there might be an assumption that as these SWC careers progressed their curiosity would be incumbered and wane; however, it is also worth noting that SWC's curiosity continued and grew the longer they coached and the more they won. The more you know, the more you realise what you don't know:

I think in the beginning when I came out and I was fresh and I went out to university to have my maths [degree], I knew everything. You couldn't beat me on anything, like in the end I knew nothing and you know that's part of learning, consistently learning. The more you know, the less you know at the same time, so I change from the arrogant guy that knew everything to the one that started to question everything and try to learn more. (Coach 17)

Informal learning as the most powerful and lasting influence

SWC frequently pointed at the significance and enduring nature of informal learning in their development (Lara-Bercial & Mallett, 2016). The two main elements reported were the importance of on-the-job learning in and through coaching praxis, and the prominent role of peer learning.

Learning in and through coaching work

With regards to on-the-job learning, SWC acknowledged its inevitability. Coach 10 reflected on the process of going from formal education into real-life coaching: "So I have had a phase in which I was reasonably 'self-made', actually after my education, being thrown in at the deep end, there you become a little bit self-made at first". Coach 9 felt being able to start coaching whilst still doing your qualifications was central to learning: "I was still a student, still at the university, finishing my diploma and things like that, but then I was already running a training group on my own". Moreover, some coaches explicitly referred to the need for emerging coaches to be allowed leeway to explore and make mistakes and to access a variety of experiences and environments.

In this regard, while some coaches debuted immediately at the high-performance level, for some SWC, their early career jobs were in low-key positions where they could explore their ideas with relatively low pressure and expectation: "Really, it was in that environment that I learned so much, I was able to try things [...] and finding out what worked [...] You know, I had a full laboratory to do whatever I wanted" (Coach 6).

Furthermore, Coach 3 emphasised the need to become self-reflective to maximise the benefits of on-the-job experiences, especially when things did not work well: "Having understood where you went wrong, having memories of similar situations that you've been in and what you did to resolve them and how that went; mistakes are a very important experience". Learning from experience was also relevant in anticipating problems and building a repertoire of ready-made solutions that could be called upon when required.

Unsurprisingly, SWC stated that *in situ* learning could be facilitated via different means. The most commonly reported and preferred mode was the influence of a significant and knowledgeable other, which they often referred to as a mentor. These mentors were positioned differently and played different roles for different coaches. For instance, for Coach 5, his mentor was one of his formal education lecturers:

> I was lucky enough to work with this man during my education at the university and later on he was also my teacher at the highest coach education of our federation. I was lucky enough to have worked with him, I have really learned a lot from him.

For Coach 1, however, his mentor was a head coach whom he assisted for several years: "Okay, I was influenced a lot by the time I spent [working] with him. Sure, that was very intensive. It couldn't have been any better". For other coaches, like Coach 4, they had brought this mentor figure right into their first coaching staff: "The best decision for me [on being appointed head coach] was that I call [NAME] and I worked with him for two years". Coach 4 also stressed that the relationship with the mentor ought to be challenging and that, ultimately, the younger developing coach still had to hold the reins and make the decisions.

This view was echoed by Coach 6 who was wary of self-interested mentors: "the mentor has to not want to be a coach, […] they can't want to coach the team or run the practices or run the drills". Indeed, the mentor role was related to guiding and thus considered different from the coaching role.

Peer learning

The second element of informal learning emphasised by SWC was the high value placed on peer learning, both as a source of affirming and challenging knowledge, but also as a catalyst to maximising on-the-job learning (Lara-Bercial & Mallett, 2016). For some coaches this happened in an organic way linked to time and place: "I was fortunate in [REGION] to grow up in a time when there were many great coaches and I grew up with my idols and colleagues" (Coach 6). For coaches with university degrees aimed solely at the development of HPC, or in systems where high-performance sport was centralised into national development centres, they had an opportunity to cross-pollinate ideas within and across sports:

> Yes, because that's what the [NATIONAL TRAINING CENTRE] provided. we don't have that now in [NEW COUNTRY]. I think that's the future, you [coaches from different sports] still deal with the same shit, it's just different skills, how do you select people, can you make it objective, when you got conflict, how do you resolve that, what's your planning, how do you behave when you go away, what's your acclimation process, how do you teach skills. (Coach 10)

Coach 7 took a step further by saying that these knowledge exchanges needed to be very carefully selected:

> I would like master classes. And I very much would like to go on short trips with a small group of people, very well chosen people and just learn from each other. The best of the best. Go for a walk, enjoy the sun and talk to each other, talk about your job with people who are also Serial Winners, people who can bring me something/ people from whom I can learn.

Notably, however, some coaches commented that sometimes it was harder to learn from coaches in the same sport as there was a culture of secrecy and withholding information to maintain a competitive edge:

I am a person who shares, I share a lot, I am not afraid to do that, but sometimes there are details you keep to yourself. Yes, the tricks of the trade [...] ultimately you want to surprise your colleagues at that important moment [in competition]. (Coach 5)

However, other coaches disagreed stating that keeping secrets was futile:

Because if you like I can take any training program during the time I was coaching the best athlete and give it to you like it doesn't matter, because if you take that and go home and do the same thing it won't work. (Coach 17)

Nevertheless, peer learning was deemed both enjoyable – "a coach lives a reasonable solitary life, it is lonely at the top, as they say, so it is pleasant to exchange ideas with a number of colleagues" (Coach 5) – and a necessary part of development as Coach 8 clearly explained:

And it's all about that to me, it's about absorbing, talking about it [...] I've been involved in, I've been involved in it since the age of three, do I know everything? No. And if I don't know everything, neither do you and neither does anybody else. And to me it's all about talking to people, exchanging views and ideas and learning from each other. And that's how you become a better coach, by communicating.

Interestingly, while being a strong advocate of learning from other coaches and from other sports, Coach 15 cautioned against the potential dangers of trying to copy other coaches or add too many new things to your own way of doing things:

What you shouldn't do is imitate, copy, and paste. There's always something to learn, for building things and making progress, but you always have to maintain your way of doing that. The chef adds salt and pepper but never loses the knack, and that's crucial.

Finally, some SWCs emphasised the power of creating internal learning networks comprising their assistant coaches and sport science support staff. Coach 7 described this as a self-perpetuating learning mechanism:

[Learning] has been an ongoing process together with my staff. Together we train each other. The discussions we have, the conversations we have, the input, the studies that come up, the research we do ourselves [...] the athlete monitoring, everything we do.

The same coach stressed how important this was given that he did not have the time to keep up with all the latest developments and literature. Coach 10 made a similar point: "I've got a philosophy also that I can't be an expert on everything and I need to get that expertise from the people around me, [how] I really learn is through my colleagues." Interestingly, for some coaches, these internal knowledge networks also included, directly or indirectly, their athletes.

Learning from the athletes was underscored by many SWC. Direct involvement included regular discussions with athletes about potential improvement avenues and changes to the programme. Coach 9 was succinct: "I think it's very important that athletes are part of the process and not just being told what they have to do. So, they understand the programme and why they are doing things". SWC believed that knowing the *why* behind the *what* is critical to fostering an athlete's autonomy.

By contrast, an example of indirect player involvement is Coach 4's explanation of how he spends a lot of time observing his players to learn new things about the sport and their capabilities: "It's very important for me that I watch my players. They are people who give me new ideas always". Similarly, Coach 13 stated that "Every great athlete has taught me lessons and [given me] experiences that I would not have had without their involvement and commitment". This is an important recognition that athletes can (and likely should) significantly contribute to coach learning in direct and indirect ways.

Internal learning as the catalyst for all other experiences

Internal learning incorporates conscious – deliberate – and unconscious – incidental – reflection on our lived experiences (Moon, 2004). Through the course of the interviews, SWC regularly commented on the importance of both types of self-reflection to foster personal development, but also as the golden thread that allowed SWC to maximise learning from all available learning opportunities – formal, non-formal, and informal.

Deliberate reflection

Deliberate or conscious reflection encompassed a broad array of activities. All coaches monitored and reviewed their athletes' and teams' performances, which contributed to evaluating and maintaining progress, but also to subsequent coach learning and development. These work tasks ranged from fully structured debriefs at key time points, to more casual, daily, and regular reflections. Coach 10 offered an example of how he went about his post-season debrief:

We'll review with the athletes and with the coaches, and I'll put all that together into a report and then I'll drag out I guess four or five key things that we want to work on for the next year. And I'll have a list of ten things, like the golden rules that we want to move on in the next year. Then we revisit them maybe four times a year with the coaches and I share them with the athletes about where we are going.

He was also able to articulate how this process supported his personal development:

So, it's really important that you review how that happened [a loss], why that happened, and what you need to rectify it. So if you've got a review improvement process you've got a strategy then for what you need to work on.

Coach 5 also emphasised the need for coaches to reflect to develop continuously and to think ahead:

In my opinion is important for coaches to continue to develop themselves. It is also very good to see; where do I stand now, what will I encounter, what competences I have by nature and then looking at that knowledge and know-how and the problems you expect to encounter, what do I need to add to myself to handle things better in the future?

Similarly, Coach 2 highlighted the need to reflect especially after negative events: "I've learned a ton by being fired … I was able to look at myself, and when you sit back after some setbacks, and you have an honest look at yourself, I think you have a chance to grow".

At the other end of the deliberate reflection, spectrum are more intimate moments where SWC reflected in solitude as Coach 1 put it "filling a whole row of notepads – you have to change this and that". Coach 3 described how this process had evolved over the years from "just a piece of paper where I used to jot down thoughts after the game, to a template with key headings that allow me to be very clinical about my reflections and analyses".

Unconscious reflection

In addition to deliberate reflection, some SWC discussed the importance of unconscious or incidental reflection and learning. Coach 3 provided the best example of this in practice discussing its never-ending nature:

Reflection is something almost automatic, something you do at moments … when you are alone, rarely a formal process, when you are alone with your memories, with your analysis, even unconsciously or involuntarily certain situations or things you have lived through come to mind. It is a fundamental process, but not necessarily structured or voluntary, or formalised. Reflection is something that is always there.

In summary, SWC engaged in a constant process of self-reflection consciously and unconsciously. Reflection was used to evaluate and improve athlete/team performance, but also to raise awareness of the gaps in knowledge or practical competence. Coaches reflected almost unconsciously during learning episodes to accommodate new knowledge and more deliberately as part of a daily training and performance-based routine to identify areas for improvement. Reflection was also central to raising the coaches' level of self-awareness about their typical behaviours and ways of dealing with events and people. This more intimate reflection, focused on the coach, was rarely highly structured nor supported by a professional mentor or coach. At times, however, this process was aided by a critical friend or long-time personal mentor.

A summary of the findings is presented in Table 3.1.

What did we learn about SWC learning journeys?

In this chapter, we discussed the learning experiences of SWC across the span of their careers. First, SWC underscored the significance of their pre-coaching experiences in shaping their coaching praxis. In line with previous research, the opportunities afforded by their own athletic careers were noted (Currie & Oates-Wilding, 2012; Rynne & Mallett, 2012). As a novel finding, however, SWCs emphasised the influence of specific characteristics of their early and proximal developmental environments such as family and community. This finding is consistent with other consultancy work we have conducted in the Australian context within McAdams' three-layered understanding of the person. These influential pre-coaching experiences were foundational to their ensuing learning journeys and specifically how they differentially engaged with formal, non-formal, and informal learning opportunities across their careers.

With regards to formal learning opportunities, SWC were found to be highly qualified both in relation to academic qualifications as well as coaching certificates and awards. They described formal learning opportunities as foundational for their subsequent learning and development (Carter & Bloom, 2009; Mallett et al., 2016; Sherwin, Campbell & Mcintyre, 2017). Notwithstanding the above, SWC indicated that formal opportunities needed to be founded upon and combined with practical, authentic coaching experiences to yield maximum outcomes for learners (Nash & Sproule, 2009; Olusoga et al., 2012). Notably, SWC spoke about the need to diversify the curriculum of formal opportunities to incorporate non-traditional topics relevant to high-performance coaching such as

TABLE 3.1 Summary of learning opportunities of SWC and their nature and impact

Pre-coaching experiences	Formal learning as a springboard	Non-formal learning as a check and challenge	Informal learning as most powerful and lasting	Internal learning as a catalyst
Early dev environments • Families' occupations, values, and settings • Early socialisation into the sport **Own athletic career** • Knowledge of the sport techniques and tactics • Knowledge of coaching methods • Knowledge of leadership and management	• Builds knowledge baseline • Supports sense-making • Useful for life lessons • Must be practically delivered and applied • Combined with real coaching experiences • Higher value of tertiary qualifications • Relevance of non-sport qualifications • Importance of broadening the curriculum	• High engagement in self-driven learning • Fuelled by personal dispositions • Serves to check, challenge, and fine-tune • Sourcing more experienced coaches • Building broad coach learning networks • Can be facilitated by: 　• Mentor 　• Knowledge translator	**On-the-job learning** • Influential • Learn from mistakes • Value of a broad range of experiences • Varies between high- and low-profile early jobs • Builds repertoire of options • Enhanced by formal and non-formal education • Requires purposeful and incidental reflection • Mentor support helpful **Peer learning** • Enjoyable • Source of new knowledge • Supports on the job learning • Importance of cross-sport learning • Not typically led by organisations but by coaches • Must be at right level • Hindered by culture of secrecy (contested nature of coaching) • Direct and indirect forms • Danger of copy/pasting • Local learning networks (own staff and athletes)	**Conscious/deliberate** • Broad range • Post-performance debriefs • Daily and ongoing • Intimate moments • Serves as performance and coach improvement • Enhances formal, non-formal, and informal learning • Raises self-awareness • Focused on future need • Draw learning from negatives • Typically unsupported or supported by critical friend **Unconscious/incidental** • Non-stop • Non-structured

organisational psychology and business management (inter- and intra-personal knowledge and competences). There seem to be opportunities for HPC education and development programmes to include more psycho-social elements in the curriculum.

In relation to non-formal learning, SWC reported the value of these opportunities as a regular opportunity to affirm and challenge one's knowledge, practice, and performance. Moreover, novel findings from our study revealed how SWC, who were deemed to be avid consumers of these types of opportunities, reported strong agency and intentionality. SWC, fuelled by an individual thirst for knowledge and personal development, were proactive in creating personal learning opportunities. While acknowledging the role that organisations may have in fostering coach development, SWC were agentic in initiating many learning opportunities. Identifying and recruiting coaches that demonstrate this commitment to learning, and the agentic power to realise it may be a *condition-sine-qua-non* for those working in high-performance sport.

Coaches also highlighted the significance of building broad coaching networks to facilitate learning (Rynne, Mallett & Tinning, 2006, 2010). SWC advocated for the central role of peer learning in the workplace setting as an enjoyable, never-ending source of new knowledge and ideas. Notably, SWC highlighted the possibilities afforded by multisport environments such as National Institutes of Sport (Rynne, et al., 2006) as well as the key role of internal local networks comprised of coaches and athletes within a particular single sport team or setting. Organically, and perhaps even systematically, exploiting the advantages of this local and internal knowledge networks seems to be worth pursuing.

Furthermore, SWC emphasised the role of informal learning as most powerful and lasting. Specifically, on the job learning was proposed as inevitably the most prevalent source of learning for coaches (Allen & Shaw, 2009; Mallett et al., 2016; Nash & Sproule, 2009). Significantly, the SWC encouraged younger coaches to gain as wide a range of experiences in the field as possible across participation domains, ages, genders, and even countries to build a broad repertoire of coaching skills. Coaches also indicated the value of spending time in less profile jobs as "laboratories for learning" their craft and, again, the value of the support that can be offered by suitable mentors. Akin to the player-loan system in professional team sport, a coach-loan equivalent may be something to consider by organisations trying to improve their succession planning.

Finally, SWC stressed the vital character of internal learning as a catalyst to maximise personal development and improve performance (e.g., Mallett et al., 2016). Two different types were identified, namely, conscious, or deliberate self-reflection (Cruz, 2014), and unconscious or incidental reflection. With regards to the former, SWC identified a broad range of instances of self-reflection, from relatively casual, low-level forms of analysis to comprehensive regular debriefs at times supported by professional mentors or selected critical friends. Another significant finding was the high level of importance of the role of mentors and knowledge translators to facilitate and accelerate learning "on-the job" and capitalise on deliberate self-reflection moments (Carter & Bloom, 2009; Fairhurst, Bloom & Harvey, 2017). Likewise, coaches talked about the pervasiveness of unconscious self-reflections, a kind of *white noise* that went unnoticed yet had a profound impact on coaches' learning. Overall, SWC portrayed self-reflection as central to raising their self-awareness, and, in turn, seeking and/or maximising other learning opportunities.

What does this mean for those supporting HPC education and development?

Based on the previous analysis and conclusions and building on our previous work (Mallett & Lara-Bercial, 2016) we would like to propose the following recommendations.

Firstly, SWC are typically highly educated people, often holding the top level of qualification provided by their federations as well as higher education degrees. Organisations supporting young HPC should encourage, facilitate, and support engagement in formal education. SWC stated, however, that they were not supportive of "token coach education" and that formal and non-formal development opportunities should be carefully thought out and pitched at the right level for the coach, and where possible individualised.

Second, SWC emphasised the pivotal role of peer learning in affirming and challenging their existing knowledge and practices. Therefore, coach developers are encouraged to find ways to enhance these opportunities where possible. Consistent with this notion of peer learning are several features currently in some coach development programmes including regular informal coach gatherings, peer observations, buddy with another coach, and study visits to other sport and non-sport settings. All these learning opportunities have the potential to contribute to coach development.

Third, SWC emphasised the importance of practically oriented learning, where knowledge is consistently translated into practical application and contextualised to authentic coaching problems. Therefore, we encourage those who design the curriculum for federation and university coaching courses to provide coaches with time, opportunities, and support to take stock of current knowledge, digest new knowledge, and look for ways to translate it into their practical contexts and problems. Individual and guided self-reflection appears critical. In a way, those developing HPC should make explicit attempts to blend formal and informal learning in seamless ways. For instance, through the careful design of problem-based learning tasks that require the application of a recently acquired knowledge base to a specific and real situation the coach is trying to resolve.

Fourth, in connection with the above, it is suggested that coach development be embedded in the reality of the job and appropriately supported via a mentor, a "more capable" assistant, peer groups, and social networks. Where appropriate, learning in and through coaching work could be facilitated by a "coach loan" system similar to that of professional teams. Emerging HPC could be "loaned out" to other organisations or countries where the coach could "cut his/her teeth" and learn on the job until they are ready to come back to the institution of origin. This could contribute to develop accountability and accelerate learning.

Finally, SWC highlighted the importance of self-reflection to maximise and accelerate learning. We would thus recommend that opportunities and mechanisms to increase the self-reflective ability of emerging HPC should be regularly built into formal, non-formal, and informal learning situations. A broad range of different options should be provided, including post-event debriefs, learning journals, checklists, self-assessment surveys, 360° feedback, facilitated reflection exercises, and the use of "critical friends".

In summary, the investigation of SWC's learning footprint reveals the idiosyncratic, individualised, and stage-dependant nature of coach learning, yet highlights key points of commonality that will allow coaches and coach developers to maximise development. In Chapter 4, we complement the coaches' learning narrative by delving into the SWC's career pathways. In doing so, we will explore the major steps that took these coaches from the time before they even considered becoming coaches to the pinnacle of their respective sports.

Note

1 Eshach (2007) defines formal learning as learning that follows a set curriculum, is formally assessed, and leads to some form of accreditation. Non-formal learning is defined as intentional, yet sitting outside of formal education, having a flexible curriculum, being non-assessed, and not leading to formal accreditation. Finally, informal learning is proposed as non-intentional, arising from our daily interactions with the environment and those within it. Alternatively, Moon (2004) places the focus on whether the learning is mediated or not. Mediated learning is facilitated by another person or a specific medium. In coaching terms, it would incorporate courses and awards, clinics and seminars, e-learning, and formal mentoring. By contrast, unmediated learning is initiated by the learner who seeks information but decides what is to be learnt and how. Examples of this in coaching include observing other coaches, reading books on a particular subject, or casual conversations with other coaches. Finally, Moon also acknowledges the existence of 'internal learning' through conscious – deliberate – and unconscious – incidental – reflection on our lived experiences.

References

Allen, J. B., & Shaw, S. (2009). Women coaches' perceptions of their sport organizations' social environment: Supporting coaches' psychological needs? *The Sport Psychologist*, *23*, 346–366.

Australian Institute of Sport (2021). *National High Performance Coach Development Strategy.* Camberra: AIS.

Blackett, A. D., Evans, A. B., & Piggott, D. (2018). "Active" and "Passive" Coach Pathways: Elite Athletes' Entry Routes Into High-Performance Coaching Roles, *International Sport Coaching Journal, 5*(3), 213–226. DOI:10.1123/iscj.2017-0053

Blackett, A. D., Evans, A., & Piggott, D. (2017). Why 'the best way of learning to coach the game is playing the game': Conceptualising 'fast-tracked' high-performance coaching pathways. *Sport, Education and Society, 22*(6), 744–758. DOI:10.1080/135 73322.2015.1075494

Carter, A. D., & Bloom, G. A. (2009). Coaching knowledge and success going beyond athletic experiences. *Journal of Sport Behavior, 32,* 419–437.

Cassidy, T. G., Potrac, P., & Jones, R. L. (2015). *Understanding sports coaching: The pedagogical, social, and cultural foundations of coaching practice (3rd ed.).* Routledge. doi: 10.4324/9780203797952

Chan, J. T., & Mallett, C. J. (2011). The value of emotional intelligence for high performance coaching. *International Journal for Sport Science and Coaching, 6,* 315–328.

Council of the European Union (2020). *Conclusions of the Council and of the Representatives of the Governments of the Member States on Empowering coaches by enhancing opportunities to acquire skills and competences.* Brussels: Council of the European Union.

Cruz, A. (2014). The coaching behaviours and philosophy of high performance secondary school basketball coaches. *Asian Journal of Physical Education & Recreation, 20*(1), 21–38.

Currie, J. L., & Oates-Wilding, S. (2012). Reflections on a dream: Towards an understanding of factors Olympic coaches attribute to their success. *Reflective Practice, 13*(3), 425–438. DOI: 10.1080/14623943.2012.670106

English Premier League (2020). *Elite coaching plan.* London: The English Premier League.

Erickson, K., Côté, J., & Fraser-Thomas, J. (2007). Sport experiences, milestones, and educational activities associated with high-performance coaches' development. *The Sport Psychologist, 21,* 302–316.

Eshach, H. (2007). Bridging in-school and out-of-school learning: Formal, non-formal, and informal education. *Journal of Science Education & Technology, 16*(2), 171–190. DOI:10.1007/s10956-006-9027-1

Fairhurst, K. E., Bloom, G. A., & Harvey, W. J. (2017). The learning and mentoring experiences of Paralympic coaches. *Disability & Health Journal, 10,* 240–246.

Galvan, H., Fyall, G., & Culpan, I. (2012). High-performance cricket coaches' perceptions of an educationally informed coach education programme. *Asia-Pacific Journal of Health, Sport and Physical Education, 3*(2), 123–140. DOI: 10.1080/18377122.2012. 700692

Gould, D., Guinan, D., Greenleaf, C., & Chung, Y. (2002). A survey of U.S. Olympic coaches: Variables perceived to have influenced athlete performances and coach effectiveness. *The Sport Psychologist, 16,* 229–250.

He, C., Trudel, P., & Culver, D. M. (2018). Actual and ideal sources of coaching knowledge of elite Chinese coaches. *International Journal of Sports Science & Coaching, 13*(4), 496–507. 10.1177/1747954117753727

Irwin, G., Hanton, S., & Kerwin, D. (2004) Reflective practice and the origins of elite coaching knowledge. *Reflective Practice, 5*(3), 425–442. DOI:10.1080/1462394042 000270718

Jiménez-Sáiz, S. L., Lorenzo-Calvo, A., & Ibañez-Godoy. (2008). Development of expertise in Spanish elite basketball coaches. *International Journal of Sport Science*, 5(17), 19–32.

Lara-Bercial, S., & Bales, J. (2022). The challenge of doing coach education and development in the 21st century: Past, present, and future trends. In K. Petry, & J. de Jong (Eds.), *Education in sport and physical activity: Future directions and global perspectives* (pp. 11–23). Routledge. doi: 10.4324/9781003002666

Lara-Bercial, S., & Mallett, C. J. (2016). The practices and developmental pathways of professional and Olympic serial winning coaches. *International Sport Coaching Journal*, 3(1), 221–239. DOI: 10.1123/iscj.2016-0083

Lara-Bercial, S., North, J., Bales, J., Petrovic, L., & Calvo, G. (2022). International Council for Coaching Excellence position statement: Professionalisation of sport coaching as a global process of continuous improvement. *International Sport Coaching Journal*, 9(2), 157–160. doi: 10.1123/iscj.2021-0097

Lyle, J. W., & Cushion, C. (2017). *Sport coaching concepts: A framework for coaching practice.* Routledge.

Lynch, M., & Mallett, C. J. (2006). Becoming a successful high performance track and field coach. *Modern Athlete and Coach*, 22, 15–20.

Mallett, C. J. (2010). High performance coaches' careers and communities. In J. Lyle, & C. Cushion (Eds.), *Sports coaching: Professionalism and practice* (pp. 119–133). London: Elsevier.

Mallett, C. J., Rynne, S. B., & Billett, S. (2016). Valued learning experiences of early career and experienced high performance coaches. *Physical Education and Sport Pedagogy*, 21(1), 89–104. DOI: 10.1080/17408989.2014.892062

Moon, J. A. (2004). *A handbook of reflective and experiential learning: Theory and practice.* Routledge.

Nash, C. S., & Sproule, J. (2009). Career development of expert coaches. *International Journal of Sports Science & Coaching*, 4(1), 121–138.

Nelson, L. J., Cushion, C. J., & Potrac, P. (2006). Formal, nonformal and informal coach learning: A holistic conceptualisation. *International Journal of Sports Science & Coaching*, 1(3), 247–259. 10.1260/174795406778604627.

Occhino, J., Mallett, C., & Rynne, S. (2013). Dynamic social networks in high performance football coaching. *Physical Education and Sport Pedagogy*, 18(1), 90–102.

Olusoga, P., Maynard, I., Hays, K., & Butt, J. (2012). Coaching under pressure: A study of Olympic coaches. *Journal of Sports Sciences*, 30, 229–239.

Parkes, J. (2018). *Coach as performer: Coach emotion, coping, and the coach-athlete-performance relationship.* PhD Thesis, School of Human Movement and Nutrition Sciences, The University of Queensland. 10.14264/uql.2018.687

Reade, I., Rodgers, W., & Spriggs, K. (2008). New ideas for high performance coaches: A case study of knowledge transfer in sport science. *International Journal of Sports Science & Coaching*, 3(3), 335–354.

Rossi, T., Rynne, S., & Rabjohns, M. (2016). Moving forwards with the aim of going backwards fast: High-performance rowing as a learning environment. *Physical Education and Sport Pedagogy*, 21(1), 55–68. DOI: 10.1080/17408989.2015. 1043254

Rynne, S. (2014). 'Fast track' and 'traditional path' coaches: Affordances, agency and social capital. *Sport, Education and Society, 19*(3), 299–313. doi:10.1080/13573322.2012. 670113

Rynne, S. B., & Mallett, C. J. (2012). Understanding the work and learning of high performance coaches. *Physical Education and Sport Pedagogy, 17*, 507–523.

Rynne, S., Mallett, C. J., & Tinning, R. (2006). High performance sport coaching: Institutes of Sport as sites for learning. *International Journal of Sport Science & Coaching, 1*, 223–234.

Rynne, S. B., Mallett, C. J., & Tinning, R. (2010). Workplace learning of high performance sports coaches. *Sport, Education and Society, 15*(3), 315–330.

Sherwin, I., Campbell, M., & Macintyre, I. (2017). Talent development of high performance coaches in team sports in Ireland. *European Journal of Sport Science, 17*(3), 271–278. doi: 10.1080/17461391.2016.1227378

Stoszkowski, J., & Collins, D. (2016). Sources, topics and use of knowledge by coaches, *Journal of Sports Sciences, 34*(9), 794–802. DOI: 10.1080/02640414.2015.1072279

Trudel, P., Milestetd, M., & Culver, D. M. (2020). What the empirical studies on sport coach education programs in Higher Education have to reveal: A review. *International Sport Coaching Journal, 7*(1), 61–73.

Trudel, P., Gilbert, W., & Rodrigue, F. (2016). The journey from competent to innovator: Using appreciative inquiry to enhance high performance coaching. *AI Practitioner, 18*(2), 40–46. DOI: 10.12781/978-1-907549-27-4-5

UKCoaching (formerly Sports Coach UK) (2012). *Coach tracking study: A four-year study of coaching in the UK.* UK Coaching.

Werthner, P., & Trudel, P. (2006). A new theoretical perspective for understanding how coaches learn to coach. *The Sport Psychologist, 20*(2), 198–212. DOI:10.1123/tsp.2 0.2.198

4

THE CAREER PATHWAYS OF SERIAL WINNING COACHES

In the previous chapter, we discussed the learning preferences and experiences of SWC across the span of their careers to date. To complement these SWC learning experiences, we provide insights into how these outliers climbed to the top of the sporting tree. Specifically, we focus this chapter on their pathways into and through coaching. To put the SWC personal histories into context, the following paragraphs provide a brief overview of the existing coach education and development literature in relation to the developmental pathways of high-performance coaches (HPC).

How do coaches become high-performance coaches?

HPC have reported unique journeys in their pursuit of a career in elite sport (e.g., Carter & Bloom, 2009; Christensen, 2014). Notwithstanding this uniqueness, researchers have identified a series of conditions that, although not applicable to every coach, describe some typical pathways and key events leading to coaching work in high-performance contexts.

Indeed, HPC have characteristically been (i) involved with their sport from an early age; (ii) socialised into that sport by a family member; (iii) competed in the same sport at a high level; and (iv) started coaching, or preparing to coach, whilst still competing (e.g., Erickson, Côté & Fraser-Thomas, 2007; Nash & Sproule, 2009). Of course, this is not the only pathway. Previous high-level athletic experiences, although very important for many, are not a conditio-sine-qua-non for coaching success (Carter & Bloom, 2009). Nevertheless, previous research shows several developmental characteristics linked to coaches' own athletic careers, or lack thereof.

DOI: 10.4324/9781003427292-6

HPC who had not been elite competitors were motivated by their perform-ance shortcomings (e.g., Carter & Bloom, 2009; Mallett & Coulter, 2016), had been influenced by close relatives (typically parents) and/or coaches to take up coaching (Sherwin, Campbell & Macintyre, 2017), and tended to hold high-level coaching qualifications and higher education degrees both in sport and other fields (Carter & Bloom, 2009; Erickson, Côté & Fraser-Thomas, 2007; Mallett, Rynne & Billett, 2016). In addition, these coaches typically served long coaching apprenticeships in grassroots sport before reaching the echelons of high per-formance (Rynne, 2014).

In contrast, HPC who had been professional athletes had spent most of their coaching career working with youth and senior elite performers (Erickson, Côté & Fraser-Thomas, 2007; Lynch & Mallett, 2006; Watts & Cushion, 2017) and were recruited for coaching roles shortly after finishing their athletic career, typically in the same programme they had competed, and without having to undergo a rig-orous selection process (Blackett, Evans & Piggott, 2018; Rynne, 2014). Within this group, there appeared to be a chasm between those who had proactively prepared for their transition into coaching well before they finished competing, and those who had taken up coaching in a more reactive manner after retirement (Blackett, Evans & Piggott, 2018; Rynne, Mallett & Tinning, 2006, 2010). From this perspective, the developmental pathway of what Blackett and colleagues termed "active coaches", those who had prepared to coach long before retiring, were akin to the more "traditional pathway" followed by non-elite athletes described by Rynne (2014) – they obtained their coaching qualifications in advance and were actively coaching before the end of their athletic career.

In sum, the career pathways of HPC, especially those who were not elite athletes, appear to be marked by early socialisation into the sport, precocious and anticipative forays into coaching, the acquisition of high-level sport qualifica-tions and tertiary degrees, and long apprenticeships. Former elite athletes cum HPC appear to have shorter and less scrutinised transitions into coaching than their non-elite counterparts yet share similar socialisation narratives.

Considering the above literature, we examined the career trajectories of this select group of individuals. This investigation into the pathways of these SWC was informed by data collected through demographic information, from a spe-cific section of the semi-structured interviews that included the life story interview.

What do the career pathways of serial winning coaches look like?

The career journeys of SWC in this study were highly idiosyncratic and personal. However, within this uniqueness and inimitability, several relatively common factors and developmental steps were identified. These elements offer a composite blueprint and representation of a typical journey of a SWC. While attempting to create a broad nomothetic account, importantly, we offer a glimpse of the variability inherent to the journey of 17 different coaches across 10 sports and 10 countries. First, a set of perceived pre-conditions for success are presented. This is followed by details of the various stages in the pathway from pre- and novice coach to Serial Winner. Then we provide additional considerations specific to the female coaches in this study (albeit small in sample size), before concluding with a synopsis of the overall feel for the journey in the words of the SWCs.

Pre-conditions for success

Data from the life story interviews revealed several personal dispositions that shaped their unique trajectories in coaching. While we are not advocating that to be a serial winning coach you require all dispositions, it seems that these SWCs possess several qualities associated with repeated success across contexts.

Leadership qualities

SWC consistently spoke about what they described as leadership qualities (e.g., knowledgeable, vocal) and opportunities for leading others that emerged from an early age and from the start of their coaching career. As previously reported by Coach 1:

> I believe I have a defining trait, one I already had as a player. I have also been a player-manager, a captain … I have always been in leading positions, I was class representative at school, too … I always did things like that, it's in me somehow. And on the pitch, I was a kind of a big mouth too, and somehow the others went along with it. It was all there.

These interests and opportunities for leading were often formalised through on-the-field coaching responsibilities or as player-assistant coaches. They reported that teammates and coaches frequently sought their help and counsel in matters relating to the sport and current performance. As explained by Coach 4, these constant "quasi-coaching" interactions led to stepping into formal coaching in a scaffolded and seamless way:

> My coaches knew that I was the player that understood more than anyone, [they] talked [to me] about tactical things […] And my teammates also understood this. I played for the national team with the best players in Europe […] and all of them were younger than me, and all of them, they would come to me to talk about tactical things. So [when I became a coach] I was really ready.

Indeed, these leadership qualities seemed to acknowledge the importance of other perceiving that you "know things" (e.g., tactical nous).

Early desire to help others and coach

Generally, SWC reported a clarity of purpose towards coaching and improving the performance of others, initially as players. Coach 7 reported this passion for helping teammates:

> I was always busy improving others […] In gym class I was that one who would [help] someone who was not able to do a somersault. I am a teacher, I am an educationalist, people interest me. I want to help people. That is just in you or it is not and I think that is a very important basis for being successful, to be a good coach.

Coach 4 described it as an early realisation that he wanted to be a coach in the future:

> [When I was] 18 years old, I started to write after every practice what we did […] and as a player I went to many coaching clinics, and coaches are like 'what are you doing here?' I didn't want to say to them that one day I would like to be a coach.

Similarly, Coach 6, a non-elite athlete, spoke of her early start coaching: "I started coaching when I was in grade eight, I coached right through till I finished university".

Identified as a potential coach

In addition, SWC spoke of the significance of someone, typically a coach or teacher, encouraging them to coach because they saw some potential in that vocational role. This encouragement was sufficient to ignite a small fire to become a coach as well as to provide the internal motivation and confidence for that kind of work. Coach 7 recalled his experience with a physical education teacher: "I was scouted fairly soon, just like for example my gym teacher in high school pushed me in the right direction to say: You should become a gym teacher, that fits you". Coach 14 stated how this identification made him feel he "had a responsibility to pass on what [he] had learned. I felt it was my responsibility to pass on all that I knew". This interest in wanting to help others shows some genuine care for others. Notably, for Coach 5, beyond initial identification as a potential coach, there was also a moment early in his career that confirmed he was on the right track:

> I was 18 or 19 years old myself, I think […] this master coach was watching that game by chance. During that game I made two important comments towards my players, and after the game he came to me and said 'that was

If you get to a point where you think you have the absolute truth, you tend not to question yourself. On the one hand, this gives you a sense of security, which is a positive, but on the other hand, I am also curious, I want to know what other things can be done, what works for others, and I like to keep a certain amount of doubt in my brain about what I do.

In contrast, SWC were also aware of the tension between constantly looking for new and better ways to do things (adaptation and innovation) and the need to maintain their perceived persona, ways of working, and a sense of stability and purpose (being true to who they are and what has been successful in the past). Coach 16 was cautious about this tension: "I'm open minded and I'm always looking for what others are doing well, but I also know what I do well. I like to integrate new things into my work, but never fully change my work". This comment suggests some "tweaking" rather than wholesale changes. Along the same lines, Coach 5 commented: "I like to keep my ideas fresh, but it does not mean you should implement everything you hear or see, there you have to make choices, but you should always keep looking for [new] things". These SWC seemed sagacious in how they did and did not play with the new understandings and clearly informed consumers of knowledge and its potential application (and consequences) in their context.

Serial insecurity

A final facilitator for SWC in attaining and sustaining their success was what we called "*Serial Insecurity*" (Lara-Bercial & Mallett, 2016). Over the course of the interviews, SWC regularly presented themselves as living on a knife's edge between a strong belief in their abilities ("*Grounded Self-Belief*") and a persistent state of doubt about whether they were good enough for the job ("*Reasonable Self-Doubt*").

The SWC's self-belief was grounded on some key elements. First and foremost, these coaches trusted their own capacity to work harder and smarter than others. Coach 2 put it in no uncertain terms:

I tell people all the time 'I'm not the smartest guy in the whole world; I have to work at it. I feel better when I work, I get confidence when I work and I know I'm prepared'. When you go to the Olympic games and you know you've been through major competitions and you've had success, it's like going to an exam – you're prepared and you know. I don't feed my family on hope; I feed my family on knowledge. I want to know I've done everything and I feel terrible when I feel like the other coach outworked me or out-prepared me, I can't stand that. I can't stand that anyone would do more in a summer than I would.

Moreover, despite the episodes of self-doubt, previous success as a coach contributed to SWC's perceptions of high confidence. For instance, Coach 14 described his complete belief in his ability to improve athletes and produce winners:

> Of course I'm confident in what I do and I know what I can do—if the material is there I can produce a winner; I'm confident that even if the guys don't have the material to win, I'm confident that they will respect [me] and when they fail, they don't blame me […] I'm arrogant enough to think that I don't know of anybody who knows more than I do about how to win. I'm not talking about all of the sciences of the sport; I'm talking about winning.

Previous success was also important to create a sense of invincibility around athletes, a way of self-presentation that instils respect and perhaps fear into the opposition:

> Once you are on a roll, it's success that breeds success. You know confidence breeds confidence. And that's the way you've got to think all the time, you know what I mean. And you then get yourself, people, other teams when you go to events, other teams just look up to you they say 'Oh, there's [COUNTRY], they are bloody good'. And psychologically you've got them where you want them. Because they know you are good. And so straight away you've got them, psychologically you've got them. You're ahead of the game. And it's about being there and the way you present yourself and the way you wait and the way you look, appearance and team gear and all the rest of it. It's that professionalism around the whole thing. (Coach 8)

Paradoxically, this *"Grounded Self-Belief"* appeared to be hand in glove with a degree of *"Reasonable Self-Doubt"*. These ongoing oscillations between confidence and doubt over time enabled these SWC to remain hungry and modest. Coach 2 was the most prominent example of this phenomenon:

> I've been on a journey that in some ways has been driven a little bit by fear of not being good enough – I want to be great, I don't know why but I do. I don't want to be great last year; I want to be great this year […] I'm scared to death about next year. I'm scared we're going down – why? I don't want us going down on my watch. There are lots of reasons. It might even be partial egomania, but I love being great – I want to be good.

Although self-doubt might trigger a lack of coaches' and athletes' self-efficacy, especially at the big event, these SWC reported how it served as a motivational tool that protected against potential complacency and arrogance:

When you are the coach of a national team, you want to prove that they were right choosing you for that position and that you are able to perform with that team or athlete … So, when that happens and you win, you should make sure it does not turn into arrogance, that is a pitfall and the other pitfall is you stop being sharp, because you must stay sharp. That curiosity and keenness should absolutely stay present at all times. (Coach 5)

This humility was also echoed by Coach 7: "I am a worrier, and many other coaches I know are, they all are, because by consciously looking for that piece of insecurity, you focus yourself on the job". This self-doubt can trigger present-moment focus rather than looking back to mitigate against conceit. For this reason, he was very keen to avoid looking back on previous successes: "I think that when someone starts to enjoy his track record … That is why I do not want to see mine, I do not think that is interesting at all, that track record is far too heavy you see".

In summary, SWC highlighted the value of balancing self-confidence and self-doubt to foster present-moment focus and subsequently remain modest and humble about their coaching achievements throughout their long careers. Indeed, as the quote from Coach 11 might infer, SWC may spend more time in "reasonable self-doubt mode" which reinforces their desire in "becoming" better rather than "celebrating" their past achievements:

The other thing is that I look at some of my colleagues—and I think you will find a lot of the coaches that are probably interviewed probably—either have huge self-opinions of themselves or huge egos, and they actually believe that that's part of the formula. In other words, you have to believe in yourself, or you have to believe you're right, or you have to be pinning against the rest of the world to prove yourself. I actually think myself that … totally differently, I think that—and I'm not trying to be silly here—I think that I'm a pretty average guy of pretty average intelligence who just works hard. I actually come at my coaching profession fairly humbly and I think that's what allows me to be successful. Because I don't think that I know everything, I don't think that I'm better than someone else, I don't think that it's because of me the athletes have won. I don't ever think of myself that way, and because I think that way, I think that's the best way for me personally to continue to improve.

These SWC tended to share a series of pre-conditions for success that included a combination of the following: i) leadership qualities focused on wanting to influence others; ii) an early desire to help others and become a coach; iii) identified potential as a coach by others; iv) atonement for perceived failure as an athlete; v) an insatiable need to improve; and vi) we termed these oscillating episodes of self-belief and self-doubt, "Serial Insecurity". These are summarised in Table 4.1.

TABLE 4.1 Pre-conditions for success in SWC

Leadership qualities	Early desire to coach and help others	Identified as a potential coach	Unfulfilled athletic career	Insatiable need to improve	Serial insecurity
Recognised by coaches and teachers	Taking on supporting teammates	Encouraged by teachers or coaches to pursue coaching	Possessing sub-elite athletic talent	Constant need to know more	**Grounded self-belief**
Recognised by teammates	Early realisation of "gift to coach"	Critical moments of realisation of potential	Underachieving as an elite athlete	Fighting off complacency	Outwork opponents
In leadership positions at early age (i.e., class rep, team captain)	Early realisation of "desire to coach" and required steps		Missed opportunities	Balance between always looking for new things and staying within one's framework and philosophy	Cover all bases
Enjoyment of being the "on-field coach"	At times forced by negative circumstances (i.e., injury, lack of talent)		Forced retirement (i.e., injury, accident)		Built on previous success
					Reasonable self-doubt
					Driven by hate/fear of losing
					Not wanting to disappoint others
					Avoiding complacency
					Sharpening the focus

What are the key steps of the serial winning coaches journey to success?

We continually emphasise throughout this book that the developmental pathways and career journeys of SWC are idiosyncratic. In this section, however, we attempt to offer two broad but contrasting pathways of these SWC; those who enjoyed an elite athletic career, and those who had been lower-level athletes or had no athletic experience. As previously stated, in total, ten SWC were former international and/or professional athletes, six had competed at national level, and only one of them had no experience of competitive sport. The analysis of the data showed that the career journeys of SWC had been substantially shaped by their athletic careers, or lack of. These different paths shaped their differential journeys in myriad ways.

Elite athletes

Personal agency was a strong driver for these former elite players in pursuing their coaching careers. Nevertheless, they also acknowledged the benefits and opportunities afforded by their past as an elite athlete. Indeed, these former elite athletes and players were headhunted for high-performance coaching jobs before or immediately after the conclusion of their competitive careers, typically by their former clubs, or the countries they represented. Coach 4 is a typical case: "I was national team captain, about to lead the team into the European championships, and the night before we are due to travel, I got a phone call from my club asking me to coach the team next year – the only condition … that I stopped playing straight away. And I did". Coach 7 had a similar story: "I had no ambition to become a coach and then I was an elite sports coach immediately […] I was immediately a head coach […] I was immediately able to work towards the Olympic Games. I started in [YEAR] and I knew I would be at the Olympics four years later".

For some of these "fast-tracked" coaches (Rynne, 2014), there was a feeling of "right time-right place" (Coach 11). For instance, Coach 14 explained the serendipitous nature of his appointment:

> I was fortunate in that I was able to step straight into the top, I didn't go through the ranks of being a coach. It was a case of circumstance. When they couldn't find no one to [coach] it, they came to me. It wasn't because I was a good coach, I had not coached in any category. It was a move from athlete to coach because nobody else was interested, nobody else would do it. So, I stepped into it.

It is worthy of discussion if this pathway in more developed countries with established sporting systems will be the means to recruit in the future.

Anecdotally, this limited preparation for working in elite sport in many developed countries has been problematic. Perhaps coach developers have become more circumspect and prefer a longer apprenticeship.

In contrast, a proportion of former elite athletes, served longer coaching apprenticeships before arriving at the elite level. Coach 10 described his voyage from school coach to international coach:

> The national federation had an apprentice coaching scheme and they [...] asked me to do it. And then I went round the schools and did the talent identification programme, and it sort of led to [more] coaching. I coached one of them from finding her in the school to be world and Olympic champion over the next 8 years.

This coach also expressed his surprise and apprehension after being asked to take the job:

> And then there was a change in the women's coach at the [NATIONAL TRAINING CENTRE] in [YEAR] and they approached me to do it, and I was only 26 at the time. And so, I had to learn fast, my little legs couldn't keep up.

We make a further distinction in the coaching journey of these former elite athletes cum SWC between those who achieved success quickly and those who took longer to reach the top. Five coaches commenced their careers with early major successes. Achieving immediate success bought these coaches credit to make bold decisions in subsequent years, and ensured they were never short of coaching jobs. Coach 4's story is the epitome of this trajectory:

> In my first year we won the national title and the [EUROPEAN CLUB COMPETITION]. And this was with a bunch of kids. After that, every club in Europe wanted me to coach there, but I stayed at my club for another two years because I needed to get better, I wasn't ready to coach a big team.

Coach 11 shared a similar account: "So I was 26 years of age, never coached before, [just] retired from [SPORT], and I put four guys on the national team. So, I was invited to go along to the World Championships".

The journeys of other SWC, who experienced later success, contrast those who enjoyed immediate triumph. The delayed success of these SWC was consistent with the notion of a "journeyman", competent and reliable rather than outstanding in their early careers and their path to glory gradual over time. This steady progress towards SWC status was reflected in a comment from Coach 2:

It's been baby steps. It would start with how I got the opportunity to go to [CLUB]; well, I got that opportunity by going to grad school and by going and taking a year off and going to [COUNTRY] and becoming a player-coach, so I could have coach on my title. That to me, is how all the steps happened. No breakthrough moments, just baby steps all along.

Serendipitous opportunities and unexpected success were not uncommon stories amongst these SWC. Coach 7 spent time working in country that did not typically achieve international success. It was the unexpected success with those sub-elite athletes that facilitated his transition into the elite: "I actually came very close to winning Gold in [COUNTRY] and that got me noticed, and also gave me the confidence that I could do it in my own country". Conversely, Coach 8 explained how he was on the verge of losing his job when success came at the eleventh hour:

We were given this five-year plan, a five-year programme and at the end, I would be judged in the fifth year. And it's those boys [points at a picture on the wall] that did it [in the fifth year], and if it wasn't for those boys, I wouldn't be sat here talking to you today. That's how crazy it all is.

A notable exception within the elite-athlete group is Coach 15, who after his athletic career in the sport, started a second career in a different sport to then return to coach his original discipline.

After I finished competing, I did other things in [OTHER SPORT], I set up my team, [even though] this was more for recreation. Luckily, because most of the time you go from coach to athlete with no transition. Without experiencing life to some extent, the constraints and the independence. In our sport everything is organised, we're well surrounded and our athletes get bed and board and their laundry done for them. They have never experienced moments in a career when they have to manage themselves, fund a project, find a coach or coach themselves. This is a shortcoming in some ways. So, I did all that with [OTHER SPORT], and I learned something through it that helped me become a successful coach.

These serendipitous pathways provide unique learning opportunities that necessitate personal agency to impact future coaching praxis. The pathways of the former elite athletes who became SWC had somewhat unique journeys as they transitioned into coaching and subsequently became SWC.

Non-elite athletes and non-athletes

For non-elite athletes and non-athletes, their journeys tended to involve an early start into coaching, and a somewhat lengthy apprenticeship spent coaching in less competitive environments, including junior sport and lower-league senior sport, or being an assistant coach in a major league. Along this pathway, a slow yet continual progression with instances of success allowed these coaches to progress towards high-performance coaching positions over time. For instance, Coach 6 (female) described a 20-year journey to elite sport, and the benefits it presented:

> I started coaching when I was at grade eight, so I was 14 years old. I coached a wide variety of sports, which I think is really important. I coached softball, baseball, hockey, track and field, basketball, volleyball. Every one of those sports brings forth a different type of athlete, a different type of environment. So, I feel like that helped me a lot in reading people and getting to know them. I coached right through till I finished university in terms of all those different sports. [Then] I did ten years as a recreation director, so had a whole lot of laboratory where I was working with and measuring coaches and I also was coaching. Coaching a wide variety of groups and teams and that type of thing so, I mean that all of those things and that was up until my early 30s that that happened. I didn't coach full-time as you will, as my full-time job until 20 years after I started coaching.

There seems to be potential merit in coaching multiple sports to better understand self and others and focus on coaching praxis.

Coach 3 had a similar experience with a 10-year apprenticeship, which culminated with him winning a major trophy in his first season as a professional coach:

> I got injured at 18 and started coaching in the youth programme for a couple of years, they then asked me to be an assistant coach with the seniors, well more like a ball boy, but I got to learn a lot, and then I took over my first head coaching job, and after a couple of years I got the chance to be an assistant coach in the top division. When the head coach left after three years they asked me to head coach at 28 and I was lucky to win at the first time of trying.

For some coaches, however, it was a case of coaching senior athletes from the beginning but having to demonstrate how they could achieve results in lower leagues/competitions. Coach 9 described his journey from lower club to the national team: "I started coaching in a bad club, but quickly showed that I could make people better and that got me other opportunities". Similarly, Coach 5 explained how, even though it was a quick process, he had to prove himself in the lower leagues: "The first year that I coached at the semi-pro level, my team won the title. A nice achievement, also a milestone, winning the title and the year after that the same team won the title again, that had never happened before. My initial period as a coach went very fast, that period was extremely successful" (Coach 5).

TABLE 4.2 Differentiated career journeys of SWC based on their athletic career

Elite athlete	*Non-elite/non-athlete*
Straight into high-performance coaching	Early start into coaching
Post career or post critical incident	Progression through the ranks from
Targeted by organisation	junior to senior sport
Right Time – Right Place	Progression from assistant coach to
Immediate success vs slow yet consistent	head coach
progression	Typically with instances of success
Served apprenticeship	leading to new positions
Small gradual steps	
Away from the limelight	
In less pressurised environments	
Unexpected success	
In a different context (non-sport or not	
their sport)	

These longer apprenticeships seem to pay dividends for these SWC and perhaps reflect their patience, commitment, and passion for coaching work. Moreover, success at all levels of coaching seems necessary for others to notice that you can coach and subsequently seek to recruit for other coaching jobs. All pathways provide unique opportunities to develop coaching craft and should be valued for providing different perspectives in how to get the best from self and others.

A summary of key elements of these distinctive journeys is presented in Table 4.2.

How did serial winning coaches make decisions about their career progression? The role of opportunity and risk

Noteworthy were the SWC's decision-making processes related to their career development. Two prominent features that emerged were an acute sense of opportunity and the ability to be comfortable with calculated levels of risk. Characteristically, these coaches' journeys were marked by a combination of being highly opportunistic as well as risk-tolerant, and probably playing the 'long game'. Opportunities had either been presented to them, a typical scenario for the former elite athletes, or had been *'manufactured'* by them through hard work and ingenuity. Perhaps more significantly though, when these opportunities manifested themselves, SWC had demonstrated a high degree of readiness, which in the main, meant they capitalised on opportunities to progress their careers. They willingly seized these opportunities with both hands again emphasising the importance of personal agency and their striving to be the best.

An example of this opportunism and risk-taking was the acceptance of coaching jobs that appeared to everyone else as potential 'poison chalices' but for some of these SWC they were challenging opportunities worthy of risk. For example, Coach 9 said of his early career choices: "I didn't want to be an assistant coach, I picked to go into a very bad club, because I thought 'I want to be a front line coach' [head coach]". Coach 2 had a similar view:

> I had a great career job [at a low level college], but instead of just being comfortable there, I was comfortable enough to take a risk with the next opportunity. I tell my kids all the time 'you have to risk yourself and put yourself out there'.

Coach 6 even left a well-paid job to take a full-time coaching position on a third of her previous salary: "But that's what you do if you want to be a coach. I couldn't pass on this opportunity".

Remarkably, this risk-taking was not dampened by the SWC's success. On the contrary, these coaches continued to take calculated risks even after becoming successful – a defining characteristic of some of these SWC. Coach 3, for instance, after winning a major trophy in his first year as a coach, rejected multiple offers to go to bigger clubs because he did not feel ready to step up at that point:

> Of course, after the first year, after many titles, they start to call me, many teams in Europe. I decided to stay one more year, to work with him [mentor assistant coach], because I understand that this is the best for me. I didn't care about the big clubs.

Likewise, Coach 15 highlighted the need to keep taking risks throughout one's career and to make the right decisions without compromising one's central beliefs:

> I believe I've taken risks and put my job on the line on several occasions. I did that fairly recently. The things that just about worked, I would have liked them to have worked better – but at the very least with sincerity and conviction, and I believe I kept my word overall. A coach cannot make decisions thinking about not losing their job, a coach has to make the decision that they think is right.

Coach 13 summarised this daring approach to career development neatly: "*This group of coaches [Serial Winners] are prepared to take the untrodden path, dare to be different, are risk takers and lateral thinkers*". It seems that there will always be some risk and serendipity in what coaching opportunities present at any time and place; however, these SWC were judicious in their decision-making appreciating the lack of certainty in outcomes but the challenge that comes with that uncertainty.

How did the journey differ for the female serial winners?

Despite many attempts to recruit multiple female SWC, the study included only two female coaches. Coach 6 coached a sport traditionally male-oriented, and typically dominated by male coaches. By contrast, Coach 16 came from a sport where female performers and coaches have been on an equal, if not higher, footing with their male counterparts for many decades. As a result, their career development journeys and experiences where significantly different.

Coach 16 did not feel her personal development or her career trajectory had been influenced by being a female. However, Coach 6 noted how, as a female coach operating in a male-oriented environment, she had encountered several additional challenges. These can be summarised into two main categories. First, she felt that she had always had to prove herself to the men in ways men themselves did not have to:

> I think being a woman in a male sport, there always had to be a good reason for my appointment. I had to be clearly better [than the men]. No-one in [sport] is going to think you are the expert when you are a woman.

Second, Coach 6 felt that as a female coach in a male-dominated sport, she had to bullet-proof herself against potential attacks from men wishing her to fail or to catch her out. This led to her becoming quite wary of sharing her feelings with those around her:

> People don't want to know their leader is weak. Or that they have weaknesses or that they're second guessing themselves or whatever [...] especially when you work with men, men don't, I mean exposing your weaknesses and saying that you need to improve in an area isn't well received with them.

As a result of these experiences, Coach 6 felt that to succeed as a woman in coaching "you just have got to have thick skin". It also highlights the lack of psychological safety in that environment, which is not conducive to thriving. Perhaps preferred "male" attributes are considered the "standard for good coaching". Male hegemony in many sports likely makes it more challenging for female coaches but hopefully over time this misuse of 'power' will abate.

How did these SWC make sense of their journeys in becoming a SWC?

Overall, there is a sense that all SWC were thoroughly prepared, showed resilience, opportunism, and serendipity in becoming a SWC. Of course, this is not to say that every coach who prepares thoroughly, overcomes difficulty and failure, creates their own opportunities, and takes purposeful risks will become a decorated coach. The combination of good fortune and opportunity was acknowledged by the coaches and played a significant part in their early success, yet they also stressed that purposeful and potentially risky career moves, together with sustained effort and learning, were pivotal in the longevity of their success. There are no shortcuts to becoming a SWC:

> Every opportunity I've had has been a dream opportunity so, it's been baby steps. Because I'd never played in the [major professional league], it took me a long time to get to the [major professional league] without ever knowing I was going there. (Coach 2)
>
> Nothing happens overnight, you don't become … from an amateur to a professional in terms of quality. One day you are an amateur and the next day you are a professional. It happens little by little, grain by grain, day by day, minute by minute, hour by hour". (Coach 14)
>
> There are no typical milestones in my coaching that had made me, because it's an on-going process, it's life. So, it's everyday improvement and this is what I believe in. (Coach 4)

The quotes of all three coaches above underscore the patience and commitment in developing one's craft and a lack of a clear pursuit to become highly successful at the elite level. They seemed more focused on becoming the best they could be in whatever coaching context.

What did we learn about SWC career pathways?

In this chapter, we have reported the idiosyncratic and idiographic accounts of career journeys of these SWC. This is an important finding. There is no single pathway in becoming a SWC. These coaches found unique ways to become a successful coach. Nonetheless, we identified several relatively common dispositional factors and trajectory points. This nomothetic approach complements the idiographic accounts to provide a more complete and nuanced understanding of the career journeys of these SWC.

SWC presented a series of pre-conditions for success. They typically possessed leadership qualities, which were recognised by teachers, coaches, and teammates and assigned them in positions of responsibility at an early age (e.g., Erickson, Côté & Fraser-Thomas, 2007; Sherwin, Campbell & Macintyre, 2017). They also exhibited an early desire to coach and help others and were cognisant of their special disposition and ability to coach. These elements led to them being identified, "earmarked", and persuaded to become coaches. Crucially, and as a novel finding, SWC also experienced critical moments which confirmed their coaching abilities and reassured them of their potential. Yet, perhaps most significantly, and a novel discovery, SWC reported unfulfilled athletic careers – a sense of not having fulfilled their performance aspirations and sporting potential – sometimes through forced retirement (i.e., injury, or a non-sport related accident); others through career mismanagement or missed opportunities (e.g., Olympic boycotts).

Furthermore, SWC demonstrated an insatiable desire to improve and know more than their competitors (Cruz, 2014; Occhino, Mallett & Rynne, 2013), coupled with an explicit yearning to mitigate against potential complacency and contentment (Olusoga et al., 2012). In this context, we were able to establish how a significant behavioural pattern of SWC was to deliberately find a functional balance between what has worked in the past (consistency and stability) and the need to innovate and take calculated risks. Finally, our study revealed novelty not previously described, a distinctive "state of mind" displayed by these coaches that we termed *Serial Insecurity* – episodic oscillations between a belief in their talent, knowledge, and capacity to succeed (*Grounded Self-Belief*), and a persistent fear of failure and of not being good enough (*Reasonable Self-Doubt*). These swings in confidence, far from debilitating, helped them to sharpen their focus daily and protect them against complacency and routine. This finding dispels the myth of the "great leader" as a "tower of strength", unfazed by the demands of the environment, and positions their performance as a recurring exercise of self-awareness and self-regulation to avoid both complacency and despair.

Unsurprisingly, early career coaches have an interest in the career journeys of others, especially in terms of their performance backgrounds as athletes, typically in the sport they coach – *How did they get there?* We found these journeys to be unique. Non-elite or non-athlete coaches typically had an early start into coaching due to their lack of success at higher levels of competition in their sport. Therefore, their journeys were typically marked by a steady progression through the rungs of the coaching ladder with key opportunities presenting themselves along the way, usually resolved successfully, and thus providing a steppingstone towards the next level of the coaching chain (e.g., Blackett, Evans & Piggott, 2018; Rynne, 2014). In contrast, elite athletes followed two different trajectories. Some of them served relatively long apprenticeships not too dissimilar to those of non-elite athletes or non-athletes. Notably, this allowed them to learn their trade incrementally, away from the pressure of high-stake positions, at times even away from their own sport with forays into other sports or the business world. In turn, some of the former elite athletes were specifically targeted by their organisation and transitioned into high-performance, high-profile jobs immediately post their athletic careers (e.g., Rynne, Mallett & Tinning, 2010). To many of them, a sense of "right time-right place" coloured their memories of their early beginnings. In some cases, these "fast-track" appointments led to immediate success; whereas for others, a lengthy period of "on-the-job apprenticeship" ensued before achieving any major coaching victories.

In this chapter, we also delved into the career decision-making processes of SWC. These coaches were found to be highly opportunistic and cautious risk-takers, combining a high work ethic with a sense of timing and ingenuity to either respond to or manufacture opportunities for career progression. This novel emphasis on the personal agency of the SWC was complemented with a preparedness to progress and an acute sense of opportunity and risk management which appeared to be key to their success. The findings, in line with previous research (Norman, Ranking-Wright & Allison, 2018), also showed that the journey might look and feel different to female coaches, especially in male-dominated sports where they may have to constantly prove themselves to their male counterparts and avoid being perceived as unknowledgeable or weak. Of course, this is speculative due to the limited sample of female SWC. Certainly, the careers of female SWC warrants future and ongoing investigation.

What does this mean for those identifying and recruiting HPC?

First, it is important to re-iterate the distinctive journeys of these SWC. In relation to any potential recommendations for identifying and recruiting HPC, there is no single pathway. Those who employ future HPC should be mindful of any potential cognitive bias that might shape their beliefs and attitudes in making these important decisions. Importantly, a passion for coaching seems a likely first step in the journey, but necessarily complemented with opportunities and personal agency.

Of interest to potential employers are that there were some trends that warrant some consideration. SWC possessed emerging leadership qualities from an early age and a genuine interest to lead, coach, and help others. Of course, those beliefs about leadership abilities were reinforced with opportunities to lead, which likely bolstered their beliefs about their leadership capabilities. Therefore, it seems appropriate to encourage those adults who shape the early sporting experiences of young athletes to provide opportunities to lead in meaningful and authentic ways. This emphasises the point that leadership development likely occurs through doing leadership work (and self and other reflection and on the quality of that work) and support. Those young athletes who have a passion for helping others seem like obvious candidates to be encouraged to become coaches.

Moreover, the analysis of the SWC's journey revealed the significant role played by ingenuity, moderate risk-taking, and resilience. In identifying, selecting, and more importantly, confirming "coaching capabilities", it seems paramount to find ways to also foster and monitor emerging coaches' ingenuity, risk-taking, and resilience to high pressure, failure, and success. Indeed, for the most part, the actual coaching environment will provide these features, but we encourage additional learning opportunities for growth by those who shape the environment.

Finally, the career pathways of SWC reveal a bias towards former elite athletes. This has been supported by multiple studies previously (e.g., Blackett, Evans &

Piggott, 2018; Rynne, 2014). The benefits afforded by a successful athletic career are undeniable both in terms of opportunity and knowledge, yet our findings revealed that it is still possible for non-elite athletes and non-athletes to become serial winners in a high-performance coaching role. Whilst their journeys are very different to those of elite athletes, head-hunters of "coaching capability" should also put mechanisms in place to monitor the performance of emerging coaches in this parallel track to ensure potential does not slip through the cracks of a system heavily weighted towards those already in it, including *hegemonic masculinity* (legitimises men's power). Diversity seems to be integral to the transformation of sport coaches and coaching. Therefore, it seems appropriate that coach developers move beyond "one size fits all" approach and acknowledge the unique learning histories of each coach and provide access to varied learning opportunities to value add to that knowledge and competencies (e.g., Mallett et al., 2016).

Note

1 R&D typically refers to Research and Development in business and industry.

References

Blackett, A. D., Evans, A. B., & Piggott, D. (2018). "Active" and "Passive" coach pathways: Elite athletes' entry routes into high-performance coaching roles. *International Sport Coaching Journal, 5*(3), 213–226. DOI: 10.1123/iscj.2017-0053

Carter, A. D., & Bloom, G. A. (2009). Coaching knowledge and success going beyond athletic experiences. *Journal of Sport Behavior, 32*, 419–437.

Christensen, M. K. (2014): Outlining a typology of sports coaching careers: Paradigmatic trajectories and ideal career types among high-performance sports coaches. *Sports Coaching Review, 2*(2), 98–113. DOI: 10.1080/21640629.2014.898826

Cruz, A. (2014). The coaching behaviours and philosophy of high performance secondary school basketball coaches. *Asian Journal of Physical Education & Recreation, 20*(1), 21–38.

Erickson, K., Côté, J., & Fraser-Thomas, J. (2007). Sport experiences, milestones, and educational activities associated with high-performance coaches' development. *The Sport Psychologist, 21*, 302–316.

Lara-Bercial, S., & Mallett, C. J. (2016). The practices and developmental pathways of professional and olympic serial winning coaches. *International Sport Coaching Journal, 3*(1), 221–239.

Lynch, M., & Mallett, C. J. (2006). Becoming a successful high performance track and field coach. *Modern Athlete and Coach, 22*, 15–20.

Mallett, C., & Coulter, T. (2016). The anatomy of a successful Olympic coach: Performer, agent, and author. *International Sport Coaching Journal, 3*, 113–127.

Mallett, C. J., & Lara-Bercial, S. (2016). Serial winning coaches: People, vision, and environment. In M. Raab, P. Wylleman, R. Seiler, A. M. Elbe & A. Hatzigeorgiadis (Eds.), *Sport and Exercise Psychology Research: From Theory to Practice* (pp. 289–322). London: Elsevier.

Mallett, C. J., Rynne, S. B., & Billett, S. (2016). Valued learning experiences of early career and experienced high performance coaches. *Physical Education and Sport Pedagogy, 21*(1), 89–104. DOI: 10.1080/17408989.2014.892062

Nash, C. S., & Sproule, J. (2009). Career development of expert coaches. *International Journal of Sports Science & Coaching, 4*(1), 121–138.

Norman, L., Rankin-Wright, A. J., & Allison, W. (2018). "It's a concrete ceiling; It's not even glass": Understanding tenets of organizational culture that supports the progression of women as coaches and coach developers. *Journal of Sport and Social Issues, 42*(5), 393–414. DOI: 10.1177/0193723518790086

Occhino, J., Mallett, C. J., & Rynne, S. (2013). Dynamic social networks in high performance football coaching. *Physical Education and Sport Pedagogy, 18*(1), 90–102.

Olusoga, P., Maynard, I., Hays, K., & Butt, J. (2012). Coaching under pressure: A study of Olympic coaches. *Journal of Sports Sciences, 30*, 229–239.

Rynne, S. (2014). 'Fast track' and 'traditional path' coaches: Affordances, agency and social capital. *Sport, Education and Society, 19*(3), 299–313. doi: 10.1080/13573322.2012.670113

Rynne, S. B., Mallett, C. J., & Tinning, R. (2006). High performance sport coaching: Institutes of Sport as sites for learning. *International Journal of Sport Science & Coaching, 1*, 223–234.

Rynne, S. B., Mallett, C. J., & Tinning, R. (2010). Workplace learning of high performance sports coaches. *Sport, Education and Society, 15*(3), 315–330.

Sherwin, I., Campbell, M. & Macintyre, I. (2017). Talent development of high performance coaches in team sports in Ireland. *European Journal of Sport Science, 17*(3), 271–278. doi: 10.1080/17461391.2016.1227378

Watts, D. W., & Cushion, C. J. (2017). Coaching journeys: Longitudinal experiences from professional football in Great Britain. *Sports Coaching Review, 6*(1), 76–93. DOI: 10.1080/21640629.2016.1238135

SECTION C

Caring Determination

5

CARING DETERMINATION – SERIAL WINNING COACHES AS LEADERS

A key goal in our study of serial winning coaches (SWC) was to identify more nuanced understandings of leadership in action in these highly contested settings. For instance, we were keen to move beyond the *what* of leadership – what coaches do – towards a greater understanding of the *how* and *why*. The study of leadership in high-performance coaching has received significant attention in the last three decades. This has translated into an array of academic research and, especially in the last five years, a vast increase in access to the views and practices of high-performance coaches (HPC) through various popular podcasts and "fly on the wall" docu-series.

There are likely many reasons for this increased interest in HP leadership. HPC are performers in their own right (Chan & Mallett, 2011; Gould et al., 2002; Parkes, 2018; Thelwell et al., 2008) and critical determinants of athlete and team performance outcomes (Greenleaf, Gould & Dieffenbach, 2001). Unsurprisingly, given their high financial investment, professional teams, and national sport programmes have wanted to better understand effective coach leadership and what this may mean for the way they recruit and support coaches (Mallett & Lara-Bercial, 2016). Likewise, the allure of elite and professional sport, fuelled by its mass media coverage, has given some HPC celebrity status and made them revered and recognised around the world. Individuals and corporations alike have become increasingly fascinated by what they can learn from HPC to better manage their businesses and increase productivity and profitability (e.g., Humphrey & Hughes, 2022; Kellet, 1999). Finally, and unfortunately, a recent string of high-profile cases of athlete maltreatment in performance settings (e.g., USA Gymnastics, British Cycling, and British Gymnastics) has led to a series of damning independent reviews showing systemic cultural failings in

DOI: 10.4324/9781003427292-8

relation to the safeguarding of high-performance athletes (UK Sport, 2017; US Department of Justice, 2021; Whyte, 2022). These poignant developments have been the catalyst for new lines of research into the ethical nature of HPC practices (e.g., Abraham et al., 2019; Cronin & Armour, 2019; Gearity & Murray, 2011; Lopez, Dohrn & Posig, 2020).

In academia, researchers have approached coach leadership from multiple perspectives. One line of research has focused on the identification of behavioural traits and implicit leadership tendencies of expert coaches (Côté et al., 1995; Côté & Sedgwick, 2003; Currie & Oates-Wilding, 2012; Lara-Bercial & Mallett, 2016; Mujika, 2017; UK Coaching, 2012; Vallée & Bloom, 2005). In the main, these studies were based on the reconstruction of the coaches' practices through semi-structured qualitative interviews, and, in a few cases, their athletes were also interviewed. Another avenue has focused on the *a posteriori* identification of coach-related success and failure factors across various Olympic campaigns (Greenleaf, Gould & Dieffenbach, 2001; Gould et al., 2002). A further line of work has set out to specifically examine leadership in Olympic coaching (Din et al., 2015) using the Integrated Research Model of Olympic Podium Performance (Din & Paskevich, 2013). Moreover, some studies have focused on specific elements of leadership and their impact on a variety of variables (i.e., emotional intelligence, Chan & Mallett, 2011; identity and meaning, Balague, 1999; coach–athlete congruence, Lorimer & Jowett, 2013; and psychological empowerment, Lee et al., 2013). Finally, a recent line of research has focused on the ethical nature of high-performance coaching, its practice, and implications (Abraham et al., 2019; Gearity & Murray, 2011; Cronin & Armour, 2019; Dohsten, Barker-Ruchti & Lindgren, 2020; Knust & Fisher, 2015; Lopez et al., 2020).

A full review of the above literature is beyond the scope of this chapter. However, in the following paragraphs, we aim to provide a synopsis of these empirical investigations.

In general, a key finding in the high-performance coaching literature is that coaching at this level goes beyond the application of technical and tactical knowledge to become "a complex and delicate process influenced by psychological, physical, social and organisational factors" (Gould et al., 1999, p. 373), which render it demanding, relational, and solution-focused (Din & Paskevich, 2013). Leadership in high-performance sport settings seems to require the deployment of a broad range of psychosocial behaviours and approaches. For instance, Côté and Sedgwick (2003) identified the development of a positive environment, accounting for individual differences, and positive rapport as central to success. Likewise, Currie and Oates-Wilding (2012) found that Olympic coaches placed great emphasis on the needs of their athletes and put these at the forefront of their planning and decision making. This humanistic perspective was also reported by Carter and Bloom (2009) in their study of

Canadian university coaches who holistically valued athletic performance as much as the all-round personal development of student–athletes. This holistic approach to leadership seems to be predicated on HPC possessing a well-defined and often explicit philosophy and vision for their coaching and athletes (Din & Paskevich, 2013; Lara-Bercial & Mallett, 2016; Vallée & Bloom, 2005).

Despite this holistic and athlete-centred philosophy, the extant research also shows that high-performance coaching is a highly dynamic and situational activity (Gould et al., 2002; Saury & Durand, 1998). HPC constantly adjust to the demands of the environment to find what works at a particular time for a particular athlete or team (Côté et al., 1995; d'Arripe-Longueville et al., 2001), which again emphasises the importance of time, place, and role. This adaptable responsiveness requires HPC to be comfortable with multiple approaches and deploy what has been termed "situational leadership" (Hersey & Blanchard, 1969). For instance, Din and Paskevich (2013) found that Olympic coaches alternated moments of collaboration and co-construction with others, such as athletes, but also with moments where decision making and action rested solely upon them. Likewise, Lee, Kim and Joon-Ho (2013) reported that both trans-actional and transformational behaviours were linked to athlete empowerment and the development of pro-social behaviours (e.g., altruism, sportsmanship, or courtesy). Notably, other researchers have identified other situational factors requiring coaches to operate in different ways; these included age and experience of athletes – younger/less experience athletes favour directive styles – and whether the team is in the middle of a winning or losing streak – during losing streaks athletes want coaches to be directive and provide solutions (Høigaard, Jones & Peters, 2008).

Indeed, what we found in the literature supports the view that there is a need for HPC to prioritise the creation of a supportive environment (Cronin & Armour, 2019; Ferrar et al., 2018; Fletcher & Sarkar, 2016; Kellet, 2009; Newton et al., 2007) that is responsive to situational demands stemming from the relational (person based), structural (organisation based) and performance (out-come based) elements of high-performance sport (Brown & Arnold, 2019; Din et al., 2015; Greenleaf et al., 2001; Lara-Bercial & Mallett, 2016). The highly competitive and small margins between winning and not, which is characteristic of high-performance sport settings, also demand coaches to ethically and effec-tively "find the line" (Abraham et al., 2019) in managing challenge and support (Fletcher & Sarkar, 2016) to drive athlete and team performance.

Along these lines and building on Noddings' seminal work on "care" (1984, 2013), Cronin and Armour (2019) have advocated for coaching to be understood as a "caring relationship" built upon Nodding's concepts of *engrossment* (atten-tional focus on the athlete), *motivational displacement* (prioritisation of the needs of the athlete above one's own), and *reciprocity* (athlete acknowledgement of the care provided by others). In addition, Cronin and Armour also draw on Batistich's notion of "caring communities" (Batistich et al., 1997) to highlight that care is contextualised and that athlete outcomes and coach behaviours are influenced by – and can influence – the surrounding environment (Cronin, Knowles & Enright, 2019; McCarthy et al., 2021).

This complexity requires coaches to possess high levels of emotional intelligence (Chan & Mallett, 2011), and the ability to notice subtle changes in the environment (Côté et al., 1995; Din et al., 2015; Kellet, 1999; Lara-Bercial & Mallett, 2016) to deploy suitable solutions and associated behaviours at any given time.

As we stated in the opening sentence of this paragraph, a primary key goal of this study was to reveal a deep understanding of leadership in action in these highly contested environments. For instance, we were keen to move beyond the *what* of leadership – what coaches do – towards a greater understanding of the *how* and *why*. This focus was motivated by the final goal of the study to facilitate the identification, recruitment, and development of the next generation of HPC. In addition, given the central role of the coach–athlete relationship in predicting performance and personal outcomes, and how often athletes have been under-represented in this type of research (Cronin & Armour, 2019; Jowett, 2017; Jowett & Clark-Carter, 2006), we intended to foreground the voices of the athletes. Interview data from 19 gold medallists who were coached to their podium success by these SWC were collected. Finally, we were also motivated to explore how leadership in high-performance coaching varied – or not – across a variety of sporting and national contexts, and thus actively targeted an international cohort from a variety of sport disciplines.

We present these findings across the next three chapters (Chapters 6–8). In the current chapter we provide an overview of coach leadership and introduce a defining feature in their approach to leadership, *Caring Determination*. The following two chapters will examine how SWC embody each of the two components of leadership (caring and determination) and how this is manifested in their daily endeavours. The final chapter will explore the antecedents of the SWC's leadership behaviours, their "why" and identify the psychosocial enablers of leadership and the benefits of the SWC's specific approach for them and their athletes.

Caring Determination

The practical manifestations of leadership reported by SWC and their athletes are as idiosyncratic and unique as their learning journeys and career pathways. Notwithstanding this variability, our analysis of these leadership behaviours – and their origin – provides grounds for the formulation of a common approach we termed Caring Determination.[1] In our 2016 paper, we defined it as:

"*The purposeful and determined pursuit of excellence based on an enduring and balanced desire to considerately support oneself and others*" (Lara-Bercial & Mallett, 2016). In our global consultancy work with practitioners, we have felt compelled to re-calibrate and create a more nuanced language that captures this defining characteristic of the SWC approach to leadership: "*The relentless pursuit of excellence balanced with a genuine and compassionate desire to support athletes and oneself*".

The notion of Caring Determination recognises that these SWC are driven by a relentless and unapologetic desire to achieve unparalleled levels of excellence in their sport. Indeed, they are obsessive in their pursuit of winning. Similarly, however, it proposed that such determination is anchored on a personal philosophy and values which privilege a humanistic view of athlete development and working relationships. The below quote from Coach 2 operationalises Caring Determination on the ground:

Treat people right. Be a person of integrity. You're allowed to be demanding but you've got to be supportive, and you've got to put them in a culture that explains why, and that allows them to grow mentally and physically. I think making people accountable is a tough job, I think going about it in a way that puts the onus on them and allows them to feel good about who they are is the key.

Caring Determination thus rests on the careful, at times precarious but fluid oscillation, between the need to make athletes uncomfortable in demanding they pursue higher challenges necessary for ongoing development and subsequent superior performance, and the provision of relative levels of care, including emotional and social support, that allows athletes to learn to cope with the associated psychosocial and physical demands. For example, Coach 7 said:

Can I be an educationalist or should I be an elite sport coach purely? And I try to put them along each other [...] When you are an educationalist, you are too soft and when you are an elite sports coach, you are perhaps too tough, I let them work together, I combine them.

Coach 11 also spoke candidly about the progression that had led him to this approach to coaching leadership:

When I was a younger coach, I was very much in dictatorial [mode] because I was a bit insecure. So, it was almost like, 'You have to do it this way. This is the one best way to do it'. Then I became very interested in athlete feedback and I almost became too democratic in my approach you might call it. Then I determined that the best way to be as a coach was to be a benevolent dictator, so a caring leader in other words. I think that is something that all coaches go through some process where they find themselves too and I know for me it works best to be a benevolent dictator. A caring—I care for the athletes I coach and the people around me – but I also know that I have to provide leadership and once in a while I have to say 'No, this is the direction we are going' or 'This is what we have to do' to lead the group. So, I think that's what you have to do to be very successful.

The athletes we interviewed corroborated this leadership approach; for example, Athlete 11 spoke at length about Coach 9's balanced approach to working with people:

No, he's not a dictator, he's very firm and he's there to help us. He recognises that we are adults and that we want to do this, and that we've got the hard job [...] He wants to help us get through it. When I say authoritarian, I mean he's not trying to be everybody's friend, he doesn't need to be everybody's friend, he respects all of his athletes, but he expects respect in return. He's just got a natural authority over people where people trust and respect him [...] and when people need motivating, he's never short of a smile for people and he'll sit down and greet them. And also [...] is he's a charming man. And he will sit down and put his arm around you or grab your shoulders and say 'yeah [name] looking strong today, let's go and do this next one'. He doesn't have to crack the whip every single time, but he can crack a big whip and he can do it with just a look or he can do it with a tongue-in-cheek comment that from anyone else you wouldn't give a shit about. But that's why I think he's got a lot of authority, because what he says carries a lot of weight and meaning for you and will get a lot out of you with a lot of impact.

Notably, our shift towards the notion of *Caring Determination* has evolved over the years. In previous writings (e.g., Lara-Bercial & Mallett, 2016), we described it as a continuum that coaches oscillate along to suit the situational context and personal needs of athletes. However, upon further review of the original interviews and countless conversations with other SWC in our coach developer work, our interpretation has shifted. Yes, SWC are able to move through a continuum spanning moments where care and support are prioritised to instances of extreme determination and demands. Yet, we have also realised that this is only the episodic manifestation of Caring Determination. At a foundational level, it appears that rather than a continuum, it is more a case of sustained determination being built on a strong base of genuine care. In other words, it is the caring and trusting nature of the coach–athlete relationship that creates the conditions for the constant challenges and demands posed by SWC on everyone around them to be met in a positive and productive way for a prolonged period. Athlete 18 (Coach 16) articulated this point well:

Yes, I think when you don't know her, what drives you to her is her professionalism and the results that she gets, and then once you are working for her, you stay there because she's an incredible human being, she cares so much, and she really makes it about the process as well as the result.

This matching of support relative to challenge is a key characteristic of these SWC. With Caring Determination defined and explained by coaches and athletes, we can now delve deeper into how this leadership approach plays out in the day-to-day interactions between these social actors. The following sections thus explore how SWC express Caring and Determination in their practice.

Note

1 In our 2015 book chapter and 2016 paper, we coined the phrase "Driven Benevolence". Over the course of multiple interactions with coaches and coach developers since, it has become apparent that Driven Benevolence does not easily translate to many languages and cultures. As such, we consulted coaches and landed on a new phrase, "Caring Determination" which has proven much easier to grasp and understand across cultures and contexts. Hence, this book will continue to use Caring Determination as the key term.

References

Abraham, A., Lyle, J. W., North, J., Lara-Bercial., S., Norris, L., Ashford, M., & Till, K. (2019). *Expert, effective and ethical coaching: Finding the line.* UK Sport.

Balague, G. (1999). Understanding identity, value, and meaning when working with elite athletes. *The Sport Psychologist, 13*(1), 89–98.

Batistich, V., Solomon, D., Watson, M., & Schaps, E. (1997). Caring school communities. *Educational Psychologist, 32*(3), 137–151. Doi: 10.1207/s15326985ep3203_1

Brown, D. J., & Arnold, R. (2019). Sports performers' perspectives on facilitating thriving in professional rugby contexts. *Psychology of Sport and Exercise, 40,* 71–81. 10.1016/j.psychsport.2018.09.008

Carter, A. D., & Bloom, G. A. (2009). Coaching knowledge and success going beyond athletic experiences. *Journal of Sport Behavior, 32,* 419–437.

Chan, J. T., & Mallett, C. J. (2011). The value of emotional intelligence for high performance coaching. *International Journal for Sport Science and Coaching, 6,* 315–328.

Côté, J., Salmela, J., Trudel, P., Baria, A., et al. (1995). The coaching model: A grounded assessment of expert gymnastic coaches' knowledge. *Journal of Sport & Exercise Psychology, 17*(1), 1–17.

Côté, J., & Sedgwick, W. A. (2003). Effective behaviors of expert rowing coaches: A qualitative investigation of Canadian athletes and coaches. *International Sports Journal, 7*(1), 62–77.

Cronin, C. & Armour, K. (2019). *Care in sport coaching: Pedagogical cases.* Abingdon: Routledge.

Cronin C., Knowles, Z. R., & Enright, K. (2019). The challenge to care in a Premier League Football Club. *Sports Coaching Review*, 9(2), 123–146. DOI: 10.1080/2164062 9.2019.1578593

Currie, J. L., & Oates-Wilding, S. (2012) Reflections on a dream: Towards an understanding of factors Olympic coaches attribute to their success, *Reflective Practice*, 13(3), 425–438. DOI: 10.1080/14623943.2012.670106

d'Arripe-Longueville, F., Saury, J., Fournier, J., & Durand, M. (2001). Coach-athlete interaction during elite Archery competitions: An application of methodological frameworks used in Ergonomics Research to sport psychology. *Journal of Applied Sport Psychology*, 13(3), 275–299, DOI: 10.1080/104132001753144419

Din, C., & Paskevich, D. (2013). An integrated research model of Olympic podium performance. *International Journal of Sports Science & Coaching*, 8(2), 431–444. DOI: 10.1260/1747-9541.8.2.431

Din, C., Paskevich, D., Gabriele, T., & Werthner, P. (2015). Olympic medal winning leadership. *International Journal of Sport Science & Coaching*, 10(4), 589–604. DOI: 10.12 60/1747-9541.10.4.589

Dohsten, J. Barker-Ruchti, N., & Lindgren. E. (2020). Caring as sustainable coaching in elite athletics: Benefits and challenges. *Sports Coaching Review*, 9(1), 48–70. DOI: 10. 1080/21640629.2018.1558896

Ferrar, P., Hosea, L., Henson, M., Dubina, N., Krueger, G., Staff, J., & Gilbert, W. (2018). Building high performing coach-athlete relationships: The USOC's National Team Coach Leadership Education Program (NTCLEP). *International Sport Coaching Journal*, 5(1), 60–70.

Fletcher, D. & Sarkar, M. (2016). Mental fortitude training: An evidence-based approach to developing psychological resilience for sustained success. *Journal of Sport Psychology in Action*, 7, 135–157.

Gearity, B. & Murray, M. A. (2011). Athletes' experiences of the psychological effects of poor coaching. *Psychology of Sport and Exercise*, 12(1), 213–221.

Gould, D., Guinan, D., Greenleaf, C., & Chung, Y. (2002). A survey of U.S. Olympic coaches: Variables perceived to have influenced athlete performances and coach effectiveness. *The Sport Psychologist*, 16, 229–250.

Gould, D., Guinan, D., Greenleaf, C., Medbery, R., & Petterson, K. (1999). Factors affecting Olympic performance of athletes and coaches from more and less successful teams. *The Sport Psychologist*, 13, 371–395.

Greenleaf, C., Gould, D., & Dieffenbach, K. (2001). Factors influencing Olympic performance: Interviews with Atlanta and Nagano US Olympians. *Journal of Applied Sport Psychology*, 13(2), 154–184. DOI: 10.1080/104132001753149874

Hersey, P., & Blanchard, K. (1969). Life cycle theory of leadership. *Training and Development Journal*, 23(5), 26–35.

Høigaard, R., Jones, G. W., & Peters, D. M. (2008). Preferred coach leadership behaviour in elite soccer in relation to success and failure. *International Journal of Sports Science & Coaching*, 3(2), 241–250. DOI: 10.1260/174795408785100581

Humphrey, J., & Hughes, D. (2022). *High performance: Lessons from the best on becoming your best*. Cornerstone.

Jowett, S. (2017). Coaching effectiveness: The coach–athlete relationship at its heart. *Current Opinion in Psychology*, 16, 154–158.

Jowett, S., & Clark-Carter, D. (2006). Perceptions of empathic accuracy and assumed similarity in the coach-athlete relationship. *British Journal of Social Psychology*, *45*(3), 617–637. DOI: 10.1348/014466605X58609

Kellet, P. (1999). Organisational leadership: Lessons from professional coaches. *Sport Management Review*, 2, 150–171.

Knust, S. K., & Fisher, L. A. (2015). NCAA division I female head coaches' experiences of exemplary care within coaching. *International Sport Coaching Journal*, *2*(2), 94–107. DOI: 10.1123/iscj.2013-0045

Lara-Bercial, S., & Mallett, C. J. (2016) The practices and developmental pathways of Professional and Olympic serial winning coaches. *International Sport Coaching Journal*, *3*(1), 221–239. DOI: 10.1123/iscj.2016-0083

Lee, Y., Kim, S.-H., & Joon-Ho, K. (2013). Coach leadership effect on elite Handball players' psychological empowerment and organizational citizenship behavior. *International Journal of Sports Science & Coaching*, *8*(2), 327–342. DOI: 10.1260/1747-9541.8.2.327

Lopez, Y. P., Dohrn, S., & Posig, M. (2020). The effect of abusive leadership by coaches on division I student-athletes' performance: The moderating role of core self-evaluations. *Sport Management Review*, *23*(1), 130–141.

Lorimer, R., & Jowett, S. (2013). Empathic understanding and accuracy in the coach–athlete relationship. In, P. Potrac, W. Gilbert, & J. Denison (Eds), *Routledge handbook of sport coaching* (pp.321–332). Routledge.

McCarthy, L., Martin, A., Slade, D., & Watson, G. (2021). Of women, by women, for women: How coaches and captains created a caring and winning culture in the New Zealand Netball Team. *The International Journal of Sport and Society*, *12*(2), 153–165. doi: 10.18848/2152-7857/CGP/v12i02/153-165.

Mujika, I. (2017). Winning the BIG Medals. *International Journal of Sports Physiology and Performance*, *12*(3), 273–274. 10.1123/IJSPP.2017-0016

Newton, M., Fry, M., Watson, D., Gano-Overway, L., Kim, M., Magyar, M., & Guivernau, M. (2007). Psychometric properties of the caring climate scale in a physical activity setting. *Revista de Psicología del Deporte*, *16*(1), 67–84.

Noddings, N. (1984). *Caring: A feminine approach to ethics and moral education*. University of California Press.

Noddings, N. (2013). *Caring: A relational approach to ethics and moral education*. University of California Press.

Parkes, J. (2018). *Coach as performer: Coach emotion, coping, and the coach-athlete-performance relationship*. PhD Thesis, School of Human Movement and Nutrition Sciences, The University of Queensland. 10.14264/uql.2018.687

Saury, J., & Durand, M. (1998). Practical knowledge in expert coaches: On-Site study of coaching in sailing. *Research Quarterly for Exercise and Sport*, *69*, 254–266. 10.1080/02701367.1998.10607692

Thelwell, R. C., Weston, N. J. V., Greenlees, I. A., & Hutchings, N. V. (2008) Stressors in elite sport: A coach perspective. *Journal of Sports Sciences*, *26*(9), 905–918. DOI: 10.1080/02640410801885933

UK Coaching (formerly Sports Coach UK) (2012). *Coach tracking study: A four-year study of coaching in the UK*. UK Coaching.

UK Sport (2017). *Report of the independent review panel into the climate and culture of the World Class Programme in British Cycling*. UK Sport.

US Department of Justice (2021). *Investigation and review of the Federal Bureau of Investigation's handling of allegations of sexual abuse by former USA Gymnastics Physician Lawrence Gerard Nassar.* US Department of Justice.

Vallée, C. N., & Bloom, G. A. (2005). Building a successful program: Perspectives of expert Canadian female coaches of team sports. *Journal of Applied Sport Psychology, 17,* 179–196.

Whyte, A. (2022). *The Whyte Review: An independent investigation commissioned by Sport England and UK Sport following allegations of mistreatment within the sport of gymnastics.* UK Sport.

Similarly, Coach 7 recognised that constant observation of his athletes was central to his practice:

I think there is a very strong sense of intuition, being able to read my athletes without talking to them, so assessing their body language, attitude, posture, choice of words [...] and especially also accepting, maybe that is the most important, especially also accepting [...] that the athletes you work with are unique and not you.

Athlete 4, however, was concerned that there was a shift towards athletes' greater sense of entitlement and what coaches can and should do for athletes:

Nowadays it is more and more about the individual, it is not about the team anymore, the team really is a collection of individuals. [...] the contact with the players is more important, like, what can a coach do for the individual [...] it is more like, what can you do for me? And not like I think as a coach: what can the individual do for me ... no, the roles are almost reversed, so you actually have to deepen more in the player and find out what is on his mind and how you can help him rather than he is helping you, [...] that is different than it was 15 years ago.

Furthermore, the value of a long-term, patient view of development was illustrated by Coach 15 when he said:

With experience we can learn how to be patient and build something that will last. The performances of a constantly evolving athlete – even at 14 or 15 years of age – build up over the long-term. [Development] needs to be viewed in terms of a career.

This view extended to the personal development of the athlete as Coach 2 explained:

That's not just about teaching the game, that's about life. The other thing is your ability to build a foundation for them to build confidence, sure in the [sport venue] but more so about life. Ideally raising a good woman and man having an impact on society, that's confidence, that's being a good person, that's understanding what's right, that's accountability. Those things all can be taught through our game because those things are all needed in the game [...] They say sport builds character; I think good people build good character.

In relation to this approach, Coach 7 highlighted that "better people make better athletes" when he said: "I have noticed that when you approach it like this [holistic approach], there is a big chance that that person will develop himself in a way that the chance of winning becomes bigger". Interestingly, Athlete 6, speaking about Coach 7, identified how his holistic approach had developed over time: "Coach 7 also knows that [the person behind the athlete matters], but he knows that rationally. It's not natural to him to be like that".

Notably, Coach 7 also explained how this athlete-centred focus at times led to the dissolution of the coach–athlete partnership for good. Indeed, coaches are encouraged to be mindful of potential incompatibility between coach and athlete:

> I cannot always be a [perfect] match for every elite athlete. I do not find that hard to take at all. No problem. I am only glad that we figured out fast enough that it was not working, so he or she is able to find another place where it is working and [they] fit, because for me it is all about the career of that athlete […] and if at some point it is not working in my team, he or she should go somewhere else as soon as possible.

Coach 11 provided a nice summation of the importance and benefits of an athlete-centred approach:

> Whether the athletes want you to keep coaching them or not is the best measure of all. Of course, if you win it's a measure of excellence, but a better measure is when athletes continue to follow you when they do not win […] when the athletes want you to continue coaching them when they lose.

In sum, within the constraints of high-performance sport, SWC display a person-first attitude focused on the athlete's wellbeing, and their long-term holistic development. This humanistic stance consistently informs coaches' decision making and programme resourcing.

Stability and dependability

A second aspect of caring revolves around SWCs' ability to create stable and dependable environments, which provide the conditions for athletes to thrive. This view was highlighted especially during the athlete interviews. The perception of the coach as trustworthy, honest, and authentic was paramount – it puts athletes' minds at rest and helps them accept, or at least endure, the inevitable frictions and conflicts inherent in high-performance sport. Moreover, these SWC were perceived to be available and most approachable that contributed to this sense of dependability. In addition, the role of the SWC as a "normaliser" was also emphasised. This was epitomised by the ability of the coach to maintain a consistent and relatively flat emotional tone, take the heat out of difficult situations, bring a sense of perspective to the challenges of elite sport, and a deliberate attempt to "keeping things fresh and fun". Indeed, SWCs were perceived as a "tower of strength" by their athletes, someone that can be relied upon consistently for comfort and support. This was manifested in the coaches' ability to radiate confidence and enthusiasm, find ways to lift athletes' spirits when down, shield and protect them from pressure, operate an accountable, yet blameless culture, and possess the inner strength to not be swayed by external influences.

Specific examples of SWC's stable and dependable behaviours were prolific through the interviews. Coach 7 identified authenticity as a key trait "My way of coaching is not artificial [...] It is a personal style. Yes, it has been refined and strengthened, but it has always been this way. I am who I am". As suggested by Athlete 1 (Coach 1), this demeanour made coaches approachable: "They [coaches] have to have this certain relaxed style [...] that's why I got on really well with him, because you could have a joke with him now and then. He simply had a certain approachability". This sentiment was echoed by Athlete 10 (Coach 9):

You want the coach to be close enough to be able to talk to him honestly and to be able to discuss things and be able to communicate well, but the coach also has to have the degree of separation whereby he can step back and be able to push you or tell you that that's wrong.

This level of approachability and authenticity is therefore also necessary to be able to take decisive actions when required: "He is very aware of the fact that it is his job to step in at the right moment, and get the team moving, and I think that is why he also looks for a personal connection with the players beforehand" (Athlete 10, Coach 9). Likewise, with regards to being available, Coach 15 pointed to his total commitment to his athletes: "Being available at all times is absolutely necessary for managing elite athletes. To produce Olympic or world champions, it's important to be 200% available". This was confirmed by Athlete 17 (Coach 16):

If you meet him after a [competition], he'll talk to you about anything, and he'll [also] talk to you privately, you know, if you ask to speak to him privately or if you just happen to be private he won't hold back.

Athlete 2 (Coach 1) expressed a similar view: "basically you can always sit down round a table and talk with him quite easily ... man-to-man and not just player-to-coach". In Athlete 7's opinion, at times Coach 7 had been intentional in hindering his own enjoyment of performance success: "He was always inclined not to enjoy the successes, but to focus completely on the people who needed help [...] he was not enjoying those successes".

Similarly, the importance of a consistent persona allows SWCs to manage the ebbs and flows of high-performance sport. Athlete 7 described Coach 7 as "very down to earth. Just a nice, sober, level-headed northerner ... a sober northerner, with both feet on the ground". Similarly, Coach 5 said: "I am not a coach that gets euphoric at great performances, but I am also not a coach that, when things are going less good, say, sinks in a swamp. I am a pretty stable person". Reinforcing the same point, Coach 3 said:

> The ability to start all over again in many occasions with energy, without putting your head down after a failure and not celebrating too much any successes, softening the emotions upwards and downwards [...] It's a way of being for a job like the one we do.

Coach 5 also felt that "You should radiate confidence towards your team: well guys, we have everything under control, we are well prepared, our plan is crisp and clear, our preparation period has been good, we have the quality, [...] it almost cannot go wrong". This need to protect the athletes was also discussed by Athlete 5 (Coach 5): "I think that one thing is very strong, you know, that he protects the group. Protecting the group and the individuals, that of course inspires confidence". In this respect, Athlete 10 (Coach 9) highlighted his coach's ability to "make sure that the responsibility is taken on by the coach as well. He feels that burden as much as we do. You feel like you are getting through things with him rather than he's blaming you".

Linked to the above was the capacity of the coach to act as a "normaliser". Athlete 8 (Coach 8) felt that a substantial component of this was the coach's disposition to provide perspective and even use some "comic relief" when appropriate: "If you were feeling a bit off colour [...] he'd enthuse you. Like he, he is not a great guy on the computer, but he did these PowerPoint presentations that when you got them, they made you laugh". Coach 8 was also hailed by Athlete 8 for his ability to "totally take all the heat out of the situation and take pressure away from us the athletes". For Athlete 14 (Coach 11), normalisation was related to the coach's ability to focus on what is really important and avoid wasting energy and emotion in what is not: "As you develop as a coach you get a really good feel for when you settle on a big thing that needs to be changed and when you have a small thing that doesn't need changing". For Athlete 10 (Coach 9), normalisation was about being able to "cope with situations that are massively volatile without them going wild, [...] he is very good at getting an environment where people say what they need to say without it getting out of control". By contrast, for Athlete 12 (Coach 10), normalisation involved,

> help[ing] me to understand what my own frame of mind needed to be for competing. He is happy to say at a point 'that performance is good enough,

you just gonna go out and do that again, [...] all we're gonna do in the Olympic final is go and race like you did.

Finally, another important element discussed at this point was the coach's ability to prevent athlete boredom. Coach 11 put it succinctly: "Variety in training will keep people motivated so try different things all the time [...] it's therapeutic, [...] there's all kinds of things you can do to keep things very motivating". The high volumes of repetitive tasks to become more expert and develop instinctive habits are necessary for athletes to become the best but some planned disruptions to that monotonous work are essential to challenge the status quo and spur athlete development.

To summarise, SWC strive to be trustworthy in the eyes of their athletes and present themselves as approachable, available, and supportive under pressure. They also display a strong ability to normalise and defuse the inherent tensions and challenges present in the high-performance environment for the benefit of those around them.

Adaptive coaching

The third component of caring stems from the coach's ability to seamlessly adapt to situational and individual demands to consistently produce positive outcomes. Coach 7 explained it lucidly: "I often call myself a chameleon coach, that I am able to change my colour everywhere [...] and mostly people in my position do the opposite, they expect everyone else to adjust to them". Acting in this manner requires vast amounts of situational awareness to continuously attune to the environment and its needs, and to react accordingly. Similarly, adaptive coaches need a high degree of individualised awareness to be able to use different coaching and relational styles with each athlete. SWCs, whilst having common boundaries, treat each person, be it an athlete or a member of staff, differently to maximise wellbeing and performance. As a result, caring adaptability translates into an enhanced capacity to adjust the programme to the physical and emotional needs of its members at any given time. Indeed, this ability to adapt to unique situations does not compromise the need to be dependable and stable.

For example, Coach 3 believed that coaching was about "small details and shades of grey" and that therefore, "adaptability and flexibility are key". In relation to dealing with different athletes, Coach 7 described how his university sports degree had taught him about a variety of teaching styles, yet he recognised that "I need all 5 styles, because the athletes are at the centre and I need to find the correct match". Likewise, Coach 4 felt that,

You must know your players, what character they have, how they are as a person because if I want to say something to X in front of everyone, maybe is good in front of the team, but if I want to say it to you, maybe it's not good in front of everybody.

Athlete 17 (Coach 14) agreed:

A lot of people think that treating everyone fairly means treating everyone the same, but that's not really the case […], if you treat them equally then that's not very fair […] well different people need to be pushed in different ways […] some people need a kick up the pants and some people need an arm around the shoulder.

This emphasises the need to differentiate between what is fair (equitable) and what is equal. Athlete 5, however, recognised that these attempts to individualise coaching were not always easy for his Coach (5):

I have noticed also that he tries to approach everybody [differently] to get the best out of them. He also finds that difficult sometimes, because sometimes […] he wants to keep 'marching to his tune', and sometimes that just does not match with a number of personalities in the group.

The above quote underscores the challenges in being consistent but being adaptable. This view extended to the ability of the coach to choose how he wanted to be perceived by the athletes. Athlete 2 (Coach 1) explained how his coach could choose "who to be on a given day, from buddy to enemy to get a reaction from the group" and how the coach could be "quite deliberately playing this". Beyond character, Coach 5 highlighted the need for "empathy, because I must be able to ... that is observation ability, you have to identify in which mood state people are at any given time". This capacity to "read the room" (Coach 1) allows SWC "to understand the delivery [modes] of your athletes. You start to figure out when to push the buttons and when to back off" (Coach 6). Athlete 6 (Coach 7) corroborated the importance of this behaviour: "that is typical of a good coach, having the assessment skills, good judgment/ empathy, to be able to do that [change tune]". This social intelligence seems central to being adaptive in how you coach – the ability to comfortably talk with others, paying attention and listening, and adapting to different social situations.

Furthermore, adaptability was also identified as key in relation to group management. Coach 7 drew a parallel with teaching: "If I am a teacher and I have different groups, and in every group, you have a different dynamic, I cannot treat this group the same as that group or that group". Similarly, Coach 1 talked about the need to be "sensitive to that: how the mood changes. And if you have that sensitivity, you will notice whether the effect [of your intervention] is moving in the right or the wrong direction". Moreover, Coach 8 spoke about the need to give groups time to digest negative results again reinforcing the need to be a socially intelligent performer:

> We've just been to a [event type] and you've had a bad result. Ok, let them think about it for a bit, don't go straight in there […] let them pack [the material] up, go and have a drink, some food whatever, and then I knew to go one hour later, get over there, […] get it off your chest.

This delayed but not too late communication in debriefing a poor result serves at least two functions. First, the delay allows for emotions to reduce to promote a conversation in which both coaches and athletes are listening and engaging. Second, too long a delay (e.g., the next day) might compromise the sleep quality that night and impede recovery, especially for those athletes who ruminate. Coach 6, however, also warned of the dangers of an excessive focus on problematic athletes or staff: "you have to be much more aware of high maintenance players and staff. So, it's kind of 'squeaky wheel gets the grease' but you can't just focus on these drama Queens and Kings or the group will suffer".

In summary, Coach 9 stressed the importance of *noticing* because "you can write everything down on paper, […] but then in the process you have to be also prepared to change, […] the programme has to always be on the edge". This learned need to be adaptive and socially intelligent likely is developed over time and requires ongoing reflective practices (guided by self and others).

In short, SWC are capable of adopting a variety of attitudes and approaches that best fit the contextual demands. Likewise, they display a significant disposition and capacity to adjust their coaching and leadership behaviours to the needs of individuals, be them personality or situationally based.

Shared leadership

Notwithstanding their strong personal visions and long-established ways of working (see Chapter 4), SWC created a collaborative culture where athletes and staff developed a sense of ownership and belonging. SWC intentionally sought to form partnerships and encouraged athletes and staff to have a voice and have their opinions heard and given due consideration. This collaborative approach contributed to establishing high levels of alignment and buy-in. The coaches' ability to compromise within the limits of their working parameters supported the creation of a co-constructed vision and fostered a sense of choice and self-determination (*autonomy*). Persuasion was valued over imposition, yet SWC were comfortable pushing back and being assertive and directive if considered appropriate. A culture of *"controlled freedom"* (Coach 4) where staff and athletes co-directed the programme within the boundaries set by the head coach was the preferred choice of leadership. This collaborative approach was informed and underpinned by the SWC's deep-seated belief that the development of self-reliant and self-sufficient individuals (athletes and staff) is a significant part of the job. These SWC prioritised leading in ways that avoided the infantilisation and overdependence of elite athletes on others. Coach 5 summarised this approach:

> I have a vision and before I start with any team whatsoever, I share that vision with my team, and I check if that vision is shared. Sometimes that will lead to some very small adjustments, I mean, of course you can not deviate completely from your vision, then it all ends, but at the level of details you can adjust things to, well, the wishes [and] needs of your players, also from the idea that they eventually feel much better with that. I think one of the most important things in being a good coach, is to continuously be open for feedback, so from that vision you always have to stay open for feedback.

Coach 3 explained how, for him, it all starts with your original stance:

> Normally, what leads to conflict is if you have a dictatorial attitude as your default mode. If something happens and I explain it to you, and you don't get it, and I explain it again and again, it gets to a point where you say, 'just do it because I say so'. Conflict comes when you say that (explicitly and implicitly) from the start without explaining things.

Athlete 7 acknowledged Coach 7's efforts to persuade rather than impose: "He is always able to substantiate why we should do this at that moment and […] when he has substantiated it like that, it is fine and I believe him and we are done [with the argument]". A foundation of honesty and openness was key for Athlete 16 (Coach 14): "He was always willing to give you his reasons for things … . Any athlete can walk up to him and say '[Coach], why do we do this?' or 'why did you do that?' and he'll give you the honest reasons". This consistency of coach and athlete perceptions is a testimony to the value of collecting data from both actors in the coach–athlete dyad. Importantly, athlete voice should be encouraged and can foster a shift from a vertical model to a more shared approach to leadership.

For Coach 3, this balance between listening to others and sticking to their personal views also applied to the management of the coaching staff and support team:

> I welcome every opinion coming from others not to discourage anyone from expressing their opinion. Those opinions add richness to the coaching staff, [you must] be receptive, listen, and show interest in what they say. Sometimes you accept a different opinion and sometimes you stand your ground and stick with your ideas, but not because you don't give a fuck [care] but with a rationale.

Athlete 3 (Coach 3) corroborated this view:

A key thing is that when he got there [to the national team], he didn't just go and say, 'this is my team now, you do as I say and that's that, this is a dictatorship!' [...] didn't get there and said, 'you can't do this or that, or you have to do this, etc'. He has respected us and our 'group things' and above all has not been a dictator, and that for a group like this ... not only as a group, but I know for certain that at the end of the day, the coaches who triumph are those who give players freedom at all levels and don't create ... I mean, dictator-type coaches like in the old days do not work anymore.

Athlete 5 (Coach 5) commented on the value of allowing the team to, in a way, run itself:

And I think for him it is a matter, not so much of prescribing certain things, but he just tries to allow a lot of it to come from the team itself. So he provides a rough framework or a rough direction the team can develop in, but how precisely the team actually develops within this framework is up to the team itself, and he encourages that. And I think that's very brave. I think a lot of coaches have a problem with that because they are afraid of it.

Coach 13 confirmed the benefits of this approach:

The best podium level coaches [...] possess great consultation and negotiation ability and are able to have the athlete buy into the process and the outcome without compromise. If this is complete, then [they] never have to make hard decisions. The structure and the buy-in makes this happen before any hard decisions are considered a possibility.

Likewise, SWCs highlighted the importance of developing self-reliant athletes. Coach 10 expressed his rationale for this: "The principle needs to be, [...] to make them as independent as they can be to make decisions. The athlete goes out there and [competes]". Similarly, Coach 8 said: "The most important aspect [of] our sport [...] is self-preparation. [...] both physically and mentally". Athlete 1 described how Coach 1 operated in this manner:

He tries to approach the players in such a way that he doesn't tell them what to do [...]. In this way he gives the player an opportunity of developing himself, questioning himself and above all also reflecting upon himself a lot. And I would say he also hopes that from these reflections the player will develop with confidence, enhance his strengths, and will become better by doing so.

Coach 11 eloquently summarised this *"shared leadership"* approach:

I actually believe … what I try to create is … you meet an athlete who knows less than you, and by the time you are in the middle of the relationship they know as much as you, and by the time they are ready to compete internationally they know more than you. So, you train people to move on [past] you and become better people, and be better, more knowledgeable, and more well prepared than you are. And that's kind of my role as a coach. So, it's a humble approach to it all.

In sum, while displaying strong convictions and established routines, SWC favour collaborative working practices which provide athletes and staff with sufficient room to co-own the performance development process. This "controlled freedom" aims to improve alignment and buy-in, as well as foster self-reliance and initiative.

The *caring* element of SWC's leadership practices revolved around a distinct and deliberate "athlete-centred" perspective focused on athletes' long-term development (performance) and wellbeing (support). A deliberate, carefully crafted collaborative atmosphere contributed to the development of buy-in and belonging from all social actors in the programme. In doing so, the creation of a stable and dependable environment wherein the coach demonstrated a high ability to adapt and react to situational and individual needs was central to success.

Having explored an understanding of the *caring* component of SWC's practice, we now focus on the second half of the leadership equation: *Determination*.

7

EXPRESSIONS OF DETERMINATION

SWC are unapologetically driven to achieve high levels of performance and success. While this is anchored on and buffered by a strong foundation of caring and support, SWC pride themselves in building an environment that continuously moves staff and athletes beyond previous levels of skill, expertise, and attainment. In this section, we explore how this is manifested daily across five key areas: Focus; Commitment; Standards; Modelling; and Resilience. Table 7.1 provides a summary of these elements.

Focus

SWC have clarity, purpose, focus, and direction for their coaching work. This clarity and purpose in what they do is supported by a clear, considered, and durable personal philosophy, which is underpinned by personal, lived values. Indeed, these coaches clearly articulated their goals and the blueprint for how, why, and what they coached. This clarity is aided by their capacity to simplify the complexity of their sport and the high-performance environment to identify priorities and maximise available human and material resources (we termed this act, *Simplexity*). Their ability to analyse the components of performance and understand strengths and areas for improvement underpinned their short, mid-, and long-term planning. As such, preparation was thorough, multi-layered, and contingency based. While taking care of the present, SWC were keen to "future-proof" the performance of their athletes by continuously exploring the evolution of their sport, pushing boundaries, and finding competitive advantages to keep them ahead of direct rivals.

In relation to having a strong philosophy, Athlete 1 talked about Coach 1's foundational beliefs as central to staying grounded: "But I think he has a certain

DOI: 10.4324/9781003427292-10

TABLE 7.1 The manifestations of determination

Focus	Commitment	Standards	Modelling passion	Resilience
Strong philosophy	Total dedication	Established ways of working	High energy	Acceptance and reframing
Clear purpose	Conviction	High demands	Work ethic	Solution-focused
Future-proof	Risk-taking	Accountability	Self-care	Realistic
Simplexity		Constant raising of the bar	Continuous learning	expectations
Strategy and processes		Perfectionism		Optimal under pressure

philosophy. And that philosophy is the one that he thinks is crucial, and when there are problems cropping up left and right, he always goes back to that". Coach 10 had similar views about the need for steadiness and knowing who you are:

I think you need to be able to go on a pathway, and then you can try something [new] here and there, but instead of jumping here and then jumping there and then jumping here, that you've got a clear way, you might then try a little bit on this side or a little bit on that side.

A central theme in this respect was the focus on the basics as explained by Athlete 9 (Coach 8):

He'll always revert back to the basics. He would just go through his list, looking at it and applying his basic fundamentals to that scenario, […] let's build it up from the bottom, basics, […] find the weaknesses, let's go and practice, practice and keep practicing.

With regards to clarity of purpose, Athlete 16 (Coach 14) emphasised the coach's clear focus on the ultimate goal of winning: "I think his attitude is very much we are here to win. You get paid, you are a professional, so we're all professionals, we're all here to win—results matter. And he sees his job as helping the athlete to win and everything he does is designed to help the athlete win". This capacity to clearly identify "what needs to be done" and focus on it was paramount for Athlete 10 (Coach 9): "I think he does know quite often when he is working with people 'this is where you need to go', and one way or another he gets you going there". Critically, these SWC had the ability to scaffold learning towards these highly aspirational goals. Indeed, they knew how to get there! Coach 1 was able to articulate this multilevel goal-directed approach:

The goal of winning is one thing, but then you have to subdivide it into specific goals for performance. We also have competitive advantages. I have a mind map I use. It is always being developed and changed, but the basic system is having a goal of winning, then most of it takes place on the level of goals for actions or performance. We always have four to five factors that we call our competitive advantages. We are simply better at those things than others; they are our strengths. They are weighted differently, too, depending on the team, on the situation. But we always try to slip that into the process. And that's always the basic model.

Linked to clarity of the big goal of winning was the notion of future proofing. Coach 9 discussed at length the vital role of knowing your sport to understand the future demands and plan accordingly:

You should know in four years' time, if you talk always about the Olympiad [as your main target], the sport overall will develop, as in times will go down, […] physically, technically, material of course, there is a big variety in what's making people go faster and performing better than four years ago. So, when you start a project then you have to first set your targets. That's why I say the vision of how your sport develops and you think 'ok, if the time is coming down by half a per cent in four years', if they are already on a very high level, then you have to think ok half a per cent going faster from A to B, what does it mean? That's what I mean about you have to have a vision about your sport, you know how you go faster from A to B, how the sport develops, so you have to be always a step ahead in your thinking and challenge yourself.

Being future focused and open to change allowed SWC to stay ahead of their competitors as highlighted by Coach 4:

Our players […] understand that as coaches we try to do things that are new to them, always staying one step ahead of the other teams. I know that some of our players talk about this. They are really happy because they know they have coaches who [are always trying to] help them a lot.

Coach 3 espoused a similar belief: "I think to stay abreast of new ideas, new ways of doing things is probably one of the secrets to continued success". Coach 2 reinforced the notion of change to remain competitive: "Over time, the formula changes, and it changes each and every single year". However, Coach 2 also emphasised the importance of, while begin flexible, "[…] knowing your way, […] In the [top professional league] you have the 30 best coaches in the world, and they all do it in their own way. One of the keys to coaching is you have to do what you do, not what someone else does". This carefully poised balance between stability and innovation was also discussed by Coach 1:

Of course, you have to make sure you don't get caught up in the wrong direction, but the motivation is actually that I am always searching for means and ways to get us moving faster in the same direction without getting caught up in the detail – the central theme must stay in the centre.

This sentiment was echoed by Coach 15: "I'm like a sponge. I am inspired daily by interesting things, [but] without simply copying and pasting, as I want to preserve my way of doing things".

Moreover, Coach 13 felt this ability to "see and know the future and [...] to place that in the now" was vital to "cut away all the peripheral issues and focus on only those things that are going to provide a winning outcome and then develop processes to achieve that outcome before the opposition".

In addition to a clear focus on the future (and the big picture) was the notion of *simplexity*. The coaches' analytic capacity to reach this point where complexity is simplified and priorities are identified and pursued is what we termed *simplexity*, which was praised by the athletes. Athlete 4 identified Coach 5's Athlete identified his use of relevant data as key to continued success: "[he coaches] based on content, [...] less from the human being, from the feeling, but more coaching based on the facts, objective observations, he analyses, yes, definitely". According to Athlete 11, this quality was also part of Coach 9's repertoire: "He loves data, pours over it, and he really makes sense of it. He sees stuff that other people just completely miss".

This capacity to simplify the complexity extended to the coaches' ability to create strategies and processes to reach their goals. For instance, my capacity to scaffold learning was supported by Coach 11 who agreed that this focus on the *"needs to do"* was central to his performance:

What I think I see for some reason very clearly are the "needs to do." So I think I'm very good at not wasting my time, like being very efficient in getting t"e "needs to be" that have to be done every day. So, I think I'm very good at narrowing in and—okay we've got this long list of things to do today and I don't get bogged down in that—I just zero in on one or two things that I think are going to make the biggest difference. So, in that sense I appear to be very well organized because I get the "needs to do" done".

This focus on "what needs to be done to maximise outcome, what I need to do to get maximum return from my programme" (Coach 5) was identified by all coaches as a critical factor for success and a vital personal skill to nurture. Coach 12 said: "I think that what I used to do, is just to get the maximum out of my resources, something like that. Human and budget also". Athlete 4 saw Coach 5 as having mastered this element and underscoring the importance of clarity of priorities, systematic and scaffolded in how you deliver:

> Yes, extreme focus, and maybe that is a characteristic. And when you link that extreme focus to his perfectionism you end up with the fact that you can only do one thing at a time, because you cannot do a few things in a half-baked way.

Coach 9 also acknowledged the benefits of achieving clarity of goals and strategy, especially to stay on track during difficult moments:

> I think you should know your endpoint and your motorway [the road you will take], see always that point there and still be aware, yes, [that] sometimes you have to go to the bypass because of some road work or something you have to, it's not that straight every time, but you always know where the motorway is.

Athlete 4 felt Coach 5 excelled in this respect, which strongly confirmed the coach's perceptions:

> We didn't do well in the World Cup, but he stayed calm, because he trusted his route, he was confident and we did not change a lot anymore, [he trusted] in his vision [...] so he dares to hold on to that, and he was proven right.

A similar point was made by Athlete 10 about Coach 9's ability to focus on what really matters and stay on track:

> He's able to plan the whole year around how to perform at that one event, say the Olympics for instance. And it takes a lot of foresight and patience to get that balance right. And you can see other nations ... they might perform much better earlier in the year [...] but they don't really get the one that matters right. And for [Coach 9], he can see the bigger picture [...] to bring the best out of his guys at the right time.

Overall, SWC demonstrate clarity of vision and purpose, the capacity to simplify the complexity of performance and focus on the big picture, and the ability to put systems and strategies in place (what, how, why, and who) to scaffold sustainable progress and success.

Commitment

As the previous section highlights, SWC display and demand full commitment to the job. In this section, we elaborate on the nuances of commitment in relation to the theme of focus. They accept, and even relish, the extreme requirements of high-performance sport; as previously reported in the NEO data (traits), these SWC were "go-getters" and intentionally pursued challenges. Long hours, anti-social schedules, and high levels of expectations and pressure are considered part of the job description and indicators that one is working at the pinnacle of the sport; emphasising the saliency of coaches' role clarity and acceptance. This understanding allows these coaches to "enjoy the grind" (Coach 2) and to achieve "a relative work-life balance" (Coach 7). SWC's unwavering commitment to excellence is fuelled by a passion for the sport and competing driven by a stubborn conviction about their understanding of their sport and the value of their working practices. This faith in "their way" underpins their capacity to fight for what they think is right and to maintain a reasonably stable and steady approach. This commitment is fuelled by passion for what, how, and why they do it. Likewise, their self-belief allows them to take calculated risks and make courageous choices that, in retrospect, have regularly provided them with a competitive advantage over their counterparts.

In relation to total dedication, Coach 15 described how he was prepared to go the extra distance and do what it takes to achieve their personally meaningful goals:

> Commitment is essential, day and night – I often turn up at [training venue] in the evening, at night, at the weekend […] when you're a coach you have to put your heart and soul into what you do. You can't have your birthday off. What our sport needs and the end goal are what matters – over and above family life included. Today I feel I still show this commitment to athletes I coach, and it is one of my strengths.

Similarly, Coach 11 felt his full commitment in his younger years had been central to his development:

> I know when I was younger, I had no issues with working on Saturdays and Sundays, I had no issues with working in the evenings, I had no issues with waking up early in the morning, I had no issues with setting aside a lot of other things in my life to further my coaching.

He was, however, uncertain about whether the new generations of coaches were prepared to make these sacrifices:

> I notice a lot of young coaches that I would not be too excited about, [they] don't see themselves as entrepreneurs. In other words someone has to go in there and do a lot of the grind work [for them] … I think a lot of people want their cake and eat it too.

It is difficult to know if these perceptions of the next generation are well-founded or perhaps these SWC have forgotten their early career behaviours. Another consideration is whether or not the next generation is fully committed but strives to have a more balanced approach to the extensive commitments of coaching 24/7. This re-calibration might be progressive and necessary in promoting coach well-being.

A key theme throughout the data found in all layers of understanding a person was passion for sport as a key driver of commitment. Athlete 5 described Coach 5's infatuation with his sport:

> He just loves the game, he is a [sport] lover […] he really loves to be on the field […] and to be busy with the sport actually, […] when you walk over to his room, then he is watching videos. […] So, he really puts in a lot of time in, but that actually comes naturally.

The SWC's commitment is also powered by a significant amount of conviction and self-belief in what they do (competence). This belief in their approach allowed these coaches to defend their position and power through other people's doubts when required. Athlete 17 made this point about Coach 10: "He is very, very determined and he doesn't back away from fighting for what he believes in […]. So, he has a very clear vision. And he absolutely follows that through". For Coach 11, reaching this level of confidence in his methodology meant he was happy to have a rolling yearly contract: "I don't want long-term contracts, I want yearly contracts because I want to be able to prove myself every year, and I don't care about a long-term contract". The volatility of coach employment has been viewed as problematic in terms of performance and well-being but in this case, it highlights that one's perspective can shape your response.

Moreover, SWC' commitment to excellence, and to the long road ahead, facilitates them tolerating high levels of calculated risk (*robust resilience*) which they see as central to enhanced performance. Coach 13 articulated this view: "This group of coaches are prepared to take the untrodden path, dare to be different, are risk takers and lateral thinkers". Coach 15 felt strongly that coaches had to be able to take the same risks as athletes: "Commitment to athletes must be total. We ask them to take risks and to commit themselves wholeheartedly – and it's important for coaches to be made from the same stuff". Coach 1 discussed this "calculated-risk" approach to trying different things in relation to match and tournament preparation: "I think it is important to be brave enough to also do something you haven't trained for before in critical games".

In summary, SWC show complete dedication to their work, fuelled by a passion for their sport and high performance, and anchored by a strong conviction in their philosophy and worldview. As a result, they are comfortable taking calculated risks in the name of progress and success.

Standards

SWC create highly structured, demanding, and all-encompassing environments, which aim to consistently draw world-class performances from all involved whether they are staff or athletes. They create a "lived culture" where "ways of working" and expectations are clearly communicated, and a high work ethic is privileged. High standards are maintained at all costs and thus, accountability and a zero-tolerance for carelessness and sloppiness are central to operationalising this approach. SWC use their persuasion skills to achieve buy-in amongst staff and athletes yet are comfortable to impose their will and make no compromises if the situation requires it. They are also (healthy) perfectionists with extreme levels of attention to detail who aim to have control over as many performance factors as possible. Healthy or adaptive perfectionists pursue performance excellence without the self-criticism and concern about others' expectations and potential judgements if they do not achieve perfect outcomes. SWC therefore leave no stone unturned in their search for perfection and getting "an edge" over their opponents. This constant "raising of the bar" provides the necessary level of on-going challenge to enhance performance, avoid complacency, and foster resilience across the board. As a result, SWC may, at times, be perceived as controlling and/or micromanaging.

With regards to "ways of working", Coach 2 recognised the value of creating a distinguishable culture:

> from how you train, [...] to how you treat the people getting on the plane, [...] to how you dress – everything [matters] to me. I don't think I'm a dictator at all, but there's a [club name] way and we expect our players to hold each other accountable in that area. We have that kind of culture.

Coach 8 based his approach on his former Navy education: "Everything was regimental. [...] Nobody would turn up late, nobody. And if they did, we [would] make an example of them. And we do things methodically. It is, [about] being disciplined, [...] not just in sport, in anything in life".

Within this disciplined and well-organised setting, high expectations and demands were present and clearly communicated. Coach 1 described the environment he tried to create: "We have very high demands, and during training they are presented either verbally or by negative vibes, going along the whole range, from shouting to complete silence. But there are always vibes and a message". He was also comfortable with the ensuing level of regular tensions emerging from this approach: "I believe that there are no 'love, peace and harmony' teams that are successful". Athlete 12 (Coach 10) explained how these demands were imposed on all within the programme and non-negotiable:

He sets very, very high standards for the support staff and they have to work very hard to keep him happy. He treats them a lot like he treats the athletes, he just sets the bar and you've got to fit into that mould. And obviously he sets high standards for the athletes and sets a very difficult training programme. There's not a lot of flexibility.

Coach 7 agreed:

[my staff] have learned to act according to my standards. And my standards are sky high. I do not accept a job half done and they all know that, and they have adjusted their standards to that. So yes, I can trust my people now, so there is no loss of energy anymore.

Athlete 12, also recognised that, despite the perceived harshness of the environment created by Coach 5, she would not like to change it:

If I was going to another Olympics, I would want Coach 5 to coach me even though I know we would have rows, and that there will be times when he would drive me up the wall [...] but I think that you need a really strong character and a really clear vision if you do something like the Olympics. Fundamentally as an athlete you have a lot to learn, so you can't expect for it to be easy and for everything to be nice all the time because you've got to go and race in a harsh environment, and no one is going to be nice to you out there. I think it's tough preparation what makes you resilient and develops the character of the athletes. I think with a more touchy feely system you could have success, but the way I see it is the reason for the repeated success, is a strong clear system.

Coach 2 emphasised the need to safeguard the culture at all times through clear accountability:

The culture can slip at any time, we've been able to not let it slip [...] we have created a level of accountability, a level of expectation for our players of what a pro does and we're relentless in that, and it's not happy-ville every day. Accountability sometimes is difficult [because it upsets people] but it's the key to success.

Coach 13 clearly described his stance as "having contempt for failure. [...] If failure is an outcome due to lack of preparation, direction, discipline, or commitment, then failure is contemptible [...] and should be addressed". Coach 1 described this position as:

Stubborn consistency – [an] extremely systematic approach to things: crazy demands, constant demands, endlessly getting on your nerves, [...] players were constantly being reminded: 'If you want something, do something!'. [...] I think you won't find anybody who is successful who is not stubborn or consistent in a certain way.

In addition, for this culture to consistently thrive over sustained periods of time there needs to be a constant raising of the bar. Coach 9 explained:

They say success breeds success ... . [but] it doesn't go automatically. You have to work with successful athletes on [finding] their new level of success, dealing with success, and setting new targets. Because if they do the same again, they will be not successful.

Coach 10 made a similar point: "I never have a view that that was good, and that's what it's got to be, you are always looking for more". Coach 14 understood that not every athlete was able to withstand these demands and acknowledged he set training at the level of the best athletes without "watering it down": "When guys see that they improve from the higher level of training they want to do it and more. But guys that don't make it complain the program's too hard and that I'm not a good coach".

Coach 17 had little time for athletes that were not prepared to raise to his level: "If they won't want to commit to that [my programme]' I'm not committing to them because I'm not the recreational coach, you can find that anywhere else' I'm pretty arsy about that". In this respect, Coach 6 reflected on the difficulty of maintaining a balance between the required extreme demands and the more enjoyable elements of sport:

I strive for excellence all the time [...] you know at times they would get frustrated because they want to move on [... ' I've always wanted balance between being tense and having fun, but I found at times that my athletes and even my staff at times couldn't find that balance.

Finally, the (healthy) perfectionism trait common amongst these SWC was central to the maintenance of these high standards. Coach 2 provided a comprehensive account of how his team took care of the minutia of the sport on a day-to-day basis:

I believe in details, that winning or losing is in the details, the minute details. For a game, one of the coaches goes through two games and he makes a presentation to me or the coaching staff with 90 clips and we narrow that down to 10 clips to show the players. I go to our last game and I go through our last game and make a presentation to them. That's for one game. You've done [the tactics] and analysed their team and your team. You've done pre-scout analysis, and you've done your own game. That's hours and hours. One of the other coaches does the scoring chances. Then we make a presentation before practice in the morning. They're doing the pre-scouts – they present it to me so we can go through it and prepare for the next opponent. You have to look after your own team before the next opponent. That goes on for 82 regular games and 10 exhibition games, and all the playoff games so it's day in day in [without reprieve]. We probably overdo it.

Athlete 5 corroborated this approach: "He [Coach 5] puts in a lot of time and effort, […] because he does not leave anything … he wants to leave nothing to chance". Athlete 6 justified Coach 7's drive for perfection along the same lines:

[At the Olympics], there's a big difference between fourth and gold. Big, big difference. It doesn't seem like that much, it's like, 'Oh they're only two seconds behind' but to make that two seconds up you need to be driven and have an enormous amount of perfectionism.

Athlete 7, also coached by Coach 7, confirmed this view:

If I could use only one word to describe him, then it will be perfectionist. And erm … yes, he leaves nothing to chance, he wants to control everything, and he will do everything for that, to have everything under control as much as possible and he does not compromise.

To what extent this behaviour can be labelled as healthy or obsessive perfectionism, we cannot say.

Athlete 11 shared a similar experience of working with Coach 9: "I don't ever get the sense that he wings anything, ever, he's always very prepared, always very considered. He seems to always have thought hard about it and thought of things that you haven't". On a lighter note, Athlete 17 provided another example of Coach 14's standard-keeping practices:

I sent him a wedding invitation, and he sent it back to me saying a wedding invitation is something very special and should not have spelling mistakes, and he corrected my spelling—And at the very end of his email he said: 'PS. Of course I would love to attend'.

Athlete 5 comprehensively described how Coach 5's perfectionism led to a constant search for an edge over the competition:

Well, we [were] playing the Olympics in [country], so [he said] we should go there. We should see what the stadium looks like, we should check out the field, [...] so we went over there, and we could not go on the field to train, but it was there. We got a tour, we saw the stadium, we climbed over a fence and went to the field to see what kind of field it was and what was the best place to train back home, which venue had a comparable field, and we did it for every tournament. He even took a piece of the field with him and did research to check out what kind of field it was and where we should train to get used to that [...] and it might help only for a half percent, but that is something. He is very good at this. Everything should be the best of the best. Nutrition [in the hotel] should be good, and when we have a hotel, it should be no more than 500m from the field, so that everything works. He wants everything organized, so that everything can be as good as possible [...] so he tries to organize everything as good as possible and he is on top of that also, he wants to know every detail and I think it is difficult for him to let go or to not want to control ... he likes to pull the strings. He just wants to know what is going on. He wants to know.

Finally, although perfectionistic by nature, SWC also understood the futility of dedicating time and energy to things they cannot control as explained by Coach 8:

What we can control, that's what we focus on [...], what we don't think about is what we can't control [...] don't worry about that. Just focus on what you can control. You've got to be [...] in a position where you are confident that you can do well [because you have taken care of all you could].

To summarise, SWC have established specific and idiosyncratic ways of working. Those with whom they work are expected to be compliant with those ways of doing. These processes are informed by the SWC's functional perfectionism and high standards and foster individual accountability and a constant improvement to avoid complacency and stagnation.

Modelling passion

SWC lead by example, which is consistent with Identity and Transformational approaches to leadership. They believe that the best way to get athletes and staff to buy into the coach's vision is by personifying the values and beliefs underpinning it. As Coach 15 put it: "I will never ask them to do something that I'm not prepared to do myself". Part of this approach includes a certain dose of impression management to ensure that athletes can never "catch you out and [they] believe you have all the answers" (Coach 4). SWC modelling their values centred around four key elements, namely, high energy, work ethic, self-care, and continuous learning. These coaches believed their job was to set the tone for others to follow. They took special care to always appear motivated and uplifted and took pride in their unique work ethic and high level of preparation as a standard for all involved. Likewise, they emphasised the need for self-care to be able to sustain high levels of effort throughout long competitive campaigns. Finally, SWC consistently displayed a disposition to continuously learn and improve fuelled by their inherent (healthy) perfectionism, which they hoped rubbed off onto others.

Coach 2 summarised the notion of "modelling": "Leadership is modelling, when you come, you work, you are prepared, you're driven, you're organized, you talk to people – those things are contagious and you set a standard". Coach 8 put it similarly:

I'd be out front, running in front of them all, and I'd have 20 youngsters behind me, running down the road at 7 am, and it's snowing or whatever. We did it, we just got on with it. And it was all part of instilling the discipline.

Central to modelling was the radiating of high energy by the coach. As Coach 3 stated:

Passion, not just how you do things, but making it contagious, being able to communicate that you really care about what you do, that you are totally dedicated to fulfilling your role, that you put maximum effort into everything. You are forgiven for your mistakes more when you are doing things with all the passion you can muster.

Coach 13 summarised it as "coaching every day as though it was my first day of coaching with the same enthusiasm and passion". Athlete 10 confirmed this was also Coach 9's modus operandi: "His passion and commitment are over-whelming, […] he's coached at the highest level and with the same enthusiasm and drive and whatever, for 30 years or something. He's given it his life".

Inextricably linked to high energy, an unmatched work ethic was another marker of powerful modelling. Coach 14 put it like this:

What I can say is that I spend more time [coaching] than anybody else. I have never missed a session, I'll be one of the first to arrive and the last to leave, and I'll never refuse to assist anybody. It often means I'm [there] for hours on end and I enjoy doing it.

Coach 15 had no doubts about the importance of displaying a faultless work ethic: "To produce Olympic or world champions, it's important to be 200%

available. Our profession is very time-consuming [...] Today I feel I still show this commitment to the athletes I coach and it is one of my strengths". In the same vein, Athlete 17 talked about Coach 14's constant presence: "He was at every workout whether it's cardio, weights or [sport], but he was at every workout". Coach 4 explained why showing athletes this work ethic was important: "If players don't trust the coach is working hard, it's best for the coach to find the door and leave".

Despite the importance of zest and displaying an exemplary work ethic, self-care was also highlighted by SWC as a significant element of modelling. For Coach 5, it was about:

> Taking care of yourself and making sure that you are fit through and through. It influences your plan for the day, but it also influences your sleep, your diet, your consumption of alcohol, all that kind of things. It's essential to me that players see how I do that.

Coach 8 explained how this area revolved around:

> being realistic about taking time out. I am a great believer of as a coach you can get burnt out for sure. It's about the number of hours, the number of days, and if you feel as if you are reaching a point where you no longer are motivated or not so enthusiastic about it, that's the time to take time out, and then come back again.

However, Coach 7 explained how this element did not come natural to him and he had to "learn the hard way, I have seriously been in bed, I have seriously been in hospital. Those were not great moments. That has been a hard lesson".

The final component of modelling identified by SWC was continuous learning, displaying positive learning behaviours in front of athletes and staff. Coach 2 explained it as a mix of honesty and opportunity: "I'd learned a ton by being fired, and what I mean by that is I was able to look at myself, and when you sit back after some setbacks, and you have an honest look at yourself, I think you have a chance to grow". In this respect, Athlete 14 talked how Coach 11 was:

> from the coaches I worked with, the one that is really willing to look at other people's coaching styles. Spends a lot of time looking at [...] what makes a good coach, what motivates athletes, what motivates coaches. He's interested in the science of coaching.

It is noteworthy that the athletes observe these pursuits of continuous learning in their coaches. It was noteworthy that these SWC were so open in modelling the importance of ongoing learning.

These influential positive learning behaviours also included owning up to your mistakes. Coach 5 offered his own experience:

Of course, at times you can be wrong. I said after a game once, 'guys, we have lost, but you did not lose, I did! I have lost, you have not lost'. In retrospect that was a beautiful moment. When you are wrong, you should dare to show your vulnerable side and to take responsibility.

In sum, SWC display high energy and a robust work ethic that is a feature of the environment. This high energy and work ethic are coupled with an unquenchable thirst for learning and self-improvement, and a proactive and pragmatic approach to self-care, which influence and inspire those around them.

Resilience

The final manifestation of determination centres around the SWC's capacity to positively meet and overcome the challenges inherent in high-performance sport. As discussed in the "*Equanimity*" section of "*Caring*", these SWC are able to accept the dynamic and volatile nature of competitive sport and reframe all the inherent tensions in a positive manner as "part and parcel of the job [...] a reminder that you are still in contention" (Coach 2). SWC interpret pressure and responsibility as the privilege of the competitor, a necessary evil that drives improved performance. They also construe failure and disappointment as central to motivation and continuous learning. This perspective facilitates their accepting of reality and owning up to mistakes so they can refocus quickly on finding alternative solutions. Paramount to this is the setting of realistic expectations and goals. While not exempt from the pain and anguish of a hard loss or a bad performance, their positive interpretation of competition, and especially negative results, allows them to recover quickly, bounce back, and distil valuable lessons. In addition, SWC accept that some elements of performance are out of their control and thus focus on the components they can impact on to maximise their chance of success. Finally, SWC are consistently capable to remain calm under pressure to make informed judgements and take important decisions relatively shielded from environmental influences.

With regards to acceptance and reframing of the nature of the high-performance environment, Coach 2 used a powerful analogy:

Pressure means you have a chance, if you didn't have a chance, you'd have no pressure. If you go to the Olympic games and there's no pressure, it means you're not expected [to win], you go there and have a good time – pressure means that you have a chance so embrace it and control it. You have to decide whether you want to carry the weight of millions of people around when you're coaching the Olympic team, or do you want them to be the wind behind the sails? You have to make that decision for yourself and handle that.

Coach 11 discussed the idea of reconsidering high-performance coaching as a privileged activity to reduce the level of stress:

I was thinking you know someone at my level gets to coach bright young athletes who are really motivated and they get to go to the Olympics and play. That's the way I've always thought about sport … So, I've never felt pressure, and when coaches talk about burnout or stress. I'm the luckiest guy in the world. My hobby is my job so how can I associate burnout or stress with that job. I just don't get preoccupied with it, I don't think about my job as being stressful so how can it become stressful?

Likewise, Coach 4 re-calibrated perceptions of pressure as positive tension:

I believe [pressure] is something that I believe is good. This is not like you know that you feel pressure, pressure, pressure, but I think it is more correct to say tension, this is something and I believe it's good for everybody.

Coach 7 agreed with the use of the word tension over pressure: "I need it, I love to have it, because that brings up the best in me […], you need tension, not stress, tension, because your body needs to feel that to bring up to best in yourself". Coach 6 made a very similar point about the saliency of perceived pressure bringing the best out of her: "I'm better under pressure […] I prefer it much better when I've got to do it. So, I think you know we're all better under pressure".
Coach 1 focused on the value of reframing hardship, loss, and disappointment as intrinsic and instrumental to learning: "Losing is important, too. It's simply part of it. You also have to experience that because you can get so much [more] out of that than from all the great games that you win". This adaptive attribution for perceived failure was central to learning from disappointment and becoming more resilient (for more on this topic see Chapter 10). For Coach 14, this capacity to learn under pressure was fundamental:

You learn ways of doing something if you are in a corner, you look for ways of getting out of that corner and those ways out of the corner is a skill isn't it. […] It's a kind of skill and I'm well aware that I have that skill and that other people don't.

Coach 7 agreed wholeheartedly:

[When] coping with setbacks, yes, mostly do not run away from it, moreover, confront yourself, walk right through it, and do not walk away, report to the front, do not hide, the sooner you are off the hook, the sooner it gets calm again and you can start up again and move on.

Similarly, Coach 3 pointed out that: "You could be very good tactically, but if you don't have the character to stick with things when things go wrong, you are not going to survive at the elite level".

This acceptance allowed SWC to be solution focused and focus on the performance process. They believed that the best antidote against pressure was the peace of mind that comes from knowing that you have done all you could to put yourself in the best possible position. They clearly understand and consistently manage pressure well in the big moments. Coach 6 said:

At the Olympic Games I slept well because I felt like […] they were as prepared as they could be. Well, I think the more prepared you are, the less pressure you've got, if you're not prepared, you're going to get more pressure because you're going to realise what you haven't covered.

Also, Coach 16 used a checklist to facilitate this process:

I have a checklist for each month, year, for four years of what I did. So, I am always checking back. When all the work is supposed to be finished for the big competition, [… ' I'm just checking, 'did I do everything?' an' I'll answer myself yes or no.

Coach 11 described the importance of:

just going through it on a day-by-day, bit-by-bit sort of approach. In other words, don't try to worry about the big picture, just deal with the little steps that get you there. I just always think well what do I need to do today?

Notably, SWC believed having realistic expectations was key to manage pressure. Coach 5 offered additional insight by describing expectations as a buffering factor: "Pressure arises when there is a difference between your performance and your expectations. So, from the start it is very important to be clear about your expectations and making sure that [they] are realistic".

Finally, being able to control one's reaction to stress to achieve optimal levels of arousal was seen as key. Coach 17 reflected on his approach:

One of my athletes, he always said to me 'how come you keep so calm?' I said, 'well I can't do anything now, right?'. When you come to the major event, there's not much I can do, if we haven't done it before I can't do it now.

So now I'm just a supporter that is looking at it and being positive, [although] inside I'm as nervous as hell because I want them to succeed.

In relation to this, Coach 3 emphasised the need to maintain a flat emotional tone to aid coping and foster longevity:

[you need] the ability to start all over again in many occasions with energy, without putting your head down after a failure and not celebrating too much any successes, softening the emotions upwards and downwards for what's to come or what has come already. It's a way of being which prepares you for the emotional rollercoaster of a job like the one we do.

Coach 9 jokingly agreed with the nature of the job: "You can't do this job without a thick skin, I mean on any given day, at least a dozen people hate you, and those are the ones that you know about".

In short, SWC are highly resilient individuals capable of accepting and re-framing the inherent tensions of high-performance sport, focused on finding solutions to the recurrent stream of challenges. They have realistic expectations, trust the performance development processes they put in place, and can maintain optimal levels of arousal even under significant internal and external pressures.

To summarise the SWC's "Caring Determination" attitude to leading their programmes, they combine an exceptional drive to achieve high levels of per-formance and success with a genuine desire to support and care for all involved. We termed this approach Caring Determination. The interviews with SWC and their athletes reveal how this caring foundation translates into four key elements: i) Athlete-centredness; ii) Stability and dependability; iii) Adaptive coaching; and iv) Shared Leadership. Likewise, through these accounts, SWC reveal extensive determination to build a culture and practice that continuously moves staff and athletes beyond previous levels of skill, expertise, and attainment. This drive is manifested daily across five key areas: i) Focus on a clear personal philosophy, purpose, and goals; ii) Commitment to the job and their vision; iii) Standards that constantly move staff and athletes beyond current levels of performance; iv) Modelling the required and desired behaviours and practices; and v) Resilience to operate under pressure and navigate the ups and downs of high-performance sport.

Considering all the above, in the following chapter we explore the founda-tional elements that drive and enable *Caring Determination*.

8

DRIVERS, ENABLERS, AND BENEFITS OF CARING DETERMINATION

We previously described the general notion and expressions of Caring Determination. To provide more depth of understanding, in this chapter we offer a glimpse into the underpinning motives that drive it to better understand the reasons why these coaches operate in the way they do.

Caring

With regards to Caring, the driver of SWC's practices and behaviours was a genuine desire to care for others. This attitude was founded on an inherent interest in people, a passion for teaching, an espoused self-perception as facilitators of other people's goals, a long-term view of human development, and a heightened sense of justice and fairness. An overview of these elements is presented in Table 8.1

Coach 11 was very clear about his commitment to people not athletes:

[the winning] I'm not very passionate about. I'm more passionate about the process and seeing a young athlete come through the system and doing well. [...] Like it sounds very corny nowadays, but building character, helping people realize their potential, helping people become better people. That's what actually really excites me and I'm very passionate about that side of it. (Coach 11)

Coach 7 went as far as to attributing his longevity as a coach to his people-based focus: "I keep on going for this long, because I feel that I have a role in the life of the athletes ... and I think that is perhaps a better role than the role of winning another gold medal".

DOI: 10.4324/9781003427292-11

TABLE 8.1 The drivers of caring

Genuine care
Interest in people
Passion for teaching
Facilitating others' goals
Long-term developmental view
Sense of justice and fairness

This interest in people was accompanied by a true passion for teaching and facilitating other people's dreams. Coach 15 said: "I started out as a coach to help athletes make their dreams come true. It wasn't about personal accomplishment but something for others". Likewise, Coach 3, talked about his passion for education: "I come from a family of teachers. The teaching gene is in me, it was inevitable". Built into this approach was a realisation and commitment to the long-term nature of development as articulated by Coach 15:

We [must] learn how to be patient and build something that will last. The performances of a constantly evolving athlete – even at 14 or 15 years of age – build up over the long-term. They need to be viewed in terms of career, accepting that they won't happen straightaway if they are to be stronger, better, and richer later on.

Finally, Caring was also buttressed by a strong sense of justice and fairness, which permeated the SWC's activities. Coach 2 emphasised how treating people well and winning was not incompatible:

I'm proud of how hard I worked and how I've treated people, [...]. What we do each and every day tells people who you are as a coach, as a professional. I like to believe that my reputation is fairly squeaky clean and one about winning with integrity.

This view also resonated strongly with Coach 11:

I love it to be fair, [...] if people say 'oh I was treated fairly and I did not make the Olympic team but I understand why', then I also feel I've been successful. [...] You know [if] there's 10 people who have made it and 10 people who haven't, and those 10 people are still mad, obviously I haven't done a very good job. So those are things that are important to me to judge whether I've been successful.

Determination

The SWC's drive to excel appeared to be fuelled by a combination of a burning, near-pathological desire to succeed arising from their past experiences, and a significant sense of duty to others. The key components are reported in Table 8.2.

Coach 2 explained his feelings about "winning": "I'm crazy about winning, I'm not a bad loser, I'm not a bad sport but I love to win […] It might even be partial egomania, but I love being great – I want to be good". Notably, the interviews revealed that, in many cases, the SWC's desire to win was inextricably tied to their own athletic experiences. Ten coaches had been international and/or professional athletes themselves, six had competed at regional/national level, while only one had no experience of competitive sport due to an early injury. Of the ten internationals, five had won medals at major events, yet only two of them had won gold. Moreover, for six of the coaches, critical life events had coloured their athletic careers (especially their conclusion), directing them towards coaching and shaping their approach therein. Coach 8, for example, had his one chance of going to the Olympics in 1980 thwarted by his country boycotting the event, while Coaches 4, 10, and 13 were involved in serious car accidents that cut their careers short. Coach 6 stated that growing up as one of the very few females playing the sport and having to endure discrimination and isolation had made her very resolute to show everyone what she was capable of. Finally, coach 8 explained how he declined the opportunity to compete at the Olympics to start a new career outside sport and had never been able to forgive himself until he returned to the sport as a coach. Thus, for many it seems that unfulfilled and unsatisfying athletic careers, at times cut short due to injuries, accidents, and even politics, left a powerful imprint on their attitude to competition as a coach. Coach 7 summarised the above point: "I am of course simply a failed elite athlete […]. Maybe that is the conclusion of this research: the most successful coaches are failed elite athletes trying to make amends". Along the same lines, Athlete 12 offered her perception of this phenomenon as it applied to Coach 10:

> I think in his own mind he still has something to prove. […] [He thinks] his achievements will get him to a level that is better than himself [as an athlete]. I think for himself to know that he is respected is really important.

TABLE 8.2 The drivers of determination

Burning desire to succeed	Sense of duty
Past athletic experiences	Duty to club/country
Critical life incidents	Duty to significant others
Serial insecurity	Duty to athletes
Passion for the sport	
Thrill of competition	

We described this driver as "Serial Insecurity" (Lara-Bercial & Mallett, 2016). These coaches lived their lives perched on a precarious balance between a "Grounded Self-Belief" in their own ability based on previous achievements and work ethic, and a "healthy" dose of "Reasonable Self-Doubt" about whether they are good enough to win again. This "Serial Insecurity", however, far from being debilitating, protected them from complacency and spurred them on to try to win again despite their previous frequent success. We re-iterate that there is a strong sense that the SWC never really atone for their perceived past failings (Mallett & Coulter, 2016; Mallett & Lara-Bercial, 2016). Coach 1 even spoke about it with trepidation: "[Every year] there is a new cycle, a different team, you always start from scratch. That's also exciting". For Coach 2, the past did not matter: "I'm scared to death about next year. I'm scared we're going down – why? I don't want us going down on my watch. I want to be great this year, not last year". Despite this, he was still able to act confidently: "I get confidence when I work and I know I'm prepared. When you go to the Olympic games and you know you've been through major competitions and you've had success, it's like going to an exam – you're prepared and you know. I don't feed my family on hope". Coach 9 also articulated this desire to continue winning despite 42 years of it:

> I have coached now for 42 years non-stop, where I didn't have the normal break time. So yes, and I feel good with it. […] the biggest challenge is as well for me to do it again, do it again, even also with the same athletes that already won. […] I don't need to do it anymore, with my age, but I still enjoy it, […] you are still sharp, you are still in the driving seat not tailing on and "he lives from the past", […] I don't want to live from the past […] I am looking forward, the next important one is my next challenge, not what I did in the past, that's for other people to write it down.

Notwithstanding the above elements related to their personal history in sport, SWC also discussed their heightened sense of purpose and duty to others as a significant driver of their determination to succeed. For some coaches, like Coach 9, this revolved around not letting down those who have supported her in the past: "The final piece for me was making sure that […] I wouldn't disappoint those people around me like my hometown, my family you know, people who believed in me". For others, like Coach 8, the pride of representing their sport and their country on the highest stage made everything worth it:

> I am very loyal as it were to the sport and to the country and I want us to be successful. Whatever we did, I just wanted to do well. It always goes back to the [Monarch], the fact that we are here to win a gold medal for [the Monarch].

Moreover, coaches like Coach 15 highlighted their commitment to both country and athletes: "I am at the service of [country denomination] athletes. It's important that coaches offer their services for the benefit of [country denomination] sport". Athlete 11 (Coach 9) corroborated this stance:

> He feels massive pressure to get it right, [because] it's people's lives. [Athletes] are there giving up their all, [all] of their twenties and some of their thirties because they love the sport. He understands [his decisions] affect people, but [...] he makes them in the best interest of [nation], but it's still tough for him.

The enablers of caring determination: cognitive and emotional flexibility

So far, in this section we have explored the general notion of *Caring Determination*, presented in its everyday manifestations, and delved into its underlying motives. Throughout this account, the behaviours of SWC have been shown to contain high doses of plasticity to respond to the ever-changing dynamic nature of the high-performance context. Over the course of the interviews, two enabling qualities of such malleability were unearthed, namely, cognitive and emotional flexibility. A summary of the main features is presented in Table 8.3.

Cognitive flexibility

Cognitive flexibility revolves around the capacity of SWC to be open-minded and lateral thinkers who are curious and solution-focused, and not overly limited by their previous experiences and personal biases. This characteristic allows them to consider multiple, even conflicting, points of view at one time, and concentrate on finding the best possible solution, even if it means acting against previously held beliefs. This fluid rather than rigid thinking, fosters their personal and professional learning and growth, supports the emergence of innovative ideas to stay ahead of others, and protects them against both complacency and

TABLE 8.3 The enablers of caring determination

Cognitive flexibility	Emotional flexibility
Open-minded	Equanimity
Lateral thinkers	Emotional regulation
Multiple viewpoints and solutions	Resilience
Flexible and responsive planning	Social competence
Innovative	Egoless (when needed)
Good learners	

boredom. It also facilitates more flexible planning and more confident and steadfast management of uncertainty and crisis. Coach 3 described the benefits of this attribute:

> I like to look after every detail, but in my experience, you have to be flexible according to the information that you are getting from the day-to-day. My starting point is a very structured planning framework, but at the same time I have learnt that being able to modify things is a key quality to have. Flexibility to make changes if the reality in front of you requires it.

Coach 9 drew a parallel with the expertise of a Chef:

> I would say a good coach is like a good cook, everybody has the same recipe and ingredients, but they are cooking different, the dish from this particular chef tastes maybe that little bit better, he doesn't just follow the recipe because it says 10 grams of salt, so he maybe put 11 grams or a little less and it tastes a bit better. You have to have that same feeling with your athletes, making the best out of their ingredients, not just following recipes.

Coach 7 also emphasised this quality as both innate and foundational to great coaching, reinforcing the importance of the "art" of coaching:

> You can educate and train whatever you want, but when you are not a coach by nature, then you will never become a coach. You can't force it. I have seen too many people coach from the books, like this is how it is written and this is how it should be done, [...] but that is not something you can fall back on. Somewhere it is within you, it is intuition, it is your other self.

Finally, Coach 16 shared the learning benefits of cognitive flexibility:

> I look at myself, what can I do better instead of pointing the finger [at others]. [...] I always believe you keep learning it doesn't matter if someone's younger or older. It doesn't matter who they are [...] I am always openminded, to assess if something I felt like, wow okay this is good, I'd like to try it. So, I always believe an open mind is important.

Emotional flexibility

Complementing cognitive flexibility, the SWC's capacity to display high levels of equanimity we termed *emotional flexibility*. This ability facilitates the acceptance of the more challenging elements of the job, the power to regulate where and how to spend the finite emotional energy at their disposal, and the resilience to bounce back from mistakes, failure, and disappointment. Moreover, emotional flexibility allows SWC to read people (individuals and groups) and situations, and to manage their emotions as well as others' thus rendering them socially and emotionally competent and confident. Lastly, emotional flexibility allows coaches to surrender their personal desires when required to focus on the needs of those around them, especially, but not exclusively, the athletes. Indeed, they put the needs of the athlete first.

Coach 3 was able to provide a specific example of emotional flexibility leading to this quality of equanimity:

> Emotions make events appear bigger or more dramatic than they really are. It helps when you put things in perspective. The impact is the same, how you react is different. Experience gives you this, a different vision, it changes how you see things; time puts things in perspective. After a loss, three hours later it feels one way, but the following morning is different.

Coach 9 offered another example of the benefits of emotional regulation:

> Well definitely you're better and better, I think you're calmer, you are more sure of your ups and downs. Yes, you're more sure of your ups and downs, I mean the details matter but you know what bridges and what battles to fight and what ones are small and big picture, and you don't need to fight that battle.

Moreover, Coach 6 alluded to the need to overcome the emotional barriers that stop coaches from accepting their own mistakes:

> Yes, and I have learned not to run away from it. Do not play the innocent but dare to admit to being wrong. Because a lot of people ... a lot of people make up a story when something goes wrong or lie about or something like that, I am averse to that.

Finally, Coach 7 referred to the importance of being able to treat different people differently within boundaries: "In a team you simply have a diversity of people, especially now, and as a professional it is very important, I should be able to adjust [...] and address a person in a way the he or she blossoms".

Notably, cognitive, emotional, and subsequent behavioural flexibility appear to be founded upon coaches' observation powers and self-awareness. SWC are able to quickly detect and notice changes within themselves, and within others and the environment in order to determine the best course of action at any given time. We discuss this ability of *noticing to inform action* further in Chapter 10.

Self-knowledge was recurrently reported by SWC as paramount to optimal performance (see Chapter 3). Coach 11 was clear in this respect: "I think one of the secrets to be successful as a coach is to be introspective. In other words, look into yourself [...] and self-analyse". Coach 15 provided additional detail:

> It's important to learn to identify one's own method of working. A coach who doesn't know who he is, with what he identifies himself, how he identifies himself, what his values are, won't make a good coach in my view as his athletes and colleagues need to know what he stands for.

In sum, cognitive and emotional flexibility support the development of adaptive coaching behaviours to suit the individual and situational demands coaches and their athletes face daily. As Athlete 14 (Coach 11) put it:

> Yeah, it just depends on the situation, and it depends on the group of athletes, it depends on ... I mean, not that he is a chameleon, but he can move through all of these different scenarios, depending on whether we're in a team that's possibly winning at the Olympics, to a team that's in a development type team. He will change his coaching and his strategy to fit the situation that's in front of him.

Benefits of caring determination for athletes

The participant athletes and coaches identified a variety of benefits to the Caring Determination approach. These can be grouped into four areas: constant growth, safety net, performance ready, and adaptability. Caring Determination was seen as equally responsible for driving continued performance improvements as well as fostering personal development beyond sport. In addition, it promoted growth from within – building an environment where athletes and staff drove each other's growth, creating a sense of collaboration and community. Moreover, all this growth took place within an environment that, whilst challenging and dynamic, provided sufficient emotional and physical safety for development to occur in a relatively healthy manner. This combination of challenge and support led to the emergence of a long-term confidence in athletes that allowed them to commit to highly demanding training programmes and thrive in the competitive arena. In addition, athletes recognised the role their coach played in getting them ready to perform through specific pre-competition interventions aimed at developing their competitive confidence. Finally, athletes highly valued their coaches' adaptability to meet their always evolving needs and their changing capabilities through a range of relational behaviours and strategies. These benefits are summarised in Table 8.4.

TABLE 8.4 Caring determination benefits for athletes

Constant growth	Safety net for mental and physical health	Performance ready	Adaptability (behavioural flexibility)
Continued performance improvement	Emotional and physical safety	Right intervention at right time	Flexible actions to meet the evolving capabilities and needs of the athlete
Support constant personal development	Confidence builder (long term)	Confidence builder (in the moment)	
Foster group internal growth			

Constant growth

The consistent and relentless demands from the SWC were portrayed by athletes as difficult to deal with yet central to improvement. Athlete 1 (Coach 1) appreciated that "he doesn't even throw me a rope to pull myself out of this mess, but makes it quite clear to me that I have to do it myself. So, he deliberately exposes me to situations involving stress and pressure, which I have to deal with". This growth extended beyond sport as attested to by Athlete 8 (Coach 8):

> For me it's the big picture and [coach name]'s influence on my life and career has been positive in a lot of ways. I think my parents think I'm very lucky to have had that opportunity, because for sure now I've achieved, I've achieved beyond what anybody maybe expected.

Athlete 16 (Coach 14) shared a similar view: "[he's played] a huge role [in my life]. I [pause] I hate to overstate this because obviously I love my family very much, but he has probably affected who I am more than any other person". This is such a powerful quote in recognising the, at times, significant influence of coaches of the development of young adults. This potential and positive influence should not be assumed.

Notably, athletes such as Athlete 1 (Coach 1) felt that SWC were also adept at allowing development to emerge from within the group:

> For him it is a matter, not so much of prescribing certain things, but he just tries to allow a lot of it to come from the team itself. So, he provides a rough framework or a rough direction the team can develop in. But how precisely the team actually develops within this framework is up to the team itself, and he encourages that. And I think that's very brave. I think a lot of coaches have a problem with that because they are afraid of it. They have a certain idea, and

they want to drum it into the team. [Coach 1] is someone who would go to hell and back to prevent that happening.

The potential of all actors in the sport setting to contribute to others' development supports the value proposition of sport as a vehicle for young people to grow (Côté, Turnnidge & Vierimaa, 2016).

Safety net for mental and physical health

The caring disposition and attitude of SWC also led to the creation of a safe climate where athletes felt protected and cared for within the constraints of a performance-driven environment. Athlete 14 explained how Coach 11 achieved this atmosphere:

> I think he keeps a pretty good perspective on winning and losing, and on training. I think when you leave the sport, the majority of the athletes— success or no success—are going to be emotionally healthy. As well as physically healthy because an elite sport is not necessarily physically healthy in terms of what you do to your body. I think one of his legacies would be to leave athletes who are emotionally and physically healthy when they leave the sport, and I don't think that that's the case with a lot of winning coaches.

This safety net was also responsible for the development of confident athletes who were prepared to invest into their careers long-term:

> Due to the fact that he expressed his confidence in me and that he also held these intensive conversations with me, he also developed me so as to open me up to these new ways of doing things, and to see the team and the coach from a different perspective. That was incredibly important for my personal development […] and it was probably also the most intensive thing I have experienced. (Athlete 2; Coach 1)

A similar view was expressed by Athlete 9 (Coach 9): "He was the facilitator in helping provide that environment and you know right from an early age I identified it as great. And we bought into it heavily". This safety net for mental and physical health creates an environment that allows people to thrive, which we will elaborate on in Chapter 11.

Performance ready when it counts the most helps athlete confidence

In addition, athletes reported that a key enabler of the Caring Determination approach was a consistent sense of being ready to perform in "critical" moments.

This was achieved partly due to the SWC's ability to intervene in key situations: "He found sensational words both in [Olympics 1] and in [Olympics 2], so he got the whole team behind him [...] he allowed it all [previous issues] to go on and then he cleared it all up in a single moment" Athlete 1 (Coach 1). Being ready to perform when it counts the most was also accomplished through the deliberate attempts by the coach to build confidence in the competitive moment. Coach 9 summarised this approach: "Even when conditions are not ideal, still you have to come strong over to the athletes and say we're fine, we have trained, we can compensate that little bit, we can still win, because you are so much better". Similarly, Coach 7 emphasised the importance of managing the lead up to the big events: "With a few weeks to go we stop working on technical development. At that point they need to trust where they are. They will perform better through high confidence than through a marginal technical improvement so close to competition". Perhaps most importantly, however, SWC were able to gain the full trust of athletes in their preparation as key to approaching events confidently: "With him you know he has done it some many times before so you just trust it 100% and give it your all. So, we always go into it feeling we can win" (Athlete 10; Coach 9).

Adaptability in approach to coaching (behavioural flexibility)

Finally, athletes felt that SWC were able to adapt their coaching in two ways. First in relation to how they were able to "read the mood of the athletes and change [their] approach to get the best out of them on a minute-by-minute basis" (Athlete 13; Coach 10); and second, with regard to being able to modify their behavioural approach to a particular athlete as they develop as an athlete and as human being. This was candidly expressed by Athlete 7 (Coach 7):

The person who has evolved the most, is me. And he has joined me in my development of course, because at first, he was a coach who was right on my tail and I needed a coach more back then, because I was young [...]. At first he was the coach, so to speak ... a coach who I was dependent on at times and now he is more a coach who says: well, you know, you are 26 now and you should do things on your own [...], so at certain moments he for example deliberately distances himself and ... yes, I think it is very smart how he handles that development, so to speak, that he ... It would be easier to hold on to the way of coaching like he did when we started to work together, but he very well takes into account your growth and he anticipates very well in that. So, he looks at ... We do not have a different understanding, but the way of coaching is different now. I mean, during my first Olympics, he had to explain things over and over again, because I ... I was a rookie, we talked about certain race elements and tactics, well, we do not have to do that anymore, that is structural/ standard now and at first we talked about the outlines and now we are talking about the details … yes, that also grows. I think that is smart, he is able to do that with everybody.

This adaptability in how you coach (behavioural flexibility), especially as the athlete develops their craft, seems to contribute to positive outcomes such as performance and personal development. We elaborate on this key point in Chapter 11.

What did we learn?

This section of our study of SWC focused on their leadership blueprint. Caring Determination, defined as "The relentless pursuit of excellence balanced with a genuine and compassionate desire to support athletes and oneself" was identified as the broad approach to encapsulate the myriad attitudes, beliefs, and behaviours forming the SWC leadership signature. In line with previous research (Din & Paskevich, 2013; Gould et al., 1999), these SWC further endorsed that HP coaching goes beyond the application of technical and tactical knowledge with psychological, social, and organisational factors playing a major role in how these SWC led, including decision-making (Barker-Ruchti, Barker & Annerstedt, 2014). The inclusion of athlete testimonies in our study allowed us to offer a deeper perspective compared to most previous research. Along with their coaches, athletes felt a vast understanding of the ins and outs of their sport was a given for any coach working at this level, and that the relational and organisational elements were the true differentiators (Brown & Arnold, 2019; Collins & Durand-Bush, 2019; Mujika, 2017; Vallée & Bloom, 2016). The creation of a positive and safe climate (Brown & Arnold, 2019; Côté & Sedgwick, 2003; McCarthy et al., 2021) centred around the holistic needs of the athlete was prioritised by SWC (Carter & Bloom, 2009; Cronin, Knowles & Enright, 2020; Currie & Oates-Wilding, 2012; Lindgren & Barker-Ruchti, 2017). Self-reliance and creativity within the boundaries of the common framework were encouraged and promoted (Cheon et al., 2015). The capacity of the SWC to situationally work along a continuum going from autocratic/assertive to collaborative/cooperative was paramount (Din & Paskevich, 2013; Dohsten, Barker-Ruchti & Lindgren, 2020; Lara-Bercial & Mallett, 2016; McCarthy et al., 2021). In agreement with existing research (Din & Paskevich, 2013; Vallée & Bloom, 2005, 2016; Weinberg et al., 2022), we confirmed that this caring approach was founded upon a clear, explicit, and publicly espoused humanistic philosophy which pervaded all aspects of the SWC's work (Coulter et al., 2016). In line with Cronin, Knowles, and Enright (2020), SWC viewed this approach as central to their work and key to their pedagogical role. SWC also recognised that, beyond the maternal dyadic (coach and athlete) notion of care proposed by

Noddings (1984; 2013) and Jowett (2017), care is also "rules-based" and enabled or constrained by the specific features of the social context and the behaviours of its actors (Cronin & Armour, 2019).

Moreover, our study delved deeper into this "way of life" by searching for the underlying motives and drivers. In the main, SWC are genuinely interested in people, have a passion for teaching, see themselves as facilitators of others' learning and success, and display an elevated sense of justice and fairness. This perspective is key to the development of sustainable high-performance practices (Dohsten, Barker-Ruchti & Lindgren, 2020). Despite the volatile and precarious nature of HP sport (Bentzen et al., 2020), SWC favour a long-term view of development for their own career as well as their athletes'. This perspective allows them to manage and deflect the pressure arising from the performance-based short-termism inherent to HP sport.

Notwithstanding the above caring approach, we also confirmed that the work of these coaches is fuelled by an unapologetic will and determination to succeed (Lara-Bercial & Mallett, 2016). SWC are highly competitive individuals driven by an unsatiable desire to do well and to win (Din et al., 2015; Hassmén et al., 2020; Vallée & Bloom, 2005). Particularly, and originally, our study elicited the sources of this urge to triumph. First, somewhat akin to the hardship-laden journey endured by some successful athletes (Collins & Macnamara, 2012), SWC described their perceived athletic failures and shortcomings and critical life incidents such as career-ending injuries and traffic accidents, as central to their motivation to win – a way of making amends (*atonement*; Mallett & Coulter, 2016; Mallett & Lara-Bercial, 2016). Remarkably, SWC's work was also powered by a unique phenomenon we termed "Serial Insecurity", the combination of "reasonable self-doubt" and "grounded self-belief" that far from being debilitating, created the momentum and drive to ward off complacency and bounce back from defeat and disappointment (Sarkar & Hilton, 2020; Weinberg et al., 2022). However, a second component to this unquenched need to win had a very different origin far from an egotistic urge to prove their worth. SWC embodied a strong sense of duty and responsibility towards their clubs, countries, athletes, and significant others that drove their daily performance. Some of these SWC did not want their athletes to experience what they experienced as athletes and sought to help them avoid that heartbreak and disappointment (Dohsten, Barker-Ruchti & Lindgren, 2020; Mallett & Coulter, 2016; Mujika, 2017).

From an athlete perspective, Caring Determination led to continued performance improvements as well as fostering personal development beyond sport (Carter & Bloom, 2009; Lara-Bercial & Mallett, 2016; Lindgren & Barker-Ruchti, 2017). In addition, it promoted growth from within – creating an environment where athletes and staff drove each other's progress (Brown & Arnold, 2019). Moreover, the environment was able to balance challenging and dynamic conditions with sufficient emotional and physical support to guarantee relatively healthy performance and wellbeing outcomes (Fletcher & Sarkar, 2016). This combination of challenge and support led to the emergence of a long-term confidence in athletes that allowed them to commit to highly demanding training programmes and thrive in the competitive arena (Dohsten, Barker-Ruchti & Lindgren, 2020). In addition, athletes recognised the role their coach played in getting them ready to perform through specific pre-competition interventions aimed at developing their competitive confidence (Cheon et al., 2015; Gould et al., 2002). Finally, athletes highly valued their coaches' adaptability to meet their always evolving needs and their changing capabilities through a "chameleonic" range of relational behaviours and strategies (Ferrar et al., 2018; Lara-Bercial & Mallett, 2016).

In conclusion, we confirmed the highly dynamic and situational nature of HP coaching (Gould et al., 2002) and the relative strength of SWC to work within, and respond to, the relational, structural, and performance-based demands and constraints of the HP environment (Din et al., 2015; Greenleaf, Gould & Dieffenbach, 2002; Kellet, 1999). World-class performance happens at the edge of chaos. In leading HP athletes and teams, SWC constantly walk a series of fine lines to preserve a precarious balance amidst many competing tensions to get the job done. These include: short- and long-term goals (Lara-Bercial & Mallett, 2016), athlete and staff challenge and support (Fletcher & Sarkar, 2016), egotistic and altruistic motivations (Mallett & Lara-Bercial, 2016), athlete support and coach wellbeing (Carson et al., 2019; Joncheray, Burlot & Julla-Marcy, 2019; Sakar & Hilton, 2020); coach control and athlete and staff creativity (Din & Paskevich, 2013; Lara-Bercial & Mallett, 2016), consistent evolution within a permanent philosophy (Din et al., 2015; Lara-Bercial & Mallett, 2016; Vallée & Bloom, 2005), job satisfaction and job insecurity (Bentzen et al., 2020), and coach self-doubt and self-belief (Lara-Bercial & Mallett, 2016). Notably, our study revealed how this capacity to live and perform in the "swampy lowlands" of elite sport coaching (Cassidy, Jones & Potrac, 2015) was powered by a combination of what we termed cognitive, emotional flexibility, and subsequent behavioural flexibility (i.e., notions of *psychological flexibility, orchestration,* and *structured improvisation,* which are discussed in more detail n Chapter 11). From a cognitive perspective, SWC demonstrated heightened levels of open-mindedness, the ability to hold multiple viewpoints at one time, think laterally, and a substantial capacity to respond to events in a swift and pliable manner (Barker-Ruchti, Barker & Annerstedt, 2014; Mujika, 2017). Emotionally, SWC showed high levels of equanimity, resilience, emotional regulation, and social competence (Sarkar & Hilton, 2020; Weinberg et al., 2022). This latent suppleness was consistently called upon to respond to the myriad challenges provided by the daily rollercoaster ride of HP sport. It also allowed SWC to normalise and reframe pressure and uncertainty as inherent, necessary, and even beneficial elements of the job (Bentzen, Kentta & Lemyre, 2020), thus extending their longevity in a profession with typically a high turnover (Bachan, Reilly & Witt, 2008; Tozetto et al., 2019).

References

Bachan, R., Reilly, B., & Witt, R. (2008). The hazard of being an English football league manager: Empirical estimates for three recent league seasons. *Journal of the Operational Research Society, 59*(7), 884–891. 10.1057/palgrave.jors.2602408

Barker-Ruchti, N., Barker, D. & Annerstedt, C. (2014) Techno-rational knowing and phronesis: The professional practice of one middle-distance running coach. *Reflective Practice, 15*(1), 53–65, DOI: 10.1080/14623943.2013.868794

Bentzen, M., Kenttä, G., & Lemyre, P. N. (2020). Elite football coaches' experiences and sensemaking about being fired: An interpretative phenomenological analysis. *International Journal of Environmental Research and Public Health, 17*(14), 5196. 10.3390/ijerph17145196

Bentzen, M., Kenttä, G., Richter, A., & Lemyre, P-N. (2020). Impact of job insecurity on psychological well- and ill-being among high performance coaches. *International Journal of Environmental Research and Public Health, 17*(19), 6939–6954. 10.3390/ijerph17196939

Brown, D. J., & Arnold, R. (2019). Sports performers' perspectives on facilitating thriving in professional rugby contexts. *Psychology of Sport & Exercise, 40*, 71–81. 10.1016/j.psychsport.2018.09.008

Carson, F., Malakellis, M., Walsh, J., Main, L. C., & Kremer, P. (2019). Examining the mental well-being of Australian sport coaches. *International Journal of Environmental Research and Public Health, 16*(23), 4601–4613. 10.3390/ijerph16234601

Carter, A. D., & Bloom, G. A. (2009). Coaching knowledge and success going beyond athletic experiences. *Journal of Sport Behavior, 32*, 419–437.

Cassidy, T. G., Potrac, P., & Jones, R. L. (2015). *Understanding sports coaching: The pedagogical, social, and cultural foundations of coaching practice (3rd ed.).* Routledge. doi: 10.4324/9780203797952

Cheon, S. H., Reeve, J., Lee, J., & Lee, Y. (2015). Giving and receiving autonomy support in a high-stakes sport context: A field-based experiment during the 2012 London Paralympic Games. *Psychology of Sport and Exercise, 19*, 59–69. 10.1016/j.psychsport.2015.02.007

Collins, J., & Durand-Bush, N. (2019). The Optimal Team Functioning Model: A Grounded Theory framework to guide teamwork in Curlin. *Journal of Applied Sport Psychology, 4*(31), 405–426, DOI: 10.1080/10413200.2018.1512536

Collins, D., & MacNamara, A. (2012). The rocky road to the top: Why talent needs trauma. *Sports Medicine, 42*(11), 907–914. DOI: 10.1007/BF03262302

Côté, J., & Sedgwick, W. A. (2003). Effective behaviors of expert rowing coaches: A qualitative investigation of Canadian athletes and coaches. *International Sports Journal, 7*(1), 62–77.

Côté, J., Turnnidge, J., & Vierimaa, M. (2016). A personal assets approach to youth sport. In K. Green, & A. Smith (Eds.), *Routledge handbook of youth sport* (pp. 243–255). Routledge.

Coulter, T., Gilchrist, M., Mallett, C., & Carey, A. (2016). Abraham Maslow: Hierarchy of coach and athlete needs. In, L. Nelson, R. Groom, & P. Potrac (Eds.), *Learning in sports coaching* (pp. 63–74). London: Routledge.

Cronin, C., & Armour, K. (2019). *Care in sport coaching: Pedagogical cases.* Abingdon: Routledge.

Cronin, C., Knowles, Z. R., & Enright, K. (2020). The challenge to care in a Premier League Football Club, *Sports Coaching Review, 9*(2), 123–146. DOI: 10.1080/2164062 9.2019.1578593

Currie, J. L., & Oates-Wilding, S. (2012) Reflections on a dream: Towards an understanding of factors Olympic coaches attribute to their success, *Reflective Practice*, *13*(3), 425–438. DOI: 10.1080/14623943.2012.670106

Din, C., & Paskevich, D. (2013). An integrated research model of Olympic podium performance. *International Journal of Sports Science & Coaching*, *8*(2), 431–444. DOI: 10.1260/1747-9541.8.2.431

Din, C., Paskevich, D., Gabriele, T., & Werthner, P. (2015). Olympic medal winning leadership. *International Journal of Sport Science & Coaching*, *10*(4), 589–604. DOI: 10.12 60/1747-9541.10.4.589

Dohsten, J., Barker-Ruchti, N., & Lindgren, E. C. (2020) Caring as sustainable coaching in elite athletics: Benefits and challenges, *Sports Coaching Review*, *9*(1), 48–70, DOI: 10.1080/21640629.2018.1558896

Ferrar, P., Hosea, L., Henson, M., Dubina, N., Krueger, G., Staff, J., & Gilbert, W. (2018). Building high performing coach-athlete relationships: The USOC's National Team Coach Leadership Education Program (NTCLEP). *International Sport Coaching Journal*, *5*(1), 60–70. 10.1123/iscj.2017-0102

Fletcher, D., & Sarkar, M. (2016). Mental fortitude training: An evidence-based approach to developing psychological resilience for sustained success. *Journal of Sport Psychology in Action*, 7, 135–157. 10.1080/21520704.2016.1255496

Gould, D., Guinan, D., Greenleaf, C., & Chung, Y. (2002). A survey of U.S. Olympic coaches: Variables perceived to have influenced athlete performances and coach effectiveness. *The Sport Psychologist*, *16*, 229–250.

Gould, D., Guinan, D., Greenleaf, C., Medbery, R., & Petterson, K. (1999). Factors affecting Olympic performance of athletes and coaches from more and less successful teams. *The Sport Psychologist*, *13*, 371–395.

Hassmén, P., Lundkvist, E., Flett, G. L., Hewitt, P. L., Gustafsson, H. (2020). Coach burnout in relation to perfectionistic cognitions and self-presentation. *International Journal of Environmental Research and Public Health*, *17*(23), 8812–8837. 10.3390/ijerph1 7238812

Joncheray, H., Burlot, F., & Julla-Marcy, M. (2019). Is the game lost in advance? Being a high-performance coach and preserving family life. *International Journal of Sports Science & Coaching*, *14*(4), 453–462. 10.1177/1747954119860223

Jowett, S. (2017). Coaching effectiveness: The coach–athlete relationship at its heart. *Current Opinion in Psychology*, *16*, 154–158.

Kellet, P. (1999). Organisational leadership: Lessons from professional coaches. *Sport Management Review*, 2, 150–171.

Lara-Bercial, S., & Mallett, C. J. (2016). The practices and developmental pathways of professional and Olympic serial winning coaches. *International Sport Coaching Journal*, *3*(1), 221–239. DOI: 10.1123/iscj.2016-0083

Lindgren, E. C., & Barker-Ruchti, N. (2017) Balancing performance-based expectations with a holistic perspective on coaching: a qualitative study of Swedish women's national football team coaches' practice experiences. *International Journal of Qualitative Studies on Health and Well-being*, *12*, sup2, DOI: 10.1080/17482631.2017.1358580

Mallett, C., & Coulter, T. (2016). The anatomy of a successful Olympic coach: Performer, agent, and author. *International Sport Coaching Journal*, *3*, 113–127.

Mallett, C., & Lara-Bercial, S. (2016). Serial winning coaches: People, vision and environment. In M. Raab, P. Wylleman, R. Seiler, A. M. Elbe, & A. Hatzigeorgiadis

(Eds.), *Sport and Exercise Psychology Research: From Theory to Practice* (pp. 289–322). Academic Press (Elsevier).

McCarthy, L., Martin, A., Slade, D., & Watson, G. (2021). Of women, by women, for women: How coaches and captains created a caring and winning culture in the New Zealand Netball team. *The International Journal of Sport and Society, 12*(2), 153–165. doi: 10.18848/2152-7857/CGP/v12i02/153-165.

Mujika, I. (2017). Winning the BIG medals. *International Journal of Sports Physiology and Performance, 12*(3), 273, 274.

Noddings, N. (1984). *Caring: A feminine approach to ethics and moral education.* University of California Press.

Noddings, N. (2013). *Caring: A relational approach to ethics and moral education.* University of California Press.

Sarkar, M., & Hilton, N. K. (2020). Psychological resilience in Olympic medal–winning coaches: A longitudinal qualitative study. *International Sport Coaching Journal, 7*(2), 209–219. 10.1123/iscj.2019-0075

Tozetto, A. B., Carvalho, H. M., Rosa, R. S., Mendes, F. G., Silva, W. R., Nascimento, J. V., & Milistetd, M. (2019). Coach turnover in top professional Brazilian football championship: A multilevel survival analysis. *Frontiers in Psychology, 10*, 1246. 10.3389/fpsyg.2019.01246

Vallée, C. N., & Bloom, G. A. (2005). Building a successful program: Perspectives of expert Canadian female coaches of team sports. *Journal of Applied Sport Psychology, 17*, 179–196.

Vallée, C. N., & Bloom, G. A. (2016). Four keys to building a Championship culture. *International Sport Coaching Journal, 3*(2), 170–177. 10.1123/iscj.2016-0010

Weinberg, R., Freysinger, V., Vealey, R., & Block, C. (2022) What does it mean to be "mentally tough" as a NCAA division I collegiate coach? *Journal of Applied Sport Psychology, 34*(2), 342–362. DOI: 10.1080/10413200.2020.1791277

Striving, Surviving, and Thriving in Elite Sport

9

STRIVING AND BECOMING A SWC

Coach in context

Context matters. Coaches and how and why they perform their craft cannot be understood without consideration of their context. This person-in-context view is analogous to the terroir (external influences) on the quality of wine produced from grapes. Quality wine can only be produced if the grapes have grown in a fertile environment (i.e., soil, climate, wind, water, and human involvement) that is predictable and stable which, in turn, enables the grapes on the vine to thrive. This metaphor is akin to appreciating and understanding the ecology in which the coach operates. We typically refer to this ecology as culture, which begs at least two key questions: *How do successful coaches develop and sustain a high-performing culture? What does it look like?*

In understanding the coach-in-context, we draw upon three concepts that capture to some extent the opportunities and challenges of coaches' work in the highly contested elite sport environment ... *human striving, surviving,* and *thriving.* We assume that these SWC, as architects and sculptors of the daily training and competition environments, have learned to create a stable and dependable *greenhouse* (terroir) for all social actors to thrive (Lara-Bercial & Mallett, 2016); however, it is important to be mindful that for most of the time the reality is that the social actors constitute a dynamical system that is always in a state of some flux. Indeed, there will be fluctuations between surviving and thriving. Furthermore, the timing of these periods of thriving might not be so predictable but certainly coaches seek to build to these peak periods when it counts the most. We preface this assumption with the notion that the likely intention of coaches is to create such a greenhouse environment; however,

DOI: 10.4324/9781003427292-13

progressing from intentions to sculpting a thriving environment is highly challenging with many moving parts.

Three core concepts related to high performance and wellbeing are striving, surviving, and thriving (e.g., Mahoney et al., 2014). Although we will initially consider each of these three concepts individually, it is worth reporting that they are co-dependent. There is some empirical support for those inter-dependencies. Firstly, striving (goal pursuits) is foundational to notions of surviving and thriving – these goals provide the fuel to behave and think in particular ways. For example, overcoming challenges (surviving) promotes a sense of competence and resilience (e.g., Fletcher & Sarkar, 2012; Sarkar et al., 2015; Sarkar & Hilton, 2020) that, in turn, can foster a sense of thriving over time. Furthermore, when people have a belief that they are learning and flourishing they re-calibrate their oft internally driven goal pursuits (e.g., Emmons, 1989) to continue their growth towards superior performances and wellbeing. These personally meaningful goal pursuits (i.e., strivings) can foster higher levels of thriving (e.g., Clark et al., 2022; Clark et al., in press; Sheldon & Elliot, 1999). In the next three chapters, we will examine the notions of striving, surviving, and thriving as reported by the coaches and athletes in this study to better understand the coach in context.

Personal strivings – *Why SWC are invested in coaching?*

In our view, striving is foundational to notions of surviving and thriving. Developmentally, personal strivings emerge in early childhood. These strivings give meaning and purpose to what we do, who we are, and who we want to become. The strivings of these SWC (2nd layer of personality) provide a framework for eventually making sense of one's lived experiences in late adolescence and early adulthood (i.e., narrative identity; 3rd layer of personality). In relation to McAdams's (1995) middle layer of personality development, we become a *motivated agent* – personal goals, values, ideologies, and cognitive style, which are shaped by social forces (e.g., McAdams, 1995; Singer, 2005) around the age of seven to nine years. Of course, as motivational and intentional lives are shaped and re-shaped in our life journey it is important to recognise they are responsive to time, place, and social role. The pursuit of successful high performance in sport cannot occur without coaches' passion and commitment for their coaching role and creating environments conducive to successful outcomes – performance and wellbeing. Examining McAdams' second layer of personality (motivated agent) enables some insights to what these coaches pursue as valued goals and therefore what drives this passion and commitment. Indeed, what are the deeper motivational forces at play that give insights into what they are striving for in everyday coaching practice? Personal strivings provide an insight into why these SWC are so passionate and committed to their coaching work. Indeed, these SWC communicate what gets them out of bed every day, as well as what they value and want to accomplish and, in some instances, want to avoid.

In personality psychology, Emmons (1989) proposes a motivational hierarchy of goals. At the most fundamental level, people have, for example, needs for *achievement* or *intimacy*. At the next hierarchical level, people have personal strivings (e.g., *not get too stressed; help others*). Personal projects, concerns, and tasks are the third level in the motivational hierarchy (e.g., *learn to deal with stress*) and at the highest level in the hierarchy, goals are focused on specific action units (e.g., *participate in a mindfulness programme; engage a more experienced coach for advice*).

In this project, we focussed on the personal strivings in Emmons' motivational hierarchy, which is captured in McAdams' second layer of personality, that is, motivated agent/characteristic adaptations (McAdams, 2013). An understanding of peoples' personal strivings and their pursuit of those strivings partially shape their personality and social behaviours (*self as motivated agent*). Insights into these serial winning coaches' personally meaningful individual strivings provide a deeper understanding of their motivational agenda, including what they value and want (Coulter et al., 2018; Emmons, 1989; Mallett & Coulter, 2016; McAdams, 2013), especially in their coaching work. Clark and colleagues (2022) recently reported the personal strivings of mentally tough footballers in understanding their personality (as motivated agents) within the context of time, place, and role (Mallett & Coulter, 2016; McAdams, 1995; McAdams, 2013), including their personal beliefs, saliency of specific goals, and the challenges in achieving these goals (Clark et al., 2022). We reiterate that there are influences from social and cultural forces in shaping what is considered acceptable in terms of what is of value and importance. In summary, these insights move beyond people's broad and de-contextualised psychological traits (*Self as actor: What kind of person am I?*) to provide insight into how individuals adapt to motivational, social-cognitive, and developmental challenges.

In the next section of this chapter, we report two sources of data about the strivings of SWC. Firstly, the data from the personal strivings exercise, which asked the SWC to respond to the stem, *On a daily basis, I typically try to ...* . It is important to note that strivings reflect intended behaviour, rather than actual behaviour, and include striving activities that are engaged on a regular basis (i.e., no one-time concerns). Secondly, we report the data from the semi-structured life story interviews with the coaches and their athletes.

Strivings: approach oriented, agentic, growth, achievement, and power

An examination of one's personal strivings (*coach as motivated agent*) considers both general themes (approach and avoidance; personal agency and communion) and motivational themes (e.g., achievement, power, affiliation, and spirituality). In what ways do these coaches engage with others and their own daily pre-occupations that elucidates a deeper understanding of their relationships and coaching work? Are these coaches more approach or avoidance oriented? Are they striving for personal interests or the interests of others (e.g., athletes) or both?

A focus on personal agentic goals in preference for others suggests some degree of self-centredness rather than a stronger sense of altruism. Previous research in sport (coaches and athletes), albeit limited, has shown that successful coaches and athletes are more likely to be approach oriented but report a more diverse mix of agency and communion strivings (Clark et al., 2022; Mallett & Coulter, 2016; Mallett & Lara-Bercial, 2016). Indeed, we expected that these SWC would reveal a diverse mix of motivational agendas because there is limited evidence that there is one "success profile" despite a belief by many in the public that one exists; therefore, we will report both individual (idiographic) and group (nomothetic) data.

A key question in the examination of SWC's personal strivings is an understanding of what those strivings might look like in everyday practice. We anticipate that the SWC will reveal some interesting and helpful insights into answering that question. Strivings capture a person's broad motivational agenda (values and wants); however, strivings are linked to intentions and goals and although that is useful to know what is less known is how these SWC survive in the highly competitive environment of elite sport in which there are limited coaching opportunities and success and failure (winning and not winning) seem to be the only criterion for judging a coach's craft and ability.

As previously reported (Mallett & Lara-Bercial, 2016), these SWC reported an approach- rather than avoidance-oriented style to their work (e.g., an optimistic explanatory style and solution focused). Indeed, they were found to seek opportunities in becoming better as people and coaches. Many of their strivings were focused on their personal agency (*self-improvement, challenge my thinking every day; have fun*) but also included the quest to help others (e.g., *build athletes' confidence daily; listen to athletes, receiving their feedback; be a leader to the team*) (Mallett & Lara-Bercial, 2016). They viewed themselves as performers and were driven by the need to be the best they could be to help athletes achieve their goals. Many of their strivings were focused on both self and their athletes (e.g., *learn something new every day*). Importantly, there were some coaches who were highly invested in developing their athletes *per se*, but equally, some also were centred on their own self-promotion, whereby the development of athletes was a mechanism for serving their own competitive needs. *Getting along to get ahead* and *becoming better to help athletes be successful* were common themes.

The most common motivational theme was centred around learning and personal growth (e.g., "engage", "support", and "learn from support staff"). The centrality of personal growth was reported as important for both coach and athlete (e.g., "permanent ongoing education"). Self-improvement was viewed as a personal responsibility for becoming the best they could be (e.g., "learn something new about my job every day"). These SWC were purposeful (e.g., "to achieve my objectives") in becoming better and fully committed to the service of athletes and support staff through ongoing support and collaborative teamwork. Although these SWC were athlete-centric focusing on their needs, they were also balanced in both their demands and expectations of athletes but with concomitant support (e.g., "demand but supportive"). Requisite for these SWC becoming better coaches was an ongoing investment in becoming better as a person and a coach and included "thinking about new ways for coaching" and "keeping abreast of contemporary coaching trends". This motivational theme of learning and personal growth is consistent with Carol Dweck's (2017) growth mindset and autonomous or internal motivation (McLean & Mallett, 2012). Indeed, these SWC view their coaching journey as them becoming better, which implies their success has been learned and the result of considerable effort.

"I think that I'm a pretty average guy of pretty average intelligence who just works hard" (Coach 11). Reflective of individuals with a growth mindset, these coaches did not view hard work or challenges as a threat to their ego and oft role modelled "high standards and hard work" and "set a certain standard, usually the first to arrive and the last to leave" (Coach 11). The synergy of the group is contingent upon high standards that are clearly shared and understood for all actors (coaches, support staff, and athletes).

The motivational theme of achievement (e.g., "be successful"; "perform to my potential") was also prominent for these SWC. Indeed, learning was central to the pursuit of achievement. This need for accomplishment was mostly internally driven (i.e., endorsed by these SWC and not overly influenced by external rewards and recognition). They valued their coaching work as highly important. The need for achievement is reflected in their strong task focus (get the job done) and with clarity of purpose (e.g., "be successful"; "have clear daily goals; achieve my key objectives"). This strong need for achievement is consistent with Deci and Ryan's (1985) psychological need for competence (McLean & Mallett, 2012). Indeed, all humans want to be viewed as competent. So, what might it mean for human striving when perceptions of competence are partially met? Is there a threshold point when people's need for competence is fully satisfied?

The motivational theme of power was also common amongst these SWC. We understand power in terms of wanting to influence others (e.g., "develop athletes' skills"; "be a leader to the team"; and "teach something to my children every day"). In terms of influencing others, these SWC were committed to a holistic development of the athletes (e.g., "have the athletes move one step closer to their performance"; "build athletes' confidence daily") by creating an adaptive environment in which athletes can thrive (e.g., "be positive within positive surroundings"). This strong desire to impact athletes' development focused on personal (e.g., values and interpersonal skills) and professional development (e.g., physical and technical).

We can confidently say that these SWC were highly ambitious and determined for success for both self and the athletes (Mallett & Lara-Bercial, 2016). Overall, these three motivational themes (learning and personal growth, achievement, and power) provide insight into the motivational agendas of these SWC who were driven by the pursuit of: (a) holistic personal growth and development for self and others; (b) the need to *get ahead* (need for achievement/ competence) by diligence in planning and preparation. Overall, we might say that these SWC were driven by the need to *get along to get ahead* (McAdams, 2015). It is noteworthy that there were differences in the saliency of these three and other motivational themes and how they shaped their daily and longer-term goals and coaching praxis. In addition to the personal strivings task, the interviews with coaches and their gold-medal and/or trophy-winning athletes and teams provided further insights into their motivational agenda.

Passion drives determination to be successful

Passion: Coaching is my identity

A key aspect of the life story interview is an understanding of the personal narratives of these SWC. *How they make sense of their past life experiences and their imagined future in creating a potentially coherent story about themselves. Indeed, it addresses a key question:* Who am I?

SWC: the biggest thing I learned there was that [National Sport Organisation] had become my identity. That moment when I wasn't on that staff and I wasn't going to be at the Olympics, that I didn't know who I was.

Interviewer: You lost who you were ...

SWC: Yes, and I swore I would never let that happen again. (Coach 6)

Many SWC found passion and enjoyment through everyday work.

I enjoy it and still don't need to do it anymore, with my age, but I still enjoy it. I enjoy it and you can always see, as long also you feel you have the right reward, also if the reward is more or less you have the feeling ok like we said from the athletes, they still respect you. And not just respect you because of what you did in the past but because of what you do on a daily basis and you come over fine, you are still sharp, you are still in the driving seat not tailing on and he lives from the past. (Coach 9)

You have to have a passion for it, for sure. Somebody asked me, I mean you saw my schedule and that's just that timeframe, it's like that all the time and someone asked me on Monday, [Coach] how do you do it like I just flew here and a two-hour time difference and I'm a bag of shit today, you know. I said well you've got to love what you do, you've got to like what you do ... So if you don't love what you do it's just not going to happen (Coach 6)

This passion for coaching work was expressed in a different way by Coach 14.

I'll never refuse to assist anybody. It often means I'm [daily training environment] on the water for hours a day and I enjoy doing it. I enjoy giving feedback. It's not hard for me; it's not work to be doing it. So, I guess you could say it's passion.

This strong motive to help others improve (and also be successful in their own right) was viewed as a passion for these SWC. This passion was reflected in their ongoing accounts of attention to detail in the little things that matter and despite the increasing pressures of administration, these SWC were, in the main, able to retain their ability to be hands on with the athletes and players because they understood the importance of doing so.

I wish I could spend more time in [daily training environment] ... But the smart coaches will never lose that personal connection down in the warehouse ... The smart manager in a plant will be down on the floor so to speak and be in touch and noting all the little details and things that are out of order and so on. (Coach 11)

Passion for some SWC extended to importance of some higher authority or purpose. Indeed, passion fuels the determination to be successful. "I'm a great supporter of, obviously of the [Monarch], and you know rightly or wrongly maybe because I was in the [military institution] for 15 years and we were looking after [Monarch] for 15 years, anyway. I am very loyal as it were to the sport and to the country and I want us to be successful. I was very, very determined to do well" (Coach 8).

Authentic care for the person

Furthermore, their passion for the development of the athlete was clearly evident:

I think I have a certain passion for what I do, I mean, it's this interesting thing though that winning side of it that I am required to do as an Olympic coach, I'm not very passionate about. I'm more passionate about the process and seeing a young athlete come through the system and doing well or doing as well as they can. Leaving the system and maybe reflecting back on it 20 years later and feeling they had a fulfilling experience and they are better for it. That side of it is sort of the passionate side of it to me. Like it sounds very corny nowadays, but building character, helping people realize their potential, helping people become better people, be better [nationality] whatever. That's what actually really excites me and I'm very passionate about that side of it. So, I enjoy that part of the process … I love the process, I love the—I think what I really look at is the whole process of helping people become better. I love it to be fair, and if people say, "oh I was treated fairly and I did not make the Olympic team but I understand why. Then I also feel I've been successful". (Coach 11)

This passion requires a genuine interest in others and is consistent with a social identity approach to leadership – making others feel special (Haslam et al., 2011).

You should become a gym teacher, that fits you. And he was right. I am a teacher, I am an educationalist, people interest me. I want to help people. I want to improve them … because I feel that I have a role in the life of the athletes … and I think that is perhaps a better role than the role of winning another gold medal … I know for sure that by choosing this line, I can make sure that she has a little bit more chance of being successful. I can make them stay with me longer and thus you are a Serial Winner. But that is really important for me and I am too much of an educationalist to see the sport that one-sided … and my boss does not want me to say this out loud, because he pays a lot of money to see gold, I do think that the foundations of my work … this justifies it better for me, because not everybody can become a champion and still has to get something out of it … But on the other hand, I have noticed that when you approach it like this, that there is a big chance that that person will develop himself in a way that the chance of winning becomes bigger as well, such a person will develop better than in a one-sided, meagre, narrow … I think that person has a better chance to win a championship … because I am me. This is me, you can educate and train whatever you want, but when you are not a coach by nature, then you will never become a coach. Then it is forced, I have seen too many people coach from the books, like this is how it is written (it is in the literature/ books) and this is how it should be done, this is how you should communicate, this is how you should manage a team and this is …, but that is not something you can fall back on. Somewhere it is in you, it is (instinct), … it is intuition, it is your other self … I am of service, I am that educationalist, I am someone with a heart for others and help someone and develop people. I am that person, for example in my football team, I am that person who gives the pass to a striker to score, I am that person who makes sure someone else is on a podium and who enjoys and is proud to see that at a distance. (Coach 7)

Most of the SWC were indeed children of parents who worked in the helping professions and perhaps these helpful intuitions, to care for others, were learned in early family life.

Determination and living espoused values

The reality of high-performance sport is that you cannot take your foot off the pedal. Although initially you might be a "hunter" in terms of pursuing success, over time some coaches might become the "hunted". *Getting ahead then staying ahead* is an ongoing challenge that does not abate (Mallett & Lara-Bercial, 2016). "You hear that very often is that success breeds success. But that's to a certain point right but you have to work for that again, every day again. It doesn't go automatically" (Coach 9). Similarly, Coach 6 commented:

> Work ethic for sure … you have to set a standard or you have to correct somebody or whatever, you can't miss that moment, you can't see something that brings your standards down and say, I'll do it later because later may not come and meanwhile they're going to observe that standard you know they're going to start acting like it. So, I'm a real component of as difficult as it might be you've got the rules, I mean I see something this morning and may not do it right this morning but I've got to do it before the day is over. I've got to deal with it and make sure that stops … . Excellence, I strive for excellence all the time.

It is one thing to strive towards implicit and explicit goals however intentions don't always shape behaviour. As reported by their athletes, these SWC lived their espoused values. In the main, these SWC were extremely committed to action supporting their strivings. They were demanding but led by example

> My standards are sky high. I do not accept a job half done and they all know that and they have adjusted their standards to that. When it is not good/good enough, it is not good/good enough, it should be done better. They all know that by now, so yes, I can trust my people by now, so there is no loss of energy anymore (Coach 7)

Two athletes coached by Coach 7 reinforced the modelling of always pursuing continual improvement:

> When you link that extreme focus to the characteristic perfectionism you end up with the fact that you can only do 1 thing at a time, because you can not do a few things in a half-baked way … You do it right or you do not, otherwise it makes no sense and that is a very good feature". (A1, Coach 7)

"Because he is very driven, very motivated, always only goes for the best, he is a perfectionist pre-eminently, if I could use only one word to describe [him], then it will be perfectionist" (A2, Coach 7).

The importance of SWC role modelling the values and associated behaviours was underscored by these SWC. A unique finding was that striving to care for self and others (probably considered an unexpected "value") was also espoused and lived despite the highly performative context and the oft-reported lack of genuine care for others in producing that success, which has been identified in many elite sporting cultures across many countries in recent times. Caring for others means being trustworthy and having integrity. It is commonly assumed that leaders are striving to be fair and demonstrate integrity, but this is not a given in a highly contested environment of elite sport: "people can also trust me, so that means I try to be open, I don't like to be the coach telling them or misleading any of those guys in a different direction ... Trying to sell the best of me to them" (Coach 9).

Furthermore, these SWC strove to be visible/present to the athletes:

But generally, I'm around all the time is one thing; so I'm visible. Sometimes the visibility is more important than the details of what you are doing so you are just—you're always in the line of vision. I think is very important. ... Being visible to the athletes involves working closely with the support staff a lot of my day is spent working with the team, like the team support staff. So, it might even be dropping in and spending five minutes with the manager making sure that she's doing the jobs that need to be done and so on. (Coach 11)

Athletes (and support staff) seem to prefer coaches to be present. The importance of physical proximity but also the social and emotional connection to others is essential.

What did we learn?

We reiterate that striving (goal pursuits) is foundational to notions of surviving and thriving. Humans are goal-oriented and goal driven (e.g., Emmons, 1989; McClelland, 1961) but these often implicit, deeper goals are personally meaningful and malleable as we journey through life. Several theories and empirical research has supported the view that our drives are fuelled by needs such as achievement, power, and affiliation (McClelland, 1961) and autonomy, competence, and relatedness (Deci & Ryan, 1985). These underlying drives are likely part of human evolution (Deci & Ryan, 1985) and learned (McClelland, 1961). Importantly, these motivational drivers provide the fuel to behave and think in particular ways in pursuit of these personally meaningful goals.

These coaches are passionately driven to be successful (achievement and accomplishment) – and they are motivated by positive incentives and oft-internal rewards (approach oriented and optimistic) – they are diligent and want to learn as much as possible (personal growth) – *get ahead and stay ahead*. They are highly committed and invested in personal learning and growth (agency) for self to satisfy their quest to master their environments (competence). Moreover, SWC are passionate and authentic about influencing others and confident they know how to influence their athletes and support staff (power) and they have a strong desire to closely relate to, and be supportive of, these athletes (communion; connection) for them to achieve successful outcomes.

Importantly, these goals are malleable and responsive to dynamic environments and self and others' expectations. These shifts in expectations are not always warranted, which underscores the volatility of the context in which they operate. For example, when athletes or teams perform above expectations, many (invested) observers elevate their expectations based on a single performance that marginalises the saliency of consistency in performance over time. The need for a clear vision as to what is possible and sufficiently challenging is central to the ongoing pursuit of becoming the best you can be: "You need to be able to predict where you want to get to. I never have a view that that was good and that's what it's got to be, you are always looking for more" (Coach 10).

In this chapter, we asked the question: So, what does it mean for human striving when perceptions of competence are met? Do we ever satisfy our need for competence? A key challenge for those SWC whose narrative identity is associated with *atonement* is that they are never likely to feel they have atoned for their perceived failings in the past because every success, although a celebration, is also a reminder of what they did not achieve that was meaningful and personal to them (e.g., Mallett & Coulter, 2016; Mallett & Lara-Bercial, 2016). This consistent reminder when their athletes win at the "big event" continues to fuel the need for some SWC to continue their pursuit of becoming the best they can be, and it seems that the goal of atonement might not ever be achieved. This reminder might explain why many SWC seldom take a long break from coaching after the "big event".

References

Clark, J., Mallett, C. J., & Coulter, T. (2022). Personal strivings of mentally tough Australian Rules footballers. *Psychology of Sport and Exercise*, *58*, 102090.

Clark, J., Mallett, C. J., Moyle, G., & Coulter, T. (2023). Competitive situations requiring mental toughness in Women's Australian Rules Football. *Journal of Sports Sciences*, *40*(21), 2412–2423. 10.1080/02640414.2022.2162239

Coulter, T. J., Mallett, C. J., & Singer, J. (2018). A three-domain personality analysis of a mentally tough athlete. *European Journal of Personality*, *32*(1), 6–29. doi:10.1002/per.2129

Dweck, C. S. (2017). From needs to goals and representations: Foundations for a unified theory of motivation, personality, and development. *Psychological Review*, *124*(6), 689–719. 10.1037/rev0000082

Deci, E. L., & Ryan, R. M. (1985). *Intrinsic motivation and self-determination in human behavior*. Plenum Press.

Emmons, R. A. (1989). The personal striving approach to personality. In L. A. Pervin (Ed.), *Goal concepts in personality and social psychology* (pp. 87–126). Erlbaum.

Fletcher, D., & Sarkar, M. (2012). A grounded theory of psychological resilience in Olympic champions. *Psychology of Sport and Exercise*, *13*(5), 669–678. 10.1016/j.psychsport.2012.04.007

Haslam, S. A., Reicher, S. D., & Platow, M. J. (2011). *The new psychology of leadership: Identity, influence and power*. Psychology Press.

Mahoney, J. W., Gucciardi, D. F., Ntoumanis, N., & Mallett, C. J. (2014). The motivational antecedents of the development of mental toughness: A self-determination theory perspective. *International Review of Sport and Exercise Psychology*, 7, 184–197.

Mallett, C., & Coulter, T. (2016). The anatomy of a successful Olympic coach: Actor, agent, and author. *International Sport Coaching Journal*, *3*, 113–127.

Mallett, C. J., & Lara-Bercial, S. (2016). Serial winning coaches: People, vision, and environment. In M. Raab, P. Wylleman, R. Seiler, A. M. Elbe, & G. Hatzigeorgiadis (Eds), *Sport and exercise psychology research: Theory to practice* (pp. 289–322). Elsevier.

McAdams, D. P. (1995). What do we know when we know a person? *Journal of Personality*, *63*, 365–396.

McAdams, D. P. (2015). *The art and science of personality development*. Guilford.

McAdams, D. P. (2013). The psychological self as actor, agent, and author. *Perspectives of Psychological Science*, *8*, 272–295.

McLean, K., & Mallett, C. J. (2012). What motivates the motivators? *Physical Education and Sport Pedagogy*, *17*(1), 21–35. DOI: 10.1080/17408989.2010.535201

McClelland, D. C. (1961). *The achieving society*. Van Nostrand.

Sarkar, M., Fletcher, D., & Brown, D. (2015). What doesn't kill me …: Adversity-related experiences are vital in the development of superior Olympic performance. *Journal of Science and Medicine in Sport*, *18*(4), 475–479. 10.1016/j.jsams.2014.06.010

Sarkar, M., & Hilton, N. K. (2020). Psychological resilience in Olympic medal-winning coaches: A longitudinal qualitative study. *International Sport Coaching Journal*, 7(2), 209–219. doi:10.1123/iscj.2019-0075

Sheldon, K. M., & Elliot, A. J. (1999). Goal striving, need satisfaction, and longitudinal well-being: The self-concordance model. *Journal of Personality and Social Psychology*, *76*(3), 482–497. 10.1037/0022-3514.76.3.482

Singer, J. A. (2005). *Personality and psychotherapy: Treating the whole person*. Guildford.

10

SURVIVING IN THE HIGHLY PERFORMATIVE ENVIRONMENT OF ELITE SPORT

It has been well documented and accepted that coaches of elite athletes and teams work in a highly contested space that is characterised by complexity, chaos, ambiguity, and pathos and that much of the work in which they engage is largely uncontrollable necessitating developed intra- and inter-personal knowledge and competencies (Côté & Gilbert, 2009) to be responsive, nimble, fluid, and adaptable (e.g., Jones & Wallace, 2005; Potrac et al., 2017). Indeed, we embrace Cushion's (2007) notion of "structured improvisation" that captures the uncontrollability and complexity in coaching praxis that requires "orchestration" from the coach to bring some order to chaos in managing the complexity and ambiguity of the coaching environment (Jones & Wallace, 2005; Potrac et al., 2017), which we believe are consistent with the notion of "psychological flexibility" (cognitive, emotional, and behavioural; Doorley, Goodman, Kelso & Kashdan, 2020; Kashdan & Rottenberg, 2010). In this highly contested landscape, how might coaches and coaching teams navigate myriad opportunities and challenges that present daily and require fluidity, adaptability, resilience, and fortitude? In addressing this important question, we consider the centrality of resilience in surviving, which seems essential to embodying holistic functioning in and through sport, before we embark on the notion of thriving in the next chapter.

Critically, coaches need to survive long enough as a coach in a specific sporting context to learn and develop their craft – like many vocations and professions, becoming more proficient requires working in the industry over time; that is, learning in and through high-performance (HP) coaching work (e.g., Rynne & Mallett, 2012; Rynne, Mallett & Tining, 2010; Tao, Rynne & Mallett, 2019). However, many coaches do not survive in this tough

DOI: 10.4324/9781003427292-14

environment in which successful performance (i.e., league trophy and gold medal) is the only valued criterion for surviving as a coach. Unfortunately, this limited insight reflects a naïve understanding of HP coaches' work. From our experience and others in the industry, those who employ professional (paid) coaches often have limited understanding and appreciation of what is coaches' work. This limited understanding prompts a reductionistic and simplistic view of coaches' craft. For example, to what extent do Board members and Administrators appreciate the degree and nuance of uncontrollability and complexity in coaching work and the time it takes for coaches to influence a specific context. Furthermore, coaches need to survive long enough to transition into the possibility of shifting from surviving to experiencing thriving, which is what coaches might implicitly seek to achieve in their pursuit of superior performance and well-being.

How might we understand the notion of surviving as a coach working in such a highly contested space? Central to surviving is the ability to cope with stressors to perform. Resilience is synonymous with coping with stressors. More recently, resilience has increasingly become a cliché in the sport context, and we focus on this construct in this chapter in relation to surviving. However, this overuse of the term resilience begs a couple of questions: How do we conceptualise (define) and operationalise (measure) psychological constructs such as resilience? Are we on the same page? These two questions segue nicely to a problem that, for decades, has plagued and continues to obfuscate psychology: *jingle-jangle fallacies*.

What is resilience?

Indeed, how to define and measure concepts and terms in social psychology is problematic. For example, there are at least 10 constructs that are similar to connection (e.g., belonging, relatedness, acceptance; see Dweck, 2017). Furthermore, there is a lack of consensus in conceptualisations and measurement of these terms/concepts/constructs (Marsh, 1994), which is problematic in making sense of research findings across various studies. These issues in conceptualisation and operationalisation (measurement) are not new problems. *Jingle fallacy* was a label for the belief that two measures with the same name indeed measure the same construct (Thorndike, 1904); whereas the belief that two scales with different names measure different constructs or two concepts are only different in name only was labelled *jangle fallacy* (Kelley, 1927). However, it is not just the measures that are problematic. A key problem is that people's beliefs about these constructs are based on unfounded and oversimplified assumptions or understandings. The myriad labels for what seems to be the same construct makes it difficult to make sense of the extant research. Several scholars have highlighted this significant issue in social psychology (e.g., Block, 1995; Hagger, 2014). Specifically, the literature on resilience and thriving, like many psychology constructs (e.g., connection, relatedness, and belonging), seems to suffer from the jingle-jangle fallacies (e.g., Brown et al., 2017). Hence, we attempt to distinguish between the two important and oft-used constructs in elite sport in this and the next chapter.

Resilience and coping in sport are important because elite athletes and their coaches are consistently required to manage and respond to myriad stressors to achieve successful sporting outcomes (Sarkar & Fletcher, 2014; Sarkar & Hilton, 2020). Therefore, the need to strive, adapt, and persist in the face of failure, overcome adversity, and self-regulate thoughts, emotions, and behaviours are necessary ingredients to not only survive, but over time potentially thrive in these demanding and complex settings (e.g., Fletcher & Sarkar, 2012).

Importance of time

A key factor in development that is often marginalised (probably because people want success today and tomorrow) is time. It takes time for learning, growth, and development to take place; however, we live in modern times in which patience seems to be a fading virtue. This lack of patience is understandable in contemporary elite sport for several reasons: (changing and potentially unrealistic) expectations of athletes, parents, and administrators, and probably coaches. Furthermore, partly because of the volatility of coach employment, it is not uncommon for coaches to feel pressure from administrators and athletes to "produce winning results" as soon as possible. There is a basic need for coaches (and athletes) to prove themselves to self and/or others. Time is a key constraint in the athlete development process, and coaches need to consider what factors are of greater importance and in what chronological sequence over an extended period. What is the priority at this point in time? For example, coaches might need to prioritise leading up – to Boards and employers. Furthermore, coaches might be tempted to expedite development (at some risk) to survive long enough to maintain their employment. Coaches need to be seen to be doing something and create visible change (often in terms of performance), which is consistent with behavioural approaches to leadership – *leaders do things*. This common dilemma to focus on shorter- rather than longer-term development might be necessary to keep your job. As Coach 10 reported, "I think I've developed now I've got a clear understanding of what's important and what's not important so I spend more time doing the important stuff and less time or let go of what's not important, so I am able to prioritise a lot better".

Noticing to inform action

Central to coaches surviving is learning in a deep but expedited manner. This also includes learning to respond flexibly and paying close attention to their athletes and the coaching environment. Indeed, the *concept of noticing*, or paying attention with the intent to learn has been reported before (e.g., Mason, 2001). This ability to flexibly respond to dynamic and evolving situations in context is necessary to foster progressive development in individual and collective performances (e.g., Jones & Wallace, 2005).

This *noticing to inform action* (Santos et al., 2013) seems logical but again what does that look like in practice and how do great coaches learn to notice? The SWC spoke about the need to be acutely aware of the context and the athlete, keenly observing situational details. It involved paying intense attention to "the world of small realities", such as how the athletes looked upon arrival to training; and interpretation of these observations in the immediate context to inform the coaches' actions (Santos et al., 2013).

> I think they learn certain patience, a certain sense of timing, and they gain wisdom … a wise older person who has dealt with situations so many times you've actually not determined the one best answer, but you have determined a pretty good answer to questions and I think that's something you gain with time. You know how to deal with all the different little stresses and all the different questions that come up and all the situations. It's almost like you've been there done that so you just sort of comes out naturally. (Coach 11)

This ability of noticing to inform action takes time but importantly requires an appreciation of the skill of seeing more (that is relevant) and how to develop that skill of noticing and responding that, in turn, is viewed as the gaining of wisdom.

> Or if something unexpected comes up—which I already alluded to—you're very well prepared to deal with it. It's not catching you with your pants down so to speak, you're ready to give an answer quickly and resolve it. I think that creates great confidence with people that work around you that you, number one, appear to be prepared and, number two, deal with all unexpected scenarios very well. (Coach 11)

Participant coaches reported being flexible based on noticing and being sensitive to each individual athlete. So, we suggest that surviving includes noticing to inform action, preparing, visualising how to respond to scenarios, using wisdom, and actively generating wisdom.

> But you can say sometimes if you see somebody really can't do it today then of course you would say 'ok, we calm down a little bit', and that's not weakness because everybody reacts a little bit different. So that's something of course you have to individualise knowing your athletes. The athletes are like gold dust, I think. Every athlete and if you have in the first place the attitude, they

are coming to you, they want to do it, that's the key basic line to me. Of course, there are days where he wants to do it but somebody in here says 'I can't do it today, I don't feel good'. Of course, there you are a little bit in discussion with athletes sometimes, 'you don't know' and that's very important you don't have to do it and there's times when 'ok, I know what he has done, back off a little bit'. That's all those small things where I think you can't just take a training programme and follow it to the letter. That's what I think. If you really want to be successful you have to be there as a coach. I see very often, also have noticed even in the [NATIONAL] team there are some coaches that are living [abroad: OTHER COUNTRY OR OTHER COUNTRY] and then they came over for a while and they go back home, I can't see that. I can't see that. So that's how I see it a little bit, how you work with a training programme. Because you have to, you can write everything down on paper, of course that is just your guideline but then in the process you have to be also prepared to change and take notice because the body is not a machine. (Coach 9)

The "art" of coaching seems to be characterised by flexibility of thought and action and being sensitive and responsive to each athlete. Indeed, this aspect of coaching work is consistent with the notions of *structured improvisation* (Cushion, 2007) and *orchestration* (Jones et al., 2012; Jones & Wallace, 2005; Potrac et al., 2017) as well as *psychological flexibility* (Kashdan, 2010; Doorley et al., 2020).

Resilience in performative environments: How is it done?

Research has supported the view that resilience is essential to elite sporting performance as it influences the relationship between stress and performance (Fletcher & Sarkar, 2012; Morgan et al., 2019). Furthermore, resilience has been suggested to benefit individual (e.g., Gonzalez et al., 2016) and team (e.g., Morgan et al., 2019) performance. *But what does resilience mean?* Resilience has been defined as "the role of mental processes and behaviour in promoting personal assets and protecting an individual from the potential negative effect of stressors" (Fletcher & Sarkar, 2012, p. 675), such as personal, organisational, and competition stressors (Sarkar & Fletcher, 2014).

Psychological resilience can be understood as both a process and an outcome of adapting to life's difficult challenges (Fletcher & Sarkar, 2013). First, *rebound resilience* is the (responsive) ability to bounce back that culminates in a return to previous levels of performance and well-being. In contrast, *robust resilience* is the (proactive) ability to develop a protective quality over time that buffers against inevitable stressors. *How might coaches support athletes to develop robust and rebound resilience that support athletes before, during, and after difficult events? Furthermore, how do coaches develop their own robust and rebound resilience?*

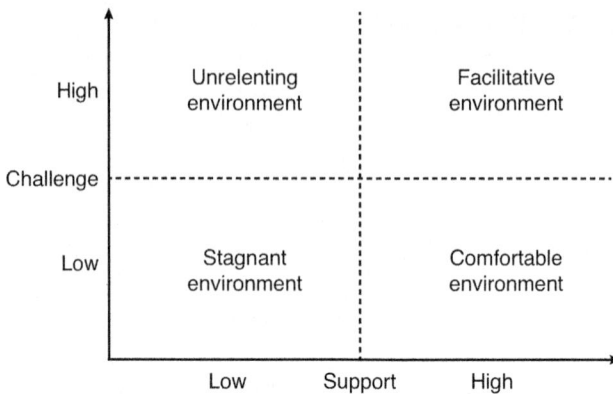

FIGURE 10.1   A challenge-support matrix (cited in Fletcher & Sarkar, 2016, p. 142 and adapted from Daloz, 1986; Sanford, 1967).

In developing individual and collective resilience, Fletcher and Sarkar (2016) underscore the importance of matching high challenge with high support, which fosters a "facilitative [high performing] environment" (e.g., athlete engagement in the process, constructive/informational feedback, psychological safety, learn mistakes and failures, sense of "us" compared with a sense of isolation, blame mentality, lack of care). Fletcher and Sarkar (2016) adapted the 2 × 2 challenge-support matrix (adapted from Daloz, 1986; Sanford, 1967), which is presented in Figure 10.1. In addition, to appreciating the challenge-support matrix, it is important to consider the development of resilience in relation to two different people: (i) the coach; and (ii) the athletes and support staff. It is noteworthy that Fletcher and Sarkar's model seems more conducive to discussion about how the coaches have developed resilience in athletes by setting up a certain facilitative environment (healthy competition, etc.). However, we are confident the same principles apply to coaches' resilience.

Developing resilience

Coping with setbacks through realistic and optimistic attributions

It was apparent in the data that early exposure to reasonable challenge fostered the development of resilience; however, what enabled this robust and rebound resilience were the personality traits and strivings of these SWC, which were likely differentially learned and inherited.

Through the self- and athlete-reported trait profiles and personal strivings, these SWC were upbeat optimists. We reiterate that two interdependent concepts that seem to be synonymous with surviving are *coping* and *resilience*.

Well number one they are a part of life. Setbacks are a part of life … You are going to have good days and bad days, you're going to have winning days and … The other thing is they make you a better person. I always feel that when you have a setback you actually re-evaluate more. (Coach 11)

The reality is that coaching experiences over time will likely represent a rollercoaster ride. Furthermore, these SWC were described as upbeat optimists and self- and athlete-reported their ability to directly manage impulsive responses to challenges. Indeed, the trait profiles suggested these SWC were clear optimists (well-being), directed individuals (impulse control), and go-getters (activity) (Mallett & Lara-Bercial, 2016). They underscored their underlying *optimistic attributions* for perceived success and failures. "I mean if I look back over my coaching career, you look at all the disappointments we've had and it's all the disappointments that turn into eventually all the successes. Because you learn from the disappointments" (Coach 8). This ability to attribute perceived failures as opportunities for learning and growth was prototypical of these SWC and likely contributed to their surviving long enough to thrive.

The pursuit of sustained success is highly aspirational, but these SWC were realistic in that striving. "Nobody is going through any sport where you are going to win everything all the time. You're not. And the only other problem is when you get to being number one, ranked number one, or you are number one, there's only one way to go, down. And you ain't going to stay up there forever you've got to be realistic about things" (Coach 8). These beliefs seemed to be developed early in their coaching careers and perhaps developed from childhood and through their own athletic experiences: "because I went straight in with the seniors so any mistakes you made were very public. And you know it's all ok, they are the experiences you learn from, and you've got to learn to put them all together and build on what you can do" (Coach 10).

It also seems that these optimistic attributions might sometimes be in tension with coaches' emotional regulatory abilities.

While on the outside I look like I am okay, but on the inside it's chaos. One of my athletes he always said to me how come you keep so calm? I said well I can't do anything, right, when you come to the major event, there's not much I can do, if we haven't done it before I can't do it now … So now I'm just a supporter that is looking at it and being positive, giving little details here and there but of no importance, so on the outside I look like I'm the coolest cucumber in the world, on the inside nervous as hell because I want them to succeed" (Coach 17).

There is no doubt that coaches and athletes and significant others will experience deep implicit emotions, especially at the big event. These intense emotions emerge because the event is important to the coach and the outcome (winning) is unpredictable. Added to these factors are the likely ruminations about whether they will keep their job.

The SWC also reported an important underlying quality or belief; that is, challenge and the associated inherent pressure and stress is essential to develop resiliency. In order to survive long enough to thrive, these SWC viewed significant challenges and the concomitant perceived pressure and stress to be perceived positively and as an opportunity for coping with these demands.

Yes, I need them [pressure and stress], I love to have them, because that brings up the best in me. That is very much typical of elite sports. Also, the top athletes have that, they even create it themselves sometimes, because when it is all going too calmly and too ... so you need tension and stress, because you (your body) need to feel that to bring up the best in yourself. (Coach 7)

Drawing upon principles underpinning stress-inoculation training (e.g., Fletcher & Sarkar, 2016; Meichenbaum, 1976), we might consider the following analogy to understand the development of resilience by these SWC:

Although people have some immunity against some diseases (traits, strivings), many of us have received a vaccine to boost our immune defences. These vaccines might be likened to small dosages of adversity that challenge our immune system that over time develops a stronger and more resilient immune system. Similarly, the adversities we face in everyday encounters in and outside of sport contribute to building this immune system that has the potential to help us when we need it most in facing future challenges in sport and other contexts.

The notion of surviving should also consider one's perspective of a situation and/or context. "You have to have some healthy way to manage the stress and keep everything in perspective" (Coach 10). This perspective-taking can influence well-being and ongoing coaching performance.

So, I've never felt pressure, and when coaches talk about burnout or—If I think I'm a missionary somewhere in Africa or I'm a brain surgeon operating on a table, that's pressure. I work with bright young people who are physically and mentally really healthy and motivated; I don't have to motivate them. And we get to play at the Olympics and I'm the luckiest guy in the world. My hobby is my job so how can I associate burnout or stress – which goes back to your question—with that job. So, I have always thought of myself as a very lucky guy who coaches great young athletes; there's no stress involved in that. (Coach 11)

It appears that for some SWC sincere gratitude for the coaching role in this context has the potential to buffer against stress in the workplace.

In terms of surviving, passion was considered central to the ongoing pursuit of success. This passion for coaching work was a key factor in relentless obsessive pursuit of mastering their coaching craft and subsequent performance success.

Passion for coaching helps SWC become resilient and survive.

Well, when you have passion about something you spend a lot of time thinking, and doing it, and exercising it. It gives you knowledge, it gives you information, and when you have a passion for what you do: that is another step of that knowledge and skill of course. You learn ways of doing something if you are in a corner, you look for ways of getting out of that corner and those ways out of the corner is a skill isn't it. It's a kind of skill and I'm well aware – dare I say – that I have skills that other people don't have. (Coach 14)

Bob Vallerand is the world-leading expert on passion, including in the sporting context. In his Dual Model of Passion (DMP) (2012), he defines passion as a strong inclination towards an activity that a person has interest in and which requires significant investment of time and energy. This passion is associated with one's sense of identity (McAdams' 3rd layer of personality) – who I am and who I am becoming. Perhaps this passion for meaning and purpose differentiates SWC from other coaches in elite sport? Two key questions might be: (i) Where does this passion emanate from?; and (ii) Is passion helpful and/or unhelpful to performance and well-being? Vallerand proposes two broad types of passion: harmonious and obsessive. The genesis of harmonious passion is internal to the person (i.e., autonomous) and central to their sense of self; whereas obsessive passion has its origins in externally controlled regulations (e.g., doing something to please others or seeking status). His extensive research has shown regular and repeated positive emotions lead to sustained psychological well-being and buffers against maladaptive psychological outcomes such as ill-being (e.g., Vallerand, 2012): "you have to have a passion for it, for sure … you've got to love what you do, you've got to like what you do … So if you don't love what you do it's just not going to happen" (Coach 6).

Aligned with this passion for coaching is the SWC perspective and gratitude for coaching.

I mean this so many good people even though I'm not a people person you've got to appreciate the people who you get … and you know you are here with

Olympians and there's so many good people and so many things that you can help them with and be a part of and then in return, they help you as well. (Coach 6)

This appreciation to work with such capable people pursuing excellence was considered to be a privilege and is consistent with the notion of harmonious passion. These positive emotions stemming from this harmonious passion will contribute to both performance and well-being. Over time, the experience of positive emotions might develop robust resilience.

Trust, performance, and well-being

The development of an adaptive-coach relationship underpins the building of trust and performance

Unsurprisingly, trust was foregrounded as essential to surviving and potentially thriving. This sense of trust was couched in terms of performance and well-being and what underpinned a trusting relationship between coach and athlete was an adaptive-coach–athlete relationship.

It seems intuitive and anecdotally pervasive that a trusting relationship underpins performance and well-being. This is not a new idea. Nevertheless, we might think about what does a trusting relationship look like? Trust in what? How did these SWC develop trusting relationships with their athletes? An athlete might trust her coach in terms of her mastering her sport but she might not trust him as a person and his integrity. "I am convinced that performance originates from a [trusting] relationship, I am convinced of that, I notice that every day" (Coach 7).

> I think the other thing is to have great people skills. And I think that when coaches are really doing well they have established this bond of trust with athletes … I think the one variable that I have to work very hard on to be successful and move forward and so on is to have a great relationship with the athletes I coach and that can branch off in all kinds of areas. How you deal on a day and day basis, how you accept their feedback, how you deal with their feedback, and how you relate to individual differences and all these things. I think that those are two things that come to mind; so, people management essentially. (Coach 11)

Trust is concerned with the relations between people and therefore central to established and lasting relationships. Is he reliable? Can I depend on that person? Is he predictable? Trust should be considered as a reciprocal process; that is, a trusting mutual relationship between coach and athlete. Effective communication (verbal and non-verbal), including feedback to each other can promote this sense of trust.

> Communication is still the biggest thing that you know, if someone understands more of what they are doing or what they need to do to get

there they take more ownership of it and they are more driven to do it. (Coach 10)

Trust and psychological safety are interdependent constructs. Psychological safety is the belief that it is ok to express concerns and beliefs without negative consequences (e.g., retribution for speaking out); i.e., a trusting relationship is foundational to psychological safety in the sport context.

Trust requires resolute belief in plan and processes

I mean you have to believe in your plan, you can't, you know there is a timeframe, a time when people would tell me, well you have to be more human now. People got to know you have weaknesses [and they] are listening. So, I did do some of that right, sort of exposed myself and that was a disaster, people don't want to know their leader is weak. Or that they have weaknesses or that they're second guessing themselves or whatever. (Coach 6)

Coaches run the risk of losing athlete trust and belief if they appear rudderless. That is not to say that coaches should not admit some errors; however, timing and impact of errors might require some forethought before acting. Nonetheless, there seems to be a need for coaches to be confident in how they go about things in everyday coaching praxis, especially in competition settings. The portrayal of confidence is not the same as arrogance or bragging but a quiet confidence in how one presents oneself in the presence of others. This confidence in oneself is likely derived by meticulous planning and preparation.

Self-doubt certainly can't come into it if you're going to lead a group … walk in like you own the place, people believe you own the place … You're not lying, you have to believe that you're in charge, you've got to believe in your process, you've got to believe and you will tweak it and you will make small adjustments. (Coach 6)

If you have to, take your responsibility, you are still responsible for what happens, so you have to stand up and be counted there when you need to be counted. And you have to have a strategy to get out of it as well. And it's also you have to back yourself in that you can do it. (Coach 10)

Athlete perceptions of their coaches influence their self-confidence. Whilst there will always be potential seeds of self-doubt, these should be challenged and put into perspective.

My explanation is part of building their confidence. I am drawing attention to it so that the people that are struggling don't think the program is wrong, or too heavy. What they are taught to think is "I was up there last week; the people that are ahead of me are doing exactly the same program" – which is why everyone has to do the program - everyone is training to the same level, those leading as well as those at the rear – "so the programme must be right. It must be what [coach] says, that I'm going through my dull spot" [*as if athlete was speaking*]. It happens consistently. (Coach 14)

Coaches employ a range of approaches to build mutual trust with the athletes for whom they are responsible. This mutual trust and respect are considered necessary to perform successfully (Potrac, 2004) and consistent with an athlete-centred philosophical approach to coaching, which we discuss later in this chapter. This mutual trust relates to coaches' planning and preparation, as well as guide and suggest ways of doing to help the athlete and develop the person behind the athlete. In this process, coaches gradually build the confidence and capabilities of the athletes to contribute to their own learning and performance. In this athlete-centred coaching approach, there is a shift towards a more collaborative style from coaches and athletes in making informed decisions in these performance settings. This increasingly collaborative approach requires the coach to show they care not just about the athlete as a performer but also as a person (Lara-Bercial & Mallett, 2016; Mallett & Lara-Bercial, 2016).

Trust is also an outcome of coach caring for the person behind the athlete

"So, it sends to them right off the bat that I'm interested in you as a person beyond just being a pawn, or an athlete … cared about the person first before they cared about them as an athlete" (Coach 11). The rhetoric of care has become a bit of a mantra in recent times but remains an elusive (leader) behaviour in many (sporting) settings. Telling athletes (and staff) you care is often perceived as meaningless and valueless. In stark contrast, showing you care is very powerful … actions certainly speak louder than words but what does care look like? As described in Chapter 6, showing you care about others probably starts with the view or belief that people matter.

> I think it is far more important that the other side (athlete) is at the centre … my position, that is a strange one, because on the one hand, as you have noticed, I am the boss of this team, simple, I am the boss, no discussion, but on the other hand I am the assistant of the career of the athlete. (Coach 7)

Furthermore, as MD previously reported, "I think the biggest thing you learn in those, when you become a full-time coach is that your athletes have lives and the sooner you figure out their life the sooner you will be happy with what you are doing". Caring means respecting and engaging the players and hearing their voices (Annerstedt & Lindgren, 2014). Showing you care includes collaborating with others and proactively engaging them in the process. "You have to explain which way you are going, you have to buy the athletes in to your project, and I think it's always, I think it's very important that athletes are part of the process and not just being told what they have to do. So, they understand the programme and why they are doing things" (Coach 9). Explaining the rationale for what athletes do and other decisions is essential to showing you care and fosters athlete performance (e.g., Mageau & Vallerand, 2003; Mallett, 2005). This ethic of care is consistent with other research on successful coaches (e.g., Annerstedt & Lindgren, 2014). As previously reported, Annerstedt and Lindgren's (2014) study on the highly successful Swedish Handball coach, Bengt Johansson, found that within the context of elite sport, which necessitates full dedication and commitment of all actors, especially the coach, a successful coach can (and should) interact with others consistently showing compassion, respect, empathy, and caring. These psycho-social qualities that might be viewed as compromising the pursuit of excellence are in indeed not binary but interdependent and essential in contributing to holistic development. According to Nel Noddings (1984; 2013), this ethic of care for self and others (and being cared for by others) is linked to one's identity and the type of person you want to be. In other words, it is central to your sense of self. It foregrounds the centrality of caring relationships in our daily lives, which is foundational to developing trust between self and others.

Athlete-centred coaching approach

The rhetoric around athlete-centred coaching has become commonplace in many western democracies. Although coaches are held responsible for athlete performance, the coach cannot independently make the athlete great and successful. These performative successes are contingent upon the athletes taking increasing responsibility and ownership for their own development and performance and the saliency of fostering one's sense of autonomy in what they do (Hodge et al., 2014; Kidman, 2005; Mageau & Vallerand, 2003; Mallett, 2005).

> We had a point of meeting formally once a week … The main reason for the meeting is that it gives them the opportunity to voice an opinion, to have a say in the programme. I encourage them to have a say in the programme because they are more likely to commit to it. If they ask for a change, they are less likely to avoid it. You see, I am putting the ball in their court. (Coach 14)

The notion that the focus is on the athlete rather than the coach is a key consideration – the athlete must become increasingly independent and responsible.

Yeah I've got some training philosophies but actually about me coaching is that it's not about me it's about them. So any, you know, it's not, my influence and I still influence them and I am not doing it they are doing it, they still need to have that independence and responsibility to go and do it. (Coach 10)

Indeed, coaching is about people. Importantly, "the athlete needs to know that the coach is on that journey with them" (Coach 10). It is a shared enterprise.

And you know, fundamentally it's still about the interaction with the coach and the athlete and that's important. The gizmo's, technology changes things, but sport is still about human endeavour and getting the most out of the person. So, I think that's one of the fundamental things that won't change actually. (Coach 10)

What did we learn?

Central to surviving is the concept of time. Once you commence your career as a coach, the clock is ticking. Self and others have expectations that can regularly change. These SWC continued to grow through their reflective coaching experiences, which helped them to survive long enough to become repeatedly successful in their craft. Clarity of what is important and prioritised helps with surviving long enough to continue coaching.

SWC were capable in developing their ability to *notice to inform action*. In other words, they learned quickly to flexibly respond to dynamic and evolving situations in context. This ability to notice to inform coaching and be responsive to individual athletes is consistent with the "art" of coaching. Furthermore, this noticing promotes self-awareness and the awareness of others that likely fosters empathy.

Two interrelated and key concepts associated with surviving are resilience and coping. Adversity is omnipresent in elite sport and the ability to buffer and rebound from adversity is necessary to survive long enough to learn, grow, and develop. How did these SWC develop resilient behaviours? Firstly, they reported realistic and optimistic attributions in understanding and making sense of successes and failures as part of the steep learning curve for these SWC. Secondly, they adopted a healthy perspective in making sense of situational and longer-term stress. Third, they were grateful for the opportunity to work with high-performing people with aspirations. Indeed, they felt privileged. Fourth, positive experiences contributed to these SWC's harmonious passion for coaching work that subsequently underpinned their resilience and ability to survive in such a highly performative context. This passion for their work was deemed to be harmonious and adaptive leading to superior performances and well-being.

The second perspective in relation to resilience is how these SWC fostered self and athlete resilience. Caring for self and others was a central theme in the data. This consistent ethic of care developed relational trust between coaches and athletes (and likely other support staff). This mutual and reciprocal trust enabled an adaptive-coach–athlete relationship to be formed and in doing so provided building blocks for resilience and survival. Constant caring for self and others enabled these SWC to build trust, which was linked to performance and well-being; however, *getting along to get ahead* is insufficient in building mutual trust. Trust also requires resolute belief in planning and preparation processes. The SWC's strong and lived ethic of care operates alongside the need to challenge the athlete and others in the daily training and competition environments to pursue performance excellence.

Finally, it was apparent that over time, SWC became more collaborative fostering athlete independence, initiative, and responsibility for performance; all of which promote psychological need satisfaction (autonomy, competence, and relatedness; Deci & Ryan, 1985; Mallett, 2005; Ntoumanis & Mallett, 2014).

In this chapter, we focused on resilience. The focus on resilience in terms of surviving is necessary to develop personal assets (robust resilience) that can over time contribute to more than overcoming adversity (rebound resilience). But these SWC did more than just survive, they were thriving and so were their athletes and support staff. Therefore, we shift our discussions from surviving to thriving in the next chapter.

References

Annerstedt, C., & Lindgren, E-C. (2014). Caring as an important foundation in coaching for social sustainability: A case study of a successful Swedish coach in high-performance sport. *Reflective Practice, 15*(1), 27–39.

Block, J. (1995). A contrarian view of the five-factor approach to personality description. *Psychological Bulletin, 117,* 187–215. 10.1037/0033-2909.117.2.187

Brown, D. J., Arnold, R., Fletcher, D., & Standage, M. (2017). Human thriving: A conceptual debate and literature review. *European Psychologist, 22,* 167–179. doi:10.1027/1016-9040/a000294

Côté, J., & Gilbert, W. (2009). An integrative definition of coaching. *International Journal of Sport Science & Coaching, 4*(3), 307–323.

Cushion, C. (2007). Modelling the complexity of the coaching process. *International Journal of Sport Science and Coaching, 3*(1), 395–401.

Daloz, L. A. (1986). *Effective teaching and mentoring: Realizing the transformational power of adult learning experiences.* Jossey-Bass.

Deci, E. L., & Ryan, R. M. (1985). *Intrinsic motivation and self-determination in human behavior.* Plenum Press. 10.1007/978-1-4899-2271-7

Doorley, J. D., Goodman, F. R., Kelso, K. C., & Kashdan, T. B. (2020). Psychological flexibility: What we know, what we do not know, and what we think we know. *Social and Personality Psychology Compass, 14*(12), 1–11. 10.1111/spc3.12566

Dweck, C. S. (2017, September 21). From needs to goals and representations: Foundations for a Unified Theory of Motivation, Personality, and Development. *Psychological Review*. Advance online publication. 10.1037/rev0000082

Fletcher, D., & Sarkar, M. (2012). A grounded theory of psychological resilience in Olympic champions. *Psychology of Sport and Exercise*, *13*(5), 669–678. 10.1016/j.psychsport.2012.04.007

Fletcher, D., & Sarkar, M. (2013). Psychological resilience: A review and critique of definitions, concepts, and theory. *European Psychologist*, *18*(1), 12–23. 10.1027/1016-9040/a000124

Fletcher, D., & Sarkar, M. (2016). Mental fortitude training: An evidence-based approach to developing psychological resilience for sustained success. *Journal of Sport Psychology in Action*, *7*(3), 135–157.

Gonzalez, S. P., Moore, E. W. G., Newton, M., & Galli, N. A. (2016). Validity and reliability of the Connor-Davidson resilience scale (CD-RISC) in competitive sport. *Psychology of Sport and Exercise*, *23*, 31–39. 10.1016/j.psychsport.2015.10.005

Hagger, M. S. (2014). Avoiding the 'déjà-variable' phenomenon: Social psychology needs more guides to constructs. *Frontiers in Psychology*, *5*, 52.

Hodge, K., Henry, G., & Smith, W. (2014). A case study of excellence in elite sport: Motivational climate in a World Champion team. *The Sports Psychologist*, *28*, 60–74.

Jones, R. L., & Wallace, M. (2005). Another bad day at the training ground: Coping with ambiguity in the coaching context. *Sport, Education and Society*, *10*, 119–134. 10.1080/1357332052000308792

Kashdan, T. B., & Rottenberg, J. (2010). Psychological flexibility as a fundamental aspect of health. *Clinical Psychology Review*, *30*(4), 865–878.

Kelley, T. L. (1927). *Interpretation of educational measurements*. World Book Co.

Kidman, L. (2005). *Athlete-centred coaching: Developing inspired and inspiring people*. Innovative Print Communications Ltd.

Lara-Bercial, S., & Mallett, C. J. (2016). The practices and developmental pathways of professional and Olympic serial winning coaches. *International Sport Coaching Journal*, *3*, 221–239. 10.1123/iscj.2016-0083

Mageau, G. A. & Robert J Vallerand, R. J. (2003) The coach–athlete relationship: A motivational model. *Journal of Sports Sciences*, *21*, 883–904. 10.1080/0264041031000140374

Mallett, C. J. (2005). Self-determination theory: A case study of evidence-based coaching. *The Sport Psychologist*, *19*, 417–429.

Mallett, C. J., & Lara-Bercial, S. (2016). Serial winning coaches: People, vision, and environment. In M. Raab, P. Wylleman, R. Seiler, A. M. Elbe, & G. Hatzigeorgiadis (Eds.), *Sport and exercise psychology research: Theory to practice* (pp. 289–322). Elsevier.

Mason, J. (2001). *Researching your own practice: The discipline of noticing* (1st Ed.). Routledge. 10.4324/9780203471876

Marsh, H. W. (1994). Sport motivation orientations: Beware of Jingle-Jangle Fallacies. *Journal of Sport & Exercise Psychology*, *16*, 365–380. 10.1123/jsep.16.4.365

Meichenbaum, D. (1976). A self-instructional approach to stress management: A proposal for stress inoculation training. In C. Spielberger, & I. Sarason (Eds.), *Stress and anxiety in modern life*. Winston.

Morgan, P. B. C., Fletcher, D., & Sarkar, M. (2019). Developing team resilience: A season-long study of psychosocial enablers and strategies in a high-level sports team. *Psychology of Sport and Exercise*, *45*, 101543. 10.1016/j.psychsport.2019.101543

Noddings, N. (1984). *Caring: A feminine approach to ethics and moral education.* University of California Press.

Noddings, N. (2013). *Caring: A relational approach to ethics and moral education.* University of California Press.

Ntoumanis, N., & Mallett, C. J. (2014). Motivation in sport: A self-determination theory perspective. In A. G. Papaioannou, & D. Hackfort (Eds.), *Routledge companion to sport and exercise psychology: Global perspectives and fundamental concepts* (pp. 67–82). Routledge.

Potrac, P. (2004). Coaches' power. In R. Jones, K. Armour, & P. Potrac (Eds.), *Sports coaching cultures: From theory to practice.* Routledge.

Potrac, P., Mallett, C., Greenough, K., & Nelson, L. (2017). Desire and paranoia: An embodied tale of emotion, identity, and pathos in sports coaching. *Sports Coaching Review, 6*(2), 142–161. 10.1080/21640629.2017.1367067

Rynne, S. B., & Mallett, C. J. (2012). Understanding the work and learning of high performance coaches. *Physical Education and Sport Pedagogy, 17,* 507–523. 10.1080/174 08989.2011.621119

Rynne, S., Mallett, C. J., & Tinning, R. (2010). The workplace learning of high performance sport coaches. *Sport, Education and Society, 15,* 315–330.

Sanford, N. (1967). The development of social responsibility. *American Journal of Orthopsychiatry, 37*(1), 22–29. 10.1111/j.1939-0025.1967.tb01063.x

Santos, V., Paes, F., Pereira, V., Arias-Carrión, O., Silva, A. C., Carta, M. G., Nardi, A. E., & Machado, S. (2013). The role of positive emotion and contributions of positive psychology in depression treatment: Systematic review. *Clinical Practice and Epidemiology in Mental Health, 9,* Article 221–237. 10.2174/1745017901309010221

Sarkar, M., & Fletcher, D. (2014). Ordinary magic, extraordinary performance: Psychological resilience and thriving in high achievers. *Sport, Exercise, and Performance Psychology, 3,* 46–60. doi: 10.1037/spy0000003

Sarkar, M., & Hilton, N. K. (2020). Psychological resilience in Olympic medal-winning coaches: A longitudinal qualitative study. *International Sport Coaching Journal, 7*(2), 209–219. DOI: 10.1123/iscj.2019-0075

Tao, Y-C., Rynne, S. B., & Mallett, C. J. (2019). Blending and becoming: Migrant Chinese high-performance coaches' learning journey in Australia. *Physical Education and Sport Pedagogy, 24,* 582–597.

Thorndike, E. L. (1904). *An introduction to the theory of mental and social measurements.* The Science Press.

Vallerand, R. J. (2012). The role of passion in sustainable psychological well-being. *Psychology of Well-Being: Theory, Research and Practice, 2,* 1. 10.1186/2211-1522-2-1

11

FROM SURVIVING TO THRIVING

Holistic Development

In addition to producing successful performance outcomes, striving, surviving, and thriving are also connected to coaches' and athletes' health and wellbeing. The health and wellbeing of coaches and athletes has become recognised as a key issue in elite sport contexts. As an architect and sculptor of the environment, coaches are responsible for the coach–athlete–performance relationship and are considered as "performers in their own right" (e.g., Gould et al., 2002; Mallett & Lara-Bercial, 2016; Parkes, 2018). For those who have experienced the highs and lows of professional and Olympic sport coaching, they will understand and appreciate the rollercoaster rides in working in the elite sport context. Coaches often ruminate about their short- and medium-term employment. It is not uncommon for coaches to ruminate about concerns, such as, *"Is a bronze medal enough to keep your coaching job?"* These potentially distracting ruminations likely compromise the coach as a performer when it counts the most. The fear of being sacked as a coach is commonplace across most countries and contributes to coach stress and burnout. Prominent scholars, such as Kenttä, Olusoga, Bentzen, and Kellmann, have investigated the problems of coach stress, exhaustion, and burnout (e.g., Altfeld et al., 2015; Bentzen et al., 2020; Kenttä et al., 2020; Olusoga et al., 2019; Olusoga & Kenttä, 2017). These maladaptive and undesirable outcomes of working in this environment are of great concern not only to coaches but also for all actors in the sporting landscape. Coaches as architects and sculptors of the sport setting differentially influence and shape the quality of the sporting experience for all actors. So, how might coaches move from striving to surviving to thriving in this highly performative environment? What do we mean by thriving?

DOI: 10.4324/9781003427292-15

Thriving is key to achieving and sustaining success

The third wave of psychology (after *Psychoanalysis* and *Behaviourism*) was labelled the humanistic movement that subsequently led to the 4th and current wave (*Positive Psychology*). Abraham Maslow led this humanistic psychology movement, with the help of influential others such as Carl Rogers (*unconditional regard*). The central tenet of this third wave was to focus on people's strengths and human growth tendencies rather than a deficit approach to human development ... in other words, shift away from a focus on what is wrong with people. It is perhaps unsurprising that Maslow pursued such an approach when you consider that much of his life was characterised by a miserable childhood; his parents provided little love to him, and he experienced poor physical health (heart attack at 39 years). He also grew up in New York during the Depression and then endured World War 2. Maslow believed that people are inherently good and driven for personal growth and to overcome challenges to achieve fulfilment (Coulter et al., 2016). A key legacy of Maslow was the notion of *self-actualisation* – people striving for personal growth, harmony, and unity that brings meaning to their lives (McAdams, 2006). Linked to this notion of personal growth and fulfilment is thriving; however, what does thriving mean and look like, especially in the context of elite sport?

Thriving in the highly contested and performative environment of elite sport is an enormous challenge. To thrive and to intentionally create an environment for others to thrive is considered helpful in producing high performance as well as contributing to the health and wellbeing of people (Benson & Scakesm, 2009; Porath et al., 2012). Nonetheless, the striving to thrive in these highly performative contexts is probably highly aspirational and to sustain that thriving over extended periods even more so. This thriving is consistent with a strengths-based approach to human development. Although thriving has been used interchangeably with terms such as growth (positive change in level of human functioning) and resilience (buffering against and overcoming adversity to perform); thriving has been considered a more holistic, integrated, and multifaceted concept (Brown et al., 2020). Several scholars have underscored the central role of holistic and fully functioning elements to realise thriving in a specific context (e.g., Brown et al., 2017; Ryan & Deci, 2017; Su, Tay & Diener, 2014). Indeed, Su, Tay and Diener (2014) suggested that "to thrive in life is not only marked by feelings of happiness, or a sense of accomplishment, or having supportive and rewarding relationships, but is a collection of all these aspects" (p. 272). Thriving is a dynamic experience of holistic functioning that over time is considered necessary for growth and subsequent higher level of functioning (Brown et al., 2020), which is not inconsistent with Maslow's concept of self-actualisation.

In recent times, there has been increased and necessary scrutiny of high-performance sport settings due to perceived toxic cultures in several developed countries that have caused, for example, significant athlete suffering. Indeed, these maladaptive cultures have tended to focus exclusively on fostering athlete performance (*win at all costs* approach) with little, if any, meaningful consideration of people's wellbeing. Unfortunately, performance and wellbeing are often considered as binary rather than interdependent outcomes. For example, this arbitrary separation is often evidenced in high-performance sport governance structures that separate these two human elements as independent remits and responsibilities that implicitly suggest they are unrelated to each other. Personal and social factors (e.g., relationships and power differentials) are central to creating an adaptive and thriving culture that fosters both performance and wellbeing for all actors in the sport setting (e.g., McHenry et al., 2020; Rouquette et al., 2021). Critically, a key challenge is for those who lead in high-performance settings to foster both optimal sport performance and adaptive health outcomes. Thriving is a concept that resonates with the optimising of health and performance outcomes. However, consistent with the previous discussion on jangle fallacies (Chapter 10) it is necessary to distinguish between some related constructs – thriving, flourishing, vitality, resilience, and growth.

What is thriving?

Recent theorising and empirical research findings have supported the view that thriving is indeed different to growth, resilience, and flourishing (e.g., Brown et al., 2017; Brown et al., 2018). In understanding what thriving is, Brown and colleagues (2018) underscored a functioning-based perspective that considers both performance and wellbeing (Sarkar & Fletcher, 2014), which differentiates thriving from other constructs such as flourishing (psychosocial and emotional wellbeing; Fredrickson, 2006). Recent research by Davis and colleagues (2021) has highlighted the mediating role of psychological need satisfaction between coach–athlete attachment (i.e., secure, anxious, and avoidance) in a sample of Swedish athletes, highlighting the saliency of psychological need satisfaction (autonomy, competence, and relatedness) and secure relationships on coach and athlete thriving. The importance of social support has been identified as critical to creating a thriving environment for all social actors (e.g., Arnold et al., 2018; Sarkar & Hilton, 2020), which begs many questions, for example, *How do coaches and colleagues provide social support to each other to promote thriving in these highly contested settings?* Indeed, in thinking about thriving we consider all social actors in a specific setting; the coach, the athletes, and the support staff and the environment in which they all interact and function on regular basis. Furthermore, at the recent European Congress for Sport and Exercise Psychology (2022), McGuire and colleagues encouraged consideration of thriving at both the individual and the collective levels, which reinforces the importance of understanding person in context.

Thriving: saliency of context

We reflect upon Alexander Den Heijer's quote, "When a flower doesn't bloom, you fix the environment in which it grows, not the flower" (https://lnkd.in/dJ5aS3w6). His quote highlights that context matters, which we continue to highlight. Coaches are key architects and sculptors of the daily training environment whose responsibility to create a context that fosters both adaptive performance and health outcomes for athletes and other social actors (e.g., Mallett & Hanrahan, 2004; Lara-Bercial & Mallett, 2016; Sarkar & Hilton, 2020; Sauvé et al., 2023). Coaches as leaders are not only responsible but should be accountable for creating an environment that is conducive to coaches, athletes, and staff thriving (e.g., Lara-Bercial & Mallett, 2016; Sauvé et al., 2023). Recent research in elite sport has shown that good leaders experience superior performance and wellbeing; furthermore, those who have good leaders also experience superior holistic outcomes (performance and wellbeing) (Fransen et al. 2017, 2020); i.e., thriving! We described these SWC's thriving environments in Lara-Bercial and Mallett (2016) as reflective of a *greenhouse* – very stable and predictable. It is also noteworthy that although the coaches are central in shaping the environment (*coach as leader*), all social actors and processes contribute in differential ways to its impact on holistic thriving.

Overall, the data supported the view that these SWC are thriving themselves; and they also intentionally strive to create environments to help their athletes/support teams to also thrive. Some essential questions include: *What are these SWC striving to achieve in their coaching work? What are some of the key challenges and adversities faced by SWC? How did they cope and learn to cope with these challenges? Do these SWC create a thriving environment? If, so, what do these environments look like?*

Learning is central to thriving: self and others

Learners and life-long learning

Understandably, elite sport is highly competitive and there are small differences between winning and not. So, what makes some settings more successful than others? Within the elite sport setting, there are ample opportunities to keep coaches, athletes, and staff seeking small gains to create and sustain their competitive edge. The oft stated, one percenters matter. "Nothing happens overnight … in terms of quality. It happens little by little, grain by grain, day by day, minute by minute, hour by hour" (Coach 14). These SWC want to *get ahead and stay ahead*, which drives their conscientiousness and passion to continue learning and exploring novel ideas (Mallett & Lara-Bercial, 2016; McAdams, 2015; Sarkar & Hilton, 2020). Unsurprisingly, learning and innovation were considered key to achieving and sustaining success and subsequent thriving: "I think to stay abreast of new ideas, new ways of doing things is probably one of the secrets to continued success or success" (Coach 11). Indeed, these SWC challenged the status quo. Central to promoting life-long learning is the creation of a learning environment in the workplace (Rynne & Mallett, 2012). The integration of new ideas from those with whom you work (and also externally) not only likely causes some disruption (which is necessary for learning to take place) but also promotes interest and novelty, mitigating against some of the necessary but mundane and highly repetitive training tasks in the sport setting.

> ... standstill means decline. You should keep developing yourself, monoto-nous and routine work, I do not think much of that at all. So that keeps ... and that is why you should try to change the people in your staff every now and then, so that freshness comes back in and new ideas come in again (Coach 2).

"In [sport] it's a big challenge so we have to create a lot of really ingenious ways to keep people motivated, and that I alluded to a lot in the last five min-utes" (Coach 11). The importance of some novelty can help coaches and athletes to be invigorated and renewed after lengthy competitive seasons that usually involve significant travel and interrupted sleep patterns. Furthermore, repeating what you did last year is unlikely to produce superior performance and wellbeing outcomes in subsequent years. Learning is not doing the same thing you can already do repeatedly.

Much of everyday work in elite sport is not predictable and new and some-times unexpected challenges emerge every day. The notion that coaches should control what you can, implicitly suggests that much of HP coaches' work is predictable ... if only it was ... which is why we acknowledge the notions of *structured improvisation, orchestration,* and *psychological flexibility* in working within this chaotic and ambiguous setting (Cushion, 2007; Doorley et al., 2020; Jones et al., 2012; Jones & Wallace, 2005; Kashdan & Rottenberg, 2010; Potrac et al., 2017). However, these often, unexpected challenges are necessary for people to thrive by learning to embrace and respond to them. This consistent exposure can contribute to buffering the potential adverse effects of future stressors (robust resilience). Indeed, in the pursuit of personal strivings, developing sufficient personal resources (assets) that act like a vaccination to these stressors and unexpected issues is part of the life-long learning necessary to thrive (Kashdan et al., 2020).

Central to thriving is the notion of coaches as life-long learners in the striving for personal growth (Maslow, 1943), transformation, and is consistent with the pursuit of *becoming* (Nietzsche, cited in Cox, 1999; Strauss, 1959). "I just know that I still haven't reached. I still don't think I've reached my potential yet so I'm still trying to learn and make myself better" (Coach 10).

The quest for life-long learning requires a humble and modest perception of what you know and can do and a realisation that there is so much more to know (*becoming*).

I actually come at my coaching profession fairly humbly and I think that's what allows me to be successful. Because I don't think that I know everything, I don't think that I'm better than someone else, I don't think that it's because of me the athletes have won. I don't ever think of myself that way, and because I think that way, I think that's the best way for me personally to continue to improve. (Coach 11)

The ongoing quest in search of better ways is consistent with the embodiment of life-long learning and thriving.

I think what I didn't lose is still when I was a very, very, young coach just coming from university I was always challenging, challenging from what I know, what I learned, from the basics, finding the niche and the small things where you can improve. Is there something we can improve on, where are people, other people missing out on. Ok that might be where we can go faster. I still think that hasn't changed to me, because that's a very important part. As I said if you lose not having a vision, having a motivation for some new things then you just come to a standstill. (Coach 9)

This enjoyable pursuit of seeking better ways is front of mind every day.

It's a constant process of learning ... You never stop learning ... I think the main point is never to stop looking in all directions. Well, I enjoy doing that because I like to read and watch basketball or the like, or I buy a book in which some symphony orchestra from Bremen talks about team building. There are so many topics. (Coach 1)

Ok you learn in a daily process, I think ... And then finding the specific, making the next notch between winning and moving [improving], that's the daily challenge. (Coach 9)

This embodiment of a life-long learner seems to be predicated on the need for some humility and limited ego as well as an understanding of competence as not only comparative but also a personal quest to constantly seek to improve and learn.

Learning from you know, like you and I today, me talking to you, you talking to me. We're, believe it or not, learning something, you know what I mean. And it's all about that to me, it's about absorbing, talking about, it's in any sport whether it's [SPORT] or [SPORT] I've been involved in, I've been involved in it since the age of three, do I know everything? No. And if I don't know everything neither do you and neither does anybody else. And to me it's all about talking to people, exchanging views and ideas, and learning from each other. And that's how you become a better coach. (Coach 8)

Success can mean a shift from hunting to being hunted. Hence, thriving is also about effectively coping with success to sustain continued success ... *getting ahead and staying ahead.*

I've seen it very often ... not every coach has had success once, but then you don't see them again because they couldn't cope with the success. To themselves and maybe then especially with the successful athlete ... That is for a good coach in the right way still celebrating, saying that there is always something so they feel special, but otherwise good teaching and good managing and fine if you want to carry on then we shouldn't lose our rules. The rules are still the rules, that's why you won. If you want to win again, ok maybe the rules might be even harder because people know you now and they want to beat you. You are a hero, and if they beat you then the new hero is there. If you want to be still the hero than you have to follow our rules. ... You have to first work with successful athletes on their new level of success, dealing with success, and setting new targets. Because if they do the same again they will be not successful so you have to be, they have to be aware as well that that's not enough. (Coach 9)

Sometimes coaches don't know what they don't know, which can be an unintended obstacle to thriving. Hubris can also become problematic for coaches.

I think in the beginning when I came out and I was fresh and I went out to university to have my maths, I knew everything. You couldn't beat me on anything, like in the end I knew nothing and you know that's part of learning, consistently learning. The more you know, the less you know at the same time, so I changed from the arrogant guy that knew everything to the one that started to question everything and try to learn more. (Coach 17)

Although there might be some merit in doing things differently (disruption) changing for the sake of change without due consideration of the impact of that change is potentially problematic. "I do what I can that will help to be the best I can be with the guys. If something comes along which is different then of course I would look to see what it is and why it's different; why it's better". (Coach 14)

The above quotes provide some support of how these SWC move from surviving to thriving. Moreover, their experiences are consistent with how we have conceptualised thriving.

Learning from others

A key source for SWC learning was other coaches. Thriving by being open to learning from other coaches, often from other sports. This cross-fertilisation of ideas and practices requires coaches to be confident in who they are and the necessity to affirm and challenge their thinking and actions.

> I mean, the best education was always if there were meetings organised sometimes very informal, coming together with other coaches, I think, from other sports. I think that was always very interesting to me to listen, to share ideas … So yes, just talking different things. That's then again bringing that together and picking the things what could be interesting for your sport, I think that's important. (Coach 9)

Seeking counsel from other coaches who have trodden a similar path to the SWC is an opportunity to refine their coaching praxis.

> There's, if someone has been a coach at a high level, you know what it is like to sit on the side … you've got that empathy and you've got that understanding about performance at that point in time … And so, if for are more pertinent or more capable of being able to say well have you thought about this, can you do that, because they've had to deal with the same situation. How they handle stress, how they handle selection, what philosophies they use, what principles they use. So, to be fair talking with those people was really interesting as well. (Coach 10)

Confidence is one thing, but to be assertive and proactive in seeking counsel from others is another step that likely separates SWC from others.

> That makes a huge difference for me, you start to think and learn from others, then when I came into the bigger scenes, I used to pick out the top ten athletes and then find out who is their coach and then I used to go up to them and say, hey my name is [Coach] I wonder if you have five minutes, I want to ask you a couple questions. I tried to painfully drag that out as long as possible, most of the time I managed to do 30 minutes or 40 minutes. Then you're sat discussing how do you do this, how do you do that, what do you think about, how should you attack this. Then write all of this down and then basically go round listening to everybody, and I think I do that still and try to find out what's their philosophy. (Coach 17)

Learning from experience

Learning from experience helps to embody thriving but it seems to be predicated on clarity of your approach for success and an open mind. Importantly, in elite sport we are often working with outliers. "You shouldn't lose your belief and your model but you have to be open minded ... It's experience as well but also in the first place as a mentality of a coach to be open minded" (Coach 9). Moreover, thriving becomes possible when coaches experience early exposure to high-performance environments, supporting the idea that seeds for future thriving are born from optimism, being proactive, and solution focused.

> What happened with me was I was thrust into a lot of early experiences. You know I was sent off to conferences by [Sport] [Nation], I was given chances to come to national camps as an observer, and I was given assistant coaching positions. And if you can offer that to a lot of young people you might find the cream will rise to the top. (Coach 11)

This early exposure to high performance early in one's coaching career provides lucidity about what ... "I was able to start at the top from the beginning/ immediately ... likely provides increased clarity about the nature of the environment and the work required to perform in that context" (Coach 7). This links to optimism, passion, and zest to become the best they can be driven by narrative identities such as *atonement* and *generativity* (Mallett & Lara-Bercial, 2016) and characteristic of people who are autonomous, purposeful, and motivated agents who plan their lives and make choices – "life is about choice, goals, and hope" (McAdams & Olson, 2010, p. 524).

Thriving from early and serendipitous exposure to high-performance environments creates learning opportunities

Several SWC reported early access to working in high-performance environments, rather than developing their coaching craft via performance pathways (e.g., elite youth). These early opportunities are not common but importantly coaches need to make the most of these prospects.

> What happened with me was I was thrust into a lot of early experiences. You know I was sent off to conferences by [sport, country], I was given chances to come to national camps as an observer, and I was given assistant coaching positions. And if you can offer that to a lot of young people you might find the cream will rise to the top. (Coach 11)

It seems that the coaches who were provided these early opportunities showed gratitude in helping the next generation of coaches:

I was only 26 at the time. And so, I had to learn fast, my little legs couldn't keep up with the treadmill there. So, women hadn't gone to the Olympics in '88 and I got them through to the Olympics in '92 … 28 my first Olympics, 26 my first world championships as a coach, so quite a young coach. So, I am quite for giving people opportunities. But some of those years were pretty tough as well. (Coach 10)

Furthermore, the early access to working with elite athletes was often seren-dipitous. "I was fortunate in that I was able to step straight into the top, I didn't go through the ranks of being a coach. It was a case of circumstance" (Coach 14).

Central to embodying thriving is the creation of an environment that facilitates this dynamic experience of holistic functioning

A facilitative environment is characterised by supportive challenge towards meaningful and realistic goals with all individuals contributing to and taking ownership of those goals. Moreover, individuals seeking challenges and craving constructive feedback in pursuit of those challenges will be fostered if there are healthy relationships between performers and leaders or coaches. This environ-ment will be characterised as a psychologically safe environment that encourages sensible risk-taking, healthy competition, with everyone supporting one another, learning from mistakes and failures, recognition, and celebration of success.

It makes sense that coaches seek to create an environment in which people, especially athletes, thrive. We reiterate that thriving is a concept that seeks to foster the optimising of health and performance outcomes (Brown et al., 2020; Lara-Bercial & Mallett, 2016; Sarkar & Hilton, 2020). Of course, this goal pursuit is expected by those within and external to the sport setting; however, in many cases there is likely an intention-behaviour gap. So, despite coaches' (and ad-ministrators') best intentions, what can we learn from the SWC as to how they create such a thriving environment?

What I try to create is … you meet an athlete who knows less than you, and by the time you are in the middle of the relationship they know as much as you, and by the time they are ready to compete internationally they know more than you. So, you train people to move on by you and become better people, and be better, more knowledgeable, and more well prepared that you are. And that's kind of my role as a coach. So, it's a humble approach to it all. (Coach 10)

This idea of nurturing others to be better does not mean pushing without embodying that you genuinely care. "The way I explain it to them is in a very positive way is that it's not like you are trying to beat up on each/everyone every day, you're trying to raise the level here by pushing each other" (Coach 10). Moreover, that I could impart as much knowledge as possible onto the [ATHLETES] but do it in a way where you are always in a positive atmosphere in positive surroundings, you know what I mean. You are always being constructive, even when it came to de-briefs, you always ended a de-brief session on a positive high, never on a negative low. (Coach 8)

Furthermore, the longer-term view of development and the attitude that coaching success can and should be partially defined as developing good people as a measure of coaching success. "I sort of rate it on whether or not the athletes that I coach have had a fulfilling experience, their self-esteem is built, and whether they've become good people 20 years down the road" (Coach 11). This striving and embodiment of positive interactions with others, including athletes was commonplace amongst these SWC. An ever-present challenge for coaches is the key constraint of time, which operates at many levels. For example, the notion of fairness in how coaches spend their time with all athletes in a squad or team is and should always be of some concern.

You're very aware of working with your top four or eight athletes and they should get the majority of your time and it will encourage the lower ranked athletes to come up … but when you are a head coach of a high-performance program you have to kind of work with your eagles so to speak, not your sparrows, and not your marginal performers so to speak. I think that is something that a lot of top coaches forget to do; they forget to work with their top performers who are eventually going to be the team so to speak. So, a lot of my day is being very aware of that, that the top performers are not neglected … you have to care for the ones that are going to win your medals at the Olympics and be very aware of spending time with them … So that's a big part of the day is to remember that. (Coach 11)

The embodiment of thriving to achieve and sustain success necessitates a complimentary, synergistic, and engaging support team

The current discourse typically focuses on the head coach rather than the coaching team – head coaches do not perform in a vacuum. We suggest a shift in the discourse to embrace all actors in the setting and as part of the broader environment in which they operate.

I can't do it on my own, so I have to bring people totally in, in my thinking, and everything … . Ok you can maybe have one success because you are a good coach and you pick the right people but to do it again of course you have a team as well, you build a team around you, and they are supporting you and cover some areas as well that are important. You can't do everything yourself ... you can do it maybe once with less people, but if you want to do it again and again you have to have a standard below as well, supporting you. (Coach 9)

You cannot do it alone ... I think that is really one of the most important things, having strong people around you and giving them the space they need to work from their own strength and that in combination with your own strength. That is what makes the difference for me ... I feel that people must be able to be creative and should find the space to make their own contribution, but within the framework/ parameters. When you step out of the framework/ do not respect the parameters, I will intervene. But when you would like to use the strength of all those people, within the framework ... and that is something I feel that I am good at, I have almost always been able to gather the right people around me. There are a lot of people that are scared of strong people around them, they are looking for people who nod yes, so to speak, and I have always looked for people that enter into discussions, because that makes you grow. I do not need people who nod yes, I need people that challenge me to do an even better job. Eventually that is what makes you stronger. (Coach 5)

The importance of valuing staff cannot be emphasised enough. This valuing of staff is often rhetorical in elite sport but not always embodied. This open communication, engagement, and valuing of staff likely fosters psychological safety in the specific setting.

Over the past two decades, coaching at the elite level has increasingly become a *team approach* and everyone's contribution has a potential un/helpful impact on others in the programme, performance, and wellbeing.

Value everybody that's in the picture and understand that, how important it is to value all of them and communicate with them [athletes and support staff]. ... the amount of staff you have to deal with and the fact that as a head coach, you've got to have your finger on the pulse of that all the time. Because every one of those staff members is going to affect your athletes' performance and every one of those can help you, to make you look sideways as well. (Coach 6)

Consistent with this view is getting the *right people on the bus*. This popular metaphor used in sport and corporate was first cited in Jim Collins' best-seller *Good to Great* (2001). It is not only getting the right people on the support team but also working with their complementary strengths (in the right seat).

The more people you have around you the more they challenge you. Of course, they want to have their say as well, they are experts in their area as well. Of course, that's, a good coach also has to be a good manager, first to motivate those guys to feel that they are part of the success but at the same time of course you sometimes also have to cut things down. (Coach 9)

The necessity for complementarity of skills (but consistent values) was reported by these SWC. For example, Coach 9 reported:

So, a team player, team sounds sometimes as if everybody is the same, but everybody is not the same and everybody has strength and weaknesses and that's what makes a good team, and a team needs that. But of course, they have to work under one, or under the same rule. There's the rules there for everybody but inside the rules there's a lot of for space for being creative to me, that's what I want, that's a key thing. So, people want to be there, they want to work with each other, that's if you can have that atmosphere and if people really want to perform they do … I think you see it, every coach has his own strengths. Some are very good and are creative and can help me as well with they have a good eye for producing video clips or whatever … People have different views how they get there, so there is a lot of space. Or as we said talking about the training programme and ok can we do it a little bit different there is space, strong enough all. There is always something to discuss.

Complementary skills but same values create potential for diversity of thought within a consistent values framework.

I've got a philosophy also that I can't be an expert in everything, and I need to get that expertise from the people around me and this is where it's getting into the other place where I really learn is through my colleagues. Because I find it really interesting working with people, you know a physio who's got a biomechanics background, a doctor who's gone into mental skills, that people that have got interesting backgrounds in fields that can bring things in and help explain complicated principles. And give some practical ways on going forward. And again I've learned a lot with that. But about the philosophy of being able to bring that into the programme but still have it in a very practical way. (Coach 10)

Unsurprisingly, it seems important that the coach strives to be visible and present in striving to support the athletes and staff and consequently accountable and on the same page:

Being visible to the athletes involves working closely with the support staff ... a lot of my day is spent working with the team, like the team support staff. So, it might even be dropping in and spending five minutes with the manager making sure that she's doing the jobs that need to be done and so on. (Coach 11)

This visibility of coaches and support staff, over time, builds the sense of being there to help others and is foundational to building stronger relations that foster trust.

The centrality of trust in serial winning coaching has been emphasised throughout this book and again we reiterate this point. In relation to thriving, athlete trust is an essential foundation; however, what seems to build trust is the coaches' ability to persuade the athlete that you can improve their performance.

What you have to do is create a trust, you have to get the athletes to believe that what you are saying is the right thing and it's going to get them there. It is not easy to do that. But one of the ways you do it is with skills, and I'm not talking about communication skills, I'm talking about actual skills, technical skills of the trade. As a young guy I was not that big and, in those days, you competed against everybody whether you were big or small and so you looked for ways, or you develop ways like that "being in a corner", you look for ways of getting the best you can out of yourself. And yes, I spent years doing that and I have been in a position where I can impart the knowledge I gained to others. People respect and they recognize it straight away. They say, "Yeah, well that's better" so they gradually get confident. And when they have that confidence, you can direct them quite simply. (Coach 14)

Trust also means that coaches are open and have integrity: "people can also trust me, so that means I try to be open, I don't like to be the coach telling them or misleading any of those guys in a different direction. Trying to sell the best of me to them" (Coach 9).

What did we learn?

Consistent with the construct of thriving these SWC focused on both adaptive performance and wellbeing outcomes; that is, holistic functioning and growth. Indeed, thriving is more than surviving through rebound resilience. It is about transformation and growth. Nevertheless, over time the building of robust resilience via personal assets to buffer the inevitable stressors is likely to provide the foundations that enable one to thrive. The ongoing pursuit of learning and becoming, passion, and enjoyment these SWC and their athletes reported is testament to their thriving.

One of the key messages in this chapter was that these coaches are thriving themselves; and they also intentionally strived to create environments to help their athletes/support teams to also thrive, which led to holistic growth. Thriving was not incidental but characterised by autonomy and intentionality. Of course, there were reports of some serendipitous luck in the SWC journeys, however, repeated success at the highest level with different athletes and contexts is not accidental. Central to thriving were two key factors: continuous learning and shaping an environment to enable people to thrive.

Learning and the notion of becoming more expert at their craft drove SWC to continually pursue opportunities to be the best they could be. What drove this pursuit of learning was wanting to *get ahead and stay ahead*. They were passionate and had a zest for their coaching work, which we suggest was highly autonomous and internally driven. They were always unsatisfied in their pursuit and in shifting from being the hunter to being hunted ensured they were always looking for a competitive advantage. This transformative learning was shaped around social relationships and involved various human sources, such as coaching staff, athletes, and other coaches. Indeed, these thriving social landscapes involved committed and intentional adaptive social relationships for all social actors (e.g., Arnold et al., 2018; Sarkar & Hilton, 2020). Furthermore, what enabled these SWC to optimise their learning was their belief in a "growth mindset" (Dweck, 2017) combined with clarity of vision and purpose.

The second key learning was centred around the environment – *context matters*. Central to embodying thriving is the creation of an environment that facilitates this dynamic experience of holistic functioning – performance and wellbeing. The embodiment of thriving to achieve and sustain success and experience necessitates a complementary, synergistic, and engaging support team. As we penned in the introduction of this chapter, Su, Tay and Diener (2014) suggested that "to thrive in life is not only marked by feelings of happiness, or a sense of accomplishment, or having supportive and rewarding relationships, but is a collection of all these aspects" (p. 272). The environment that is shaped by SWC enables those social actors within that setting to experience the dynamic shaping and re-shaping of holistic functioning over time that contributes to superior functioning and personal growth (Brown et al., 2020). This "greenhouse" that is created includes all social actors thriving (Lara-Bercial & Mallett, 2016): the coach, athletes, and support staff. The passion of these SWC and the enjoyment and satisfaction they and the athletes and support staff experienced in such a highly contested space is testament to their approach and embodiment of leadership – *caring determination*. The remit of coaches as leaders includes the expectation and embodiment of individual and collective accountability and responsibility. Social and emotional support enables people to develop their personal qualities or resources that, in turn, help to promote learning and build trust over time.

In the next chapter, we synthesise the findings into some key take-home messages that might be helpful in shaping future high-performance coach development.

References

Arnold, R., Edwards, T., & Rees, T. (2018). Organizational stressors, social support, and implications for subjective performance in high-level sport. *Psychology of Sport and Exercise, 39*, 204–212.

Altfeld, S., Mallett, C. J., & Kellmann, M. (2015). Coaches' burnout, stress, and recovery over a season: A longitudinal study. *International Sport Coaching Journal, 2*, 137–151. 10.1123/iscj.2014-0113.

Brown, D. J., Arnold, R., Standage, M., Turner, J. E., & Fletcher, D. (2020). The prediction of thriving in elite sport: A prospective examination of the role of psychological need satisfaction, challenge appraisal, and salivary biomarkers. *Journal of Science and Medicine in Sport, 24*, 373–379.

Brown, D. J., Arnold, R., Fletcher, D., & Standage, M. (2017). Human thriving: A conceptual debate and literature review. *European Psychologist, 22*, 167–179. doi:10.102 7/1016-9040/a000294.

Brown, D. J., Arnold, R., Reid, T., & Roberts, G. (2018). A qualitative inquiry of thriving in elite sport. *Journal of Applied Sport Psychology, 30*, 129–149. doi:10.1080/1 0413200.2017.1354339.

Benson, P., & Scakesm, P. (2009). The definition and preliminary measurement of thriving in adolescence. *The Journal of Positive Psychology, 4*, 85–104. doi: 10.1080/1743 9760802399240

Bentzen, M., Kenttä, G., Richter, A., & Lemyre, P-N. (2020). Impact of job insecurity on psychological well- and ill-being among high performance coaches. *International Journal of Environmental Research and Public Health, 17*, 6939. 10.3390/ijerph17196939.

Coulter, T., Gilchrist, M., Mallett, C., & Carey, A. (2016). Abraham Maslow: Hierarchy of coach and athlete needs. In L. Nelson, R. Groom, & P. Potrac (Eds.), *Learning in sports coaching* (pp. 63–74). Routledge.

Cox, C. (1999). *Nietzsche: Naturalism and Interpretation.* University of California Press. ISBN 0-520-21553-2.

Cushion, C. (2007). Modelling the complexity of the coaching process. *International Journal of Sport Science and Coaching, 3*(1), 395–401.

Davis, L., Brown, D. J., Arnold, R., & Gustafsson, H. (2021). Thriving through relationships in sport: The role of the parent–athlete and coach–athlete attachment relationship. *Frontiers in Psychology (Movement Science and Sport Psychology),* 10.3389/ fpsyg.2021.694599

Doorley, J. D., Goodman, F. R., Kelso, K. C., & Kashdan, T. B. (2020). Psychological flexibility: What we know, what we do not know, and what we think we know. *Social and Personality Psychology Compass, 14*(12), 1–11. 10.1111/spc3.12566

Dweck, C. S. (2017, September 21). From needs to goals and representations: Foundations for a Unified Theory of Motivation, Personality, and Development. *Psychological Review.* Advance online publication. 10.1037/rev0000082

Fransen, K., Haslam, S. A., Steffens, N. K., Mallett, C. J., Peters, K., & Boen, F. (2020). Making 'us' better: High-quality athlete leadership relates to health and burnout in professional Australian football teams. *European Journal of Sport Science*, *20*(7), 953–963. 10.1080/17461391.2019.1680736

Fransen, K., Haslam, S. A., Mallett, C. J., Steffens, N. K., Peters, K., Boen, F. (2017). Is perceived athlete leadership quality related to team effectiveness? A comparison of three professional sports teams. *Journal Science and Medicine in Sport*, *20*, 800–806. 10.1 016/j.jsams.2016.11.024

Fredrickson, B. L. (2006). Unpacking positive emotions: Investigating the seeds of human flourishing. *The Journal of Positive Psychology*, *1*, 57–59. doi: 10.1080/1743976050051 0981

Gould, D., Dieffenbach, K., & Moffett, A. (2002). Psychological characteristics and their development in Olympic champions. *Journal of Applied Sport Psychology*, *14*, 172–204. 10.1080/10413200290103482.

Jones, R., Morgan, K., & Harris, K. (2012). Developing coaching pedagogy: Seeking a better integration of theory and practice. *Sport, Education and Society*, *17*(3), 313–329.

Jones, R. L., & Wallace, M. (2005). Another bad day at the training ground: Coping with ambiguity in the coaching context. *Sport, Education and Society*, *10*(1), 119–134.

Kashdan, T. B., Disabato, D. J., Goodman, F. R., Doorley, J. D., & McKnight, P. E. (2020) Understanding psychological flexibility: A multimethod exploration of pursuing valued goals despite the presence of distress, *Psychological Assessment*, *32*(9), 829–850.

Kashdan, T. B., & Rottenberg, J. (2010). Psychological flexibility as a fundamental aspect of health. *Clinical Psychology Review*, *30*(4), 865–878.

Kenttä, G., Bentzen, M., Dieffenbach, K., & Olusoga, P. (2020). Challenges experienced by women high-performance coaches: Sustainability in the profession. *International Sport Coaching Journal*, *7*, 200–208. 10.1123/iscj.2019-0029.

Lara-Bercial, S., & Mallett, C. J. (2016). The practices and developmental pathways of professional and Olympic serial winning coaches. *International Sport Coaching Journal*, *3*, 221–239. doi: 10.1123/iscj.2016-0083

Mallett, C. J., & Hanrahan, S. J. (2004). Elite athletes: What makes the "fire" burn so brightly? *Psychology of Sport and Exercise*, *5*, 183–200.

Mallett, C. J., & Lara-Bercial, S. (2016). Serial winning coaches: People, vision, and environment. In M. Raab, P. Wylleman, R. Seiler, A. M. Elbe & G. Hatzigeorgiadis (Eds.), *Sport and exercise psychology research: Theory to practice* (pp. 289–322). Elsevier.

Maslow, A. H. (1943). A theory of human motivation. *Psychological Review*, *50*(4), 370–396. doi: 10.1037/h0054346

McAdams, D. P. (2006). *The person: A new introduction to personality psychology* (4th ed.). Wiley.

McAdams, D. P. (2015). *The art and science of personality development*. Guildford Press. doi: 10.5860/choice.192399.

McAdams, D. P., & Olson, B. D. (2010). Personality development: Continuity and change over the life course. *Annual Review of Psychology*, *61*, 517–542. 10.1146/ annurev.psych.093008.100507.

McHenry, L. K., Cochran, J. L., Zakrajsek, R. A., Fisher, L. A., Couch, S. R., & Hill, B. S. (2022/2020). Elite figure skaters' experiences of thriving in the coach-athlete relationship: A person-centered theory perspective. *Journal of Applied Sport psychology*, *34*. 10.1080/10413200.2020.1800862

Olusoga, P., Bentzen, M., & Kentta, G. (2019). Coach burnout: A scoping review. *International Sport Coaching Journal*, *6*, 42–62. 10.1123/iscj.2017-0094.

Olusoga, P., & Kenttä, G. (2017). Desperate to quit: A narrative analysis of burnout and recovery in high-performance sports coaching. *The Sport Psychologist*, *31*, 237–248. 10.1123/tsp.2016-0010.

Porath, C., Spreitzer, G. M., Gibson, C., & Garnett, F. G. (2012). Thriving at work: Toward its measurement, construct validation, and theoretical refinement. *Journal of Organizational Behavior*, *33*, 250–275. doi: 10.1002/job.756

Parkes, J. (2018). *Coach as performer: Coach emotion, coping, and the coach-athlete performance relationship*. Doctoral thesis, The University of Queensland.

Potrac, P., Mallett, C., Greenough, K., & Nelson, L. (2017). Desire and paranoia: An embodied tale of emotion, identity, and pathos in sports coaching. *Sports Coaching Review*, *6*(2), 142–161. 10.1080/21640629.2017.1367067

Rouquette, O. Y., Knight, C. J., Lovett, V. E., & Heuzé, J. P. (2021). Effect of parent responsiveness on young athletes' self-perceptions and thriving: An exploratory study in a Belgian French-Community. *Psychology of Sport and Exercise*, *52*, 101801. doi: 10.1016/j.psychsport.2020.101801

Ryan, R. M., & Deci, E. L. (2017). *Self-determination theory: Basic psychological needs in motivation, development, and wellness*. Guilford Press.

Rynne, S. B. & Mallett, C. J. (2012). Understanding the work and learning of high performance coaches. *Physical Education and Sport Pedagogy*, *17*, 507–523. DOI: 10.1080/17408989.2011.621119.

Sarkar, M., & Fletcher, D. (2014). Ordinary magic, extraordinary performance: Psychological resilience and thriving in high achievers. *Sport, Exercise, and Performance Psychology*, *3*, 46–60. doi: 10.1037/spy0000003

Sarkar, M., & Hilton, N. K. (2020). Psychological resilience in Olympic medal-winning coaches: A longitudinal qualitative study. *International Sport Coaching Journal*, *7*(2), 209–219. DOI: 10.1123/iscj.2019-0075

Sauvé, J. L., Waldhauser, K. J., Wilson, B., Bundon, A., & Beauchamp, M. R. (2023). What supports and what thwarts Olympic athlete well-being?: Coach and organizational perspectives, *Journal of Applied Sport Psychology*. DOI: 10.1080/10413200.2023.2166156

Strauss, L. (1959). *What is political philosophy and other studies*. University of Chicago Press.

Su, R., Tay, L., & Diener, E. (2014). The development and validation of the comprehensive inventory of thriving (CIT) and the brief inventory of thriving (BIT). *Applied Psychology: Health and Well-Being*, *6*, 251–279. doi: 10.1111/aphw.12027

12
LEARNING FROM SWC TO INFORM HP COACH DEVELOPMENT

This chapter serves as a corollary for the book and indeed addresses the question, "So what?". We draw upon the findings presented in the previous chapters and our own extensive experiences as coaches and coach developers to explore answers to the question of "so what"? The intended outcome is that we give the reader pause to think whether any of this affirms or challenges their views regarding high-performance coaches and how some come to be so successful. In this book, we garnered rich insights into these SWC and their athletes – the thoughts, feelings, and behaviours that have contributed to their repeated success. Indeed, we wanted to foreground their voices and those of their athletes. We provided rich nuance and practical insights into many concepts to bring the accounts to life and this book provided a format whereby we could offer a depth of detail that is not possible in other forms of writing. In doing so, we shaped the stories into a coherent narrative with the aim of generating interest and reflection for the reader with respect to both understanding and practice.

In our experience, individuals will connect to the accounts in this book in differential ways, usually influenced by one's life history. This is something that we acknowledge and embrace. We also anticipate that people will engage in conversations with others in making sense of what is contained in this text, particularly regarding how it does and does not connect with them in their context. Our intention is to underscore the central role of the coach in the sport setting and seek to enhance the quality of coaching that, in turn, will foster the personal and group (psycho-social) outcomes for those involved in elite sport (Côté & Gilbert, 2009). Sport has the potential to be a unique vehicle to contribute to adaptive youth/young adult development (Côté, Turnnidge, & Vierimaa, 2016; Lara-Bercial & McKenna, 2022), but this does not happen in

DOI: 10.4324/9781003427292-16

some mechanised and linear way. Such positive outcomes are dependent on the skilled and intentional actions of high-quality coaches. Across the chapters of this book, we have made use of the insights generously provided by the SWC (and their athletes) to explain how they have positively contributed to both performance and wellbeing outcomes (i.e., *thriving*).

The SWC possess tremendous clarity of vision and purpose that enables them to focus on what really matters to achieve exceptional and sustained high-performance levels. They know what it takes to win and never lose sight of it. They are also highly skilled across various areas of work – fostering learning, planning, managing, etc. – and have few weak spots. Their elevated levels of awareness – of self and others – allow them to consistently improve themselves as well as read others and the environment so that they may respond efficiently and effectively to what is needed in that situation. Most importantly, however, SWC excel in their ability to foster and maintain interpersonal relationships, which enable them to drive athletes towards extraordinary levels of success while deliberately – and relatively – safeguarding their wellbeing. Over time, all the above attributes contribute to building a substantial level of credibility that generates high levels of trust and contributes to their sustained success.

Although we do not endorse the notion that one size fits all or that there is such a thing as a success profile, in this research it was possible to identify some personal qualities and environments that were shaped to foster thriving in the highly contested context of elite sport. We say again, these SWC were not all the same. Nevertheless, we can say with some confidence that there are some shared aspects we think are interesting and informative to progressing HP coach development and coaching praxis. We view these shared aspects as opportunities for learning from these highly successful coaches to affirm and challenge coaches and coach developers seeking to produce successful outcomes in elite sport.

First and foremost, these SWC love their work. They have passion for what they do and importantly, they have clarity of what is their work and how they can become better at it. We reiterate that elite sport is a highly contested context and to survive and thrive requires passion for what you do. These SWC enjoyed the challenges that are present in everyday coaching work. They were optimistic go-getters who were solution focused and viewed challenges and obstacles as opportunities for learning and subsequent growth for self and others. Indeed, some viewed their job as a privilege.

Second, these SWC were cognisant that they were in the "people business". Indeed, for these SWC coaching was relational, which is unsurprising and rhetorically commonplace. Coaches are expected to possess professional knowledge related to technical, tactical, and physical nous. This knowledge and associated competencies are assumed. However, the relationships you create will determine a large part of your success and especially your sustainability over time. Your moral values and your genuine care for people matter. In the earlier chapters, there is substantive evidence that shows how care is embodied by these SWC as a foundation to coaching praxis. These "hows" of coaching move beyond the typical rhetoric about care whereby coaches and leaders say they care but their actions are not consistent with that expressed care. Followers are usually adept in recognising this inconsistency between rhetoric and behaviour. Central to the stories of the SWC is that care is understood and lived in tandem with determination to achieve. These SWC provided ample evidence that they were obsessive about the pursuit of winning; however, this was not at the expense of one's wellbeing. The notion of *caring determination* provides depth of understanding to what drives these SWC but it is more than rhetoric. These SWC provide rich examples that are accessible and practical that we hope will resonate with coaches (and leaders in other contexts).

Third, SWC continued to invest in relationships over time. We can see this through the positioning of caring determination not as something to be achieved, but rather something for leaders to continually strive for. Importantly for those reading this book, caring determination is something that all can strive for rather than just something these SWC coaches just have. We underscore, however, the significant challenges in developing adaptive relationships in specific sport settings. Forming adaptive relationships in everyday life is challenging but in the context of elite sport we believe there are additional layers of challenge that make this capability essential to survive and thrive. Developing and sustaining adaptive relationships with key stakeholders are not easy, but the underpinning knowledge and skills are learnable qualities. Over time, those who invest in developing intra- and inter-personal knowledge and competencies will benefit from that investment. So, to be so adept at navigating this aspect of coaches' work is testament to the qualities of these SWC. This capability becomes challenging for those coaches transitioning from being a one-person support team to a coach who is provided with additional human resources. The additional responsibilities include nurturing the development of other staff and building a cohesive support team for athletes, who likely have different motives, ways of doing, and beliefs about how things should operate. In this transition, it is imperative that coaches be provided appropriate support as the coach's work has changed, becoming more complex and messy.

Fourth, and related to the above, is the high level of self-awareness and self-knowledge possessed by the SWC. The importance of these characteristics does not represent a new insight. It is well-known that fostering self-awareness requires self-reflection and 360-degree feedback from respected confidantes; however, the reality is that it is often a messy, vulnerable, and uncomfortable process and experience in the cauldron of HP sport. As coach developers, we often advise HP coaches to be clear about who you are (identity, philosophy, and values; *autobiographical author*), what you want (strivings; *motivated agent*), where your red lines are (accountability), what are you prepared to do and not do (acceptance of roles; responsibilities), and what you stand for (lived values). Nonetheless, we fully support the importance of knowledgeable others (critical friends) to affirm and challenge HP coaches. Our caveat is that early- and mid-career coaches drive this partnership, rather than others being imposed upon them.

Fifth, we underscore the importance of self-care. We encourage coaches to find their inner "Homer Simpson" (i.e., *grounded realist*). The lives of HP coaches are typically hectic and chaotic and out of sync with mainstream society in the weekly schedule; so, the regular scheduling of quality time with family and friends and doing other tasks is necessary to survive and thrive. HP coaches should take full responsibility for this to include non-coaching work in everyday life. What this balance looks like in practice and whether or not it is being achieved is up to the individual coach and the important people in their lives; it remains relative to the person in context. Moving from talking about it to doing it is not negotiable.

Sixth, the SWC were highly responsive to the dynamic environments in which they operated. HP coaches understandably attempt to control as many variables as possible attempt to predict the performance outcome; however, in reality, it is a fallacy to think we can predict. The more HP coaches accept and subsequently operate with the knowledge that much will always remain uncontrollable, unpredictable, messy, chaotic, and ambiguous, the more likely they will survive and thrive in a highly contested environment. The notions of orchestration, structured improvisation, and psychological flexibility (cognitive, emotional, and subsequently behavioural) were all ways of understanding how the HP coaches navigate and respond to environments in which they work. Structure and frameworks for operating are essential but HP coaches need to be fluid within those frames. Some appropriate questions in the pursuit of success might be: *What is necessary now to perform at my best? What do my athletes need from me right this moment? What do I keep doing, change, and adapt to the current situation?*

Finally, the SWC had access to and availed themselves of resources and support to nourish their ongoing development. As noted above, HP coaches typically function in a messy environment. *Context matters*. Not only are HP coaches the architects and sculptors of that environment they are part of a larger context and culture that also shapes and re-shapes how they function. Organisational support, stability, and predictability are essential for HP coaches to create a thriving environment. HP coaches are themselves organisational resources that require nourishment and support to continue to develop their craft. Some SWC were afforded a chance to develop their craft in low-pressure environments – countries where the sport was slightly underdeveloped or in the lower leagues – to then return to the "big stage" when ready. A "coach loan" system to this effect – akin to young players from "big" clubs going to play for "lower" teams to foster development – might be worth considering in some cases. Importantly, other organisational resources (human, financial) can support and/or undermine the quality of HP coaches' work.

High-performance coach development as a wicked problem

The work of HP coaches has progressed over the past few decades and reflecting transformations in society and sport itself has become increasingly more demanding and complex. Nevertheless, in many countries across different sports and at various levels of operation, the vocation of sports coaching has made significant strides over the same period. It takes time to develop programmes to build capacity and capability with a workforce that is comprised of a mix of volunteer and paid workers. We also need to be cognisant of different cultures, countries, and sports with varied access to resources (e.g., human, technology, and financial) when engaging in discussions about capacity and capability. Indeed, some countries are quite sophisticated with respect to coach education and development whereas others are less so. The journeys navigated by individual personnel in specific sports and countries in developing the current and next generation of coaches are also quite idiosyncratic, with many moving parts and countless synergistic and competing forces at play. We consider it important to acknowledge and more fully engage with such complexities in order to inform future directions.

High-performance coach development is essential to the ongoing preparation of those who are responsible for athlete and team success on the "big stage"; however, the *what*, *why*, and *how* of coach development are problematic. Globalisation, new technologies, and the pursuit of professionalism have modernised coach development resulting in a series of trade-offs, conundrums, and consequences that cannot easily be understood or undone. Indeed, contemporary coach development appears to exhibit the characteristics of "wicked problems" in that it is difficult to define and interpret, is subject to competing and uncertain causes, and generates further issues even when the solutions applied are well-intentioned (Sam, 2009; Vaughan et al, 2019). Wicked problems are characterised by high complexity, difficulty in defining the problem, and context specificity (Rittel & Weber, 1973). The contextual nature of coaching necessitates that coach development efforts reflect a consideration of the uniqueness of the sport, the diversity and transiency of participants especially in team sports, and the socio-cultural influences that shape how problems are understood. Like many wicked problems, there is often a view that there is "a" solution to the problem; however, it is more useful to consider a potential solution as being better or worse than another solution as opposed to considering solutions to be absolutely right or wrong. Such an approach acknowledges the situatedness of the solutions and that our assessment of their relative worth is dependent upon our beliefs and values at a particular time (Rittel & Weber, 1973; Vaughan et al., 2019). This is important because as alluded to earlier, attempts to provide solutions to wicked problems might also inadvertently cause unintended consequences (Gilchrist & Mallett, 2020) thus causing the wicked problem to undergo some transformation over time.

Central to addressing the challenges of high-performance coach development is clearly defining the problem in the first place because how a problem is defined will shape possible solutions (Rittell & Weber). One aspect of the wicked problem of coach development in the context of this book is how can HP coach development be shaped so that *caring determination* is a more prominent feature in sport coaching globally? While we do not seek to provide fully formed answers or solutions to this wicked problem, in what remains of this book we endeavour to make sense of the research to date (including our own on SWC) and consider how future research might continue to provide guidance to inform policy and practice in HP coach development.

Responding (partly) to the wicked problem of HP coach development through getting the right people

A key message from this study is that *one size does not fit all*. There is not a single success profile despite continued attempts by many to pursue one. These SWC experienced different journeys and pathways in becoming who they are. They were driven by different strivings and athletic backgrounds and underlying plots (e.g., *atonement, generativity*). Once again, we re-iterate the importance of context. Understanding the context is central to coaches surviving long enough to thrive. This is all ultimately necessary if athletes are to benefit from the caring determination of their coaches.

The focus here is on quality people in HP coaching. In exploring this focus, we discuss what constitutes quality evidence and on what bases decisions might be made regarding the identification, recruitment, support, and release of HP coaches. We appreciate that getting the right people is messy and complex.

Get the right people on the bus (Collins, 2001) is a well-known metaphor in corporate leadership. Jim Collins' message in *Good to Great*, is that before espousing a vision, it is necessary to identify who are the right people and get them "on the bus". Relatedly, if the wrong people are already on the bus they must be moved on. Once you have the right people then you can create the vision with everyone facing forward and going in the same direction. Indeed, this idea sounds manageable and straightforward; however, identifying and recruiting is one of the most challenging tasks for all organisations – sport, corporate, and government.

Let us consider a typical high-performance sporting context. There is a raft of complicated questions that must be answered in seeking to get the right people on the bus. For example, how well do administrators (those who employ and sack coaches) know and understand what coaches actually do? How do employers evaluate the quality of a coach's work? Who does and who should advocate for coaches? Is there alignment between coaches, support staff, Administrators, and Board members? Does the organisation have a coach succession plan? Although there have been attempts to answer these questions in some HP coach identification and recruitment processes, we can say with some confidence that the appointment of HP coaches remains typically indiscriminate, unsystematic, serendipitous, and often characterised by confirmation/ unconscious bias. Indeed, who knows who is not an uncommon practice. Finding the right coach is time-consuming, expensive, and the process typically lacks rigour (McEntire & Greene-Shortridge, 2011). So, how can we improve the process through a focus on quality?

We endorse a more comprehensive approach to understanding the person beyond their athlete and coach CV, and time-honoured trait-based profiling systems. A key challenge associated with the seemingly ubiquitous "profiling" exercises across and beyond sport is the rigour in generating quality evidence and making plausible understandings to inform decisions about coaches (e.g., identification, recruitment, development, and release). There are reasons why prominent researchers worldwide do not use personality tools that lack satisfactory peer-reviewed psychometric support (e.g., DiSC Personality Profiling, MBTI, Hogan's Personality Inventory). Essentially, they are not measuring what they say they measure. We advocate the use of empirically supported tools to assist coaches and those who intend to recruit, support, and evaluate them in understanding who they are at a deeper level and promote self-reflection and self-awareness, which the SWC considered as key to success (Mallett & Lara-Bercial, 2016).

Even when using psychometrically supported tools measuring the well-established and empirically supported *Big 5-factor* model (e.g., NEO, HEXACO), we offer caution. Although such tools provide more rigorous and trustworthy insights into a person, on their own they remain somewhat limited in what they tell us about personality and behaviour. The strength of traits or dispositions is that they are normative and de-contextualised, but this also represents their weakness. Personality is more complex than a reliance on traits. Furthermore, how we behave depends on who we are with; context does matter. It is for this reason that in our work with SWC we made use of theoretically, conceptually, and empirically supported tools that not only related to traits, but also to other layers of personality including the person as a motivated agent (i.e., Personal Strivings matrix) and the person as an autobiographical author (i.e., Life Story Interview). To follow up on that multi-layered understanding of the SWC, we interviewed them and their athletes to access insights into better understanding the context in which they operate (see Figure 2.1 in Chapter 2).

Regardless of what data are generated beyond the CV, a fundamental issue is what employers do with that information in terms of their decision making. From our perspective, any data should provide the stimulus for a conversation with coaches, support staff, and athletes. In this study, we found these successful coaches to be moderate risk-takers, athlete-centred, visionary, capable leaders of self and others, lifelong learners, resilient, and able to create a thriving environment for all actors (Mallett & Lara-Bercial, 2016). This begs the question how do those who employ coaches access this type of information when recruiting a coach? We acknowledge how challenging this task is. Perhaps, and this might already happen in some instances, yet not systematically, a round of 360-degree feedback pre-recruitment, where information about the prospective coach is gathered from a wide range of people that have worked with the coach (athletes, parents, support staff, performance directors, programme administration staff, etc.), could add depth to the recruitment process. This could be aided by the inclusion of some of the multi-layered tools we used in this research which provided significant additional texture to the understanding of the person behind the coach.

Nevertheless, it is imperative that those who employ and evaluate coaches have deep insights into what is coaches' work, their role in supporting their ongoing learning and development, and make systematic and values-based decisions that move beyond reliance on winning and losing ratios (Mallett & Côté, 2006).

Responding (partly) to the wicked problem of HP coach development through a focus on integrated learning

The primary aim of HP coach development is to enrich the personal and professional growth of HP coaches (Mallett, Rynne, & Trudel, 2020). In contributing to the growth of HP coaches, a key influence in the first decade of this century was the broad adoption of Coombes and Ahmed's (1974) classification of learning by many researchers: formal, informal, and non-formal. In responding to the "wicked problem" that is HP coach development, we recommend an integrated approach embracing all forms of learning including those that may be categorised as formal, informal, and non-formal. In our view, the reality that one single learning approach can foster caring determination is not substantiated.

Although we endorse an integrated approach, researchers have reported coaches' preference for informal learning. Unfortunately, many have interpreted that finding as being discrete rather than forming part of an idiosyncratic blend of all forms of learning across one's coaching journey (Mallett et al., 2009). All forms of learning should be valued for their potential contribution to coach development (Cushion et al., 2010; Lara-Bercial & Mallett, 2016; Mallett et al., 2009; Mallett, Rynne, & Billett, 2016; Trudel & Gilbert, 2006). These SWC embraced all forms of learning in differential ways as reported in Chapter 3. The emphasis on informal learning has merit (at least in part due to the variability of time that is necessary to develop your craft – in any vocation) and in more recent times, the role of digital media has also been influential. The impact of informal learning on the development of caring determination was evidenced by the SWC in several ways; for example, learning to become more fluid in how they coached was achieved partly through self-reflection and noticing to inform action. However, it was clear that informal learning alone was insufficient to foster this central characteristic of the SWC success. These SWC pursued non-formal and formal learning in developing their craft (see Chapter 3). Indeed, all forms of learning were valued in the obsessive pursuit to be the best – this was their competitive advantage.

In becoming a SWC, and developing the characteristic of caring determination, there was strong evidence of foundational higher education providing a solid foundation to develop their coaching craft. This formal education underpinned their ongoing learning through non-formal and informal means. The notion of formal education as a central pillar to coach learning is not new. The Eastern European countries developed university coaching degrees in the 1940s. In Brazil, it is typically a legal pre-requisite to have completed a four-year Physical Education degree to become a coach – of course there are exceptions to that rule. Nonetheless, whilst higher education provides the foundation, access to higher education is not always possible (proximity, financial costs) and the potential for paid coaching work is limited. The impact of formal learning on the development of caring determination was evidenced by the SWC in several ways, including learning some "coaching skills" as well as gaining a greater understanding of the human condition and "what makes people tick". However, it was clear that formal learning alone was insufficient to foster this central characteristic of the SWC success. Other forms of learning were also engaged in developing their craft.

Non-formal learning is also a common feature of sporting systems worldwide. Typically taking the form of short courses run by state, national, and international sporting bodies, and sometimes universities, non-formal offerings have contributed to the development of caring determination in myriad ways; for example, affirming and challenging their coaching practices. Of course, and as reiterated several times so far, without an integrated approach to learning it is likely that these outcomes would be weaker or may not have been realised at all. Notwithstanding the need for coach agency in driving their own learning (determination), deliberately fostering a seamless recurring stream of formal, informal, and non-formal learning opportunities appears paramount.

However, despite its promotion there remains limited understanding of coach learning and development (e.g., access; impact on coach behaviours; informal, non-formal, and formal learning; and context) and within multiple paradigms of thinking and methodologies for coming to know. This raises serious problems when we are advocating an integrative approach to learning in HP coach development. As such, the question remains: How do we best support coaches to acquire new forms of (integrative) knowledge within their domain so that they can continually shape how they coach and subsequently their athletes' outcomes? This is a key and enduring question (Kjær, 2019). Like Walker, Thomas and Driska (2018), we are of the opinion that whilst we need to recognise uniqueness, complexity, and context, there are likely some guiding principles and concepts that are common to coach development more broadly. We encourage coaches and coach developers to play creatively and responsively with these guiding principles and concepts in specific sports and contexts to foster adaptive outcomes for all actors in the sporting landscape. These guiding principles were presented in Chapter 3.

In playing with these principles, it is also worthwhile keeping in mind the finding that in becoming the best they could be, the stories of the SWC resonated with adult learning principles. This was particularly so with respect to experiential and self-directed learning (e.g., Trudel, Gilbert, & Werthner, 2010). The SWC and their athletes reported the situatedness of their learning, which was partially driven by working collaboratively with athletes to problem-solve in the moment as well as over time. Self-directed and guided self-reflection was central to optimising the learning opportunities in a variety of forms including informal, formal, and non-formal situations. The result was not only the affirmation of existing quality practices but also the fostering of behavioural change where appropriate (transformational learning and practice). More importantly, the lifelong pursuit of learning and *becoming* underpinned the SWC success in terms of performance and the wellbeing of self and others in their setting. An internal thirst for continuous learning, work ethic, and healthy perfectionism, of course, seems to be a central component of determination.

Fostering caring determination in (HP) coaching

In underscoring *caring determination* as the central tenet of this book, we consider how we can foster this approach to leadership in the development of HP coaches and coaches more broadly. We promote the idea that caring determination should become a more pervasive feature in HP coach development and indeed in all coach development programmes, regardless of context.

Becoming the best requires some sense of balance between what some people might view as opposing forces – high challenge (determination to be the best) and high care. There might be a belief that if you focus on one, the other likely suffers. However, it is possible to pursue and achieve athlete needs for high challenge (determination) and care. Indeed, these SWC built a foundation of care first. This foundational ethic of care (terroir) enabled these SWC to obsessively pursue becoming a better performer (determination-based coaching behaviours). Therefore, care and determination (challenge) are not binary – one should not be compromised at the expense of the other. Both care and determination are essential to thriving and should be pursued by HP coaches.

These SWC moulded an environment in which all social actors thrived. Indeed, these SWC behaved in ways that supported both performance and wellbeing. Many SWC evolved in their capacity to be more emotionally and socially supportive, whereas others seemed to be influenced by family and their own coaches to be caring for self and others – they learned the importance of caring and pursuing meaningful goals in childhood. Not all coaches experience this epiphany, and some do so late in their careers. The sooner we can re-shape people's beliefs to embrace caring determination, more athletes (and coaches, support staff) will experience the espoused potential of sport to foster adaptive outcomes. This shift in thinking and behaviour requires a holistic, evidence-based, and comprehensive approach to coach development.

References

Coombes, P. H., & Ahmed, M. (1974). *Attacking rural poverty: How non-formal education can help*. John Hopkins University Press.

Collins, J. (2001). *Good to great*. Collins Business. ISBN: 9780712676090

Côté, J., & Gilbert, W. (2009). An integrative definition of coaching effectiveness and expertise. *International Journal of Sports Science & Coaching, 4*, 307–323.

Côté, J., Turnnidge, J., & Vierimaa, M. (2016). A personal assets approach to youth sport. In K. Green, & A. Smith (Eds.), *Routledge handbook of youth sport* (pp. 243–255). Routledge.

Cushion, C., Nelson, L., Armour, K., Lyle, J., Jones, R., Sandford, R., & O'Callaghan, C. (2010). Coach learning and development: A review of literature. UK Sports Coach.

Gilchrist, M., & Mallett, C. J. (2020). Contemporary approaches to sport leadership. In Maurizio, B., Filho, E., & Terry, P. C. (Eds.), *Advancements in mental skills training* (pp. 236–248). Routledge.

Kjær, J. B. (2019). The professionalization of sports coaching: A case study of a graduate soccer coaching education program. *Journal of Hospitality, Leisure, Sport & Tourism Education, 24*, 50–62. 10.1016/j.jhlste.2018.11.001

Lara-Bercial, S., & McKenna, J. (2022). Roots to grow and wings to fly: An ethnography of psychosocial development in adolescent performance sport. *Sports, 10*(4), 48. doi: 10.3390/sports10040048

Mallett, C. J., & Côté, J. (2006). Beyond winning and losing: Guidelines for evaluating high performance coaches. *The Sport Psychologist. 20*, 213–221.

Mallett, C. J., & Lara-Bercial, S. (2016). Serial winning coaches: People, vision and environment. In M. Raab, P. Wylleman, R. Seiler, A-M. Elbe, & A. Hatzigeorgiadis (Eds.), *Sport and exercise psychology research: Theory to practice* (pp. 289–322). Elsevier.

Mallett, C. J., Rynne, S. B., & Billett, S. (2016). Valued learning experiences of early career and experienced high performance coaches. *Physical Education and Sport Pedagogy, 21*(1), 89–104.

Mallett, C. J., Rynne, S. B., & Trudel, P. (2020). The continuing education of the coach: A lifelong journey. In D. Gould, & C. J. Mallett (Eds.), *The sports coaching handbook* (pp. 239–258). Human Kinetics.

Mallett, C. J., Trudel, P., Lyle, J., & Rynne, S. (2009). Formal versus informal coach education. *International Journal of Sport Science & Coaching, 4*, 325–334.

McEntire, L. E. & Greene-Shortridge, T. M. (2011). *Recruiting and selecting leaders for innovation: How to find the right leader. Advances in Developing Human Resources, 13*(3), 266–278.

Rittel, H. W., & Weber, M. M. (1973). Dilemmas in a general theory of planning. *Policy Sciences, 4*(2), 155–169.

Sam, D. L., & Berry, J. W. (2009). Adaptation of young immigrants: The double jeopardy of acculturation. In I. Jasinskaja-Lahti, & A. T. Mähönen (Eds.), *Identities, Intergroup Relations, and Acculturation* (pp. 191–205). Gaudeamus.

Trudel, P., & Gilbert, W. (2006). Coaching and coach education. In D. Kirk, D. Macdonald, & M. O'Sullivan (Eds.), *Handbook of physical education* (pp. 516–539). Sage.

Trudel, P., Gilbert, W., & Werthner (2010). Coach education effectiveness. In J. Lyle, & C. Cushion (Eds.), *Sport coaching: Professionalisation and practice* (pp. 135–152). Elsevier.

Vaughan, J., Mallett, C. J., Davids, K., Potrac, P., & López-Felip M. (2019). Developing creativity in football and life: A wicked transdisciplinary problem. *Frontiers in Psychology (Movement Science and Sport Psychology), 10*. 10.3389/fpsyg.2019.02090

Walker, L. F., Thomas, R., & Driska, A. P. (2018). Informal and nonformal learning for sport coaches: A systematic review. *International Journal of Sports Science & Coaching, 13*(5), 694–707. 10.1177/1747954118791522

INDEX

Note: *Italicized* and **bold** page numbers refer to figures and tables.

accessed learning opportunities, ranking of 39
accountability 8, 53, 93, 110, 111, 114, 184, 190
active coaches 58
adaptability, in approach to coaching **129**, 131–132
adaptive coaching 8, **92**, 97–99, 120, 128
adaptive-coach relationship, development of 162–163
agreeableness 17, 24, 29n1
Allport, G. 15
altruism 28, 83, 134, 144
Annerstedt, C. 165
approachability 95
Armour, K. 83, 84
athlete-centred coaching approach 165–166
athlete-centredness 91–94, **92**
athlete interviews 25, 26, 94
athletes-cum-coaches 4
athletic career 22, 36, 40–42, 49, **50**, 57, 58, 61, **66**, 67, **71**, 74, 75, 77, 123
atonement 28, 29, 65, 133, 151, 178, 193; for underachievement, as an athlete 61–62
authentic care for the person 147–149
authenticity 95
autobiographical author 5, 19, 25, 26, 190

autonomy 28, 29, 47, 99, 150, 165, 167, 172, 184

Bales, J. 4
Batistich, V. 84
behaviour, understanding 20–21, *21*
behavioural flexibility 9, 127, **129**, 131–132, 134, 191
behavioural signature 7, 17
Big Five personality traits 17
Blackett, A. D. 58
Bloom, G. A. 82–83
Braun, V. 26
business manager 91

career advisor 91
career pathways of SWC 57–77; elite athletes 67–69, **71**; female serial winners 73; non-athletes 69–71, **71**; non-elite athletes 69–71, **71**; opportunity and risk, role of 71–72; pre-conditions for success 59–66, **66**, 74–75
caring 121–122; communities 84; determination *see* caring determination: drivers of **122**; expressions of *see* caring, expressions of: relationship 83
caring, expressions of 91–102, **92**; adaptive

coaching 97–99; athlete-centredness 91–94; shared leadership 99–102; stability and dependability 94–97

caring determination 81–87, 121–134, 184, 190, 193; adaptability, in approach to coaching 131–132; for athletes, benefits of 128–132, **129**; cognitive flexibility 125–126, **125**; constant growth 129–130; definition of 84–85; emotional flexibility **125**, 126–128; in HP coaching, fostering 197–198; performance ready 130–131; safety net for mental and physical health 130

Carter, A. D. 82–83

CED see Coach Education and Development (CED) programme

characteristic adaptations 16–19, 143

Clarke, V. 26

coach: and athlete, relationship between 84, 94; in context 141–142; as leader 173

Coach Education and Development (CED) programme 35, 38

coaching capabilities 76, 77

coaching work, learning in and through 44–45

"coach loan" system 53

cognitive flexibility 125–126, **125**, 134, 191

Collins, J.: Good to Great 181, 193

commitment **104**, 107–109

competence 9, 28, 29, 48, 49, 51, 109, 146, 150, 151, 167, 172, 175; psychological need for 145; social 134

conscientiousness 17, 24, 29n1, 173

constant growth 129–130, **129**

context, coach in 141–142

controlled freedom 99

coping: with setbacks through realistic and optimistic attributions 158–161

Côté, J. 82

Coulter, T. 21

Cox, K. S. 17

Cronin, C. 83, 84, 132

Currie, J. L. 82

Cushion, C. 153

Davis, L. 172

Deci, E. 145; Intrinsic Motivation and Self-Determination in Human Behavior 28

deliberate reflection 37, 47–48

dependability **92**, 94–97, 120

determination 123–126, 149–150; caring see caring determination: drivers of **123**; expressions of see determination, expressions of

determination, expressions of 103–120, **104**; commitment 107–109; focus 103–107; modelling passion 114–117; resilience 117–120; standards 110–114

Diener, E. 171, 184

Din, C. 83

dispositional traits 16–18

DMP see Dual Model of Passion (DMP)

Driven Benevolence 87n1

Dual Model of Passion (DMP) 161

Dweck, C. 145

dynamic social networks 37

early developmental environment 39, **50**

elite athletes 3, 4, 20, 40, 41, 58, 60, 61, 67–69, **71**, 75–77, 94, 95, 100, 123, 153, 155, 179

elite sport, surviving in HP environment of 153–167

Emmons, R. A. 24, 143

emotional flexibility **125**, 126–128, 134, 191

emotional intelligence 82, 84

engrossment 83

Enright, K. 132

equanimity 117, 126, 127, 134

Eshach, H. 39, 53n1

European Congress for Sport and Exercise Psychology 172

extraversion 17, 24, 29n1

Eysenk, H. J. 15

female serial winners, career pathways of 73

Fletcher, D. 158

focus 103–107, **104**

formal learning, definition of 53n1

generativity 26, 178, 193

Gilbert, W. 37

grounded realists (aka, Homer Simpson) 28, 191

grounded self-belief 63, 64, 75, 124, 133
growth mindset 145, 184

Haslam, A. 20
Heijer, A. D. 173
high-performance coaches (HPC) 3, 5–10,
    35, 188–198; caring determination
    80, 83, 84; characteristics of 57;
    education and development,
    current limitations of 38; education
    and development, supporting
    52–53; identification of 76–77;
    learning journeys of 36–38;
    recruitment of 76–77; wicked
    problem 10, 192–197
holism 15; holistic development 170–185;
    holistic understanding of self and
    others 19–20
HPC see high-performance coaches (HPC)

ICCE see International Council for
    Coaching Excellence (ICCE)
IGLA see Innovation Group of Lead
    Agencies (IGLA)
individual differences 15–16
informal learning 43–47, **50**; definition of
    53n1; learning in and through
    coaching work 44–45; peer
    learning 45–47
Innovation Group of Lead Agencies
    (IGLA) 4–6
integrated framework of personality 5,
    16–20; autobiographical author 19;
    holistic understanding of self and
    others 19–20; motivated agent 18;
    social actor 17–18
Integrated Research Model of Olympic
    Podium Performance 82
internal learning **50**, 53n1; deliberate
    reflection 47–48; unconscious
    reflection 48–49
International Council for Coaching
    Excellence (ICCE) 4–6

jangle fallacy 154, 172
jingle fallacy 154
Johansson, B. 165
Joon-Ho, K. 83
journeyman 68–69
Jowett, S. 133

Kim, S.-H. 83
Knowles, Z. R. 132

Lara-Bercial, S. 28, 173; *Serial winning
    coaches: People, vision, and
    environment* 27
leadership: coaching 85–86; qualities 59;
    shared **92**, 99–102; situational 83
learners 173–177
learning: from experience 178; life-long
    173–177; from others 177
Lee, Y. 83
Levak, R. W. 26
life counsellor 91
life-long learning, thriving and 173–177
Lindgren, E-C. 165
living espoused values 149–150

Mallett, C. J. 28, 37, 173; *Serial winning
    coaches: People, vision, and
    environment* 27
Maslow, A. 171
McAdams, D. 7, 26, 142; integrated
    framework of personality 5, 16–20;
    three-layered understanding of the
    person 49; *"What do we know when
    we know a person?"* 14, 20
McGuire, C. 172
mediated learning 53n1
mental health, safety net for **129**, 130
modelling passion **104**, 114–117
Moon, J. A. 53n1
motivated agent 5, 18, 26, 27, 142, 190;
    coach as 143; self as 143
motivation 15; motivational displacement
    83; motivational hierarchy 143
MPIC see Multilevel Personality In
    Context (MPIC) model
Multilevel Personality In Context (MPIC)
    model 20
Murray, H. A. 14, 15

narrative identity 5, 16, 18, 19, 26, 142,
    151, 178
NEO-FFI-3 23–25
NEO-PI-3 24
neuroticism 17, 24, 29n1
Noddings, N. 83, 165
non-athletes 69–71, **71**, 75, 77
non-elite athletes 58, 60, 69–71, **71**, 75, 77

non-formal learning 42–43, **50**; definition of 53n1
noticing to inform action 155–157

Oates-Wilding, S. 82
Occhino, J. 37
openness to experience 17, 24, 29n1
orchestration 134, 153, 157, 174, 191

Pals, J. L. 17, 18, 21
Paskevich, D. 83
passion 146–147, 161–163
peer learning 39, 43, 45–47, **50**, 51, 52
performance ready **129**, 130–131
personalities of SWC 14–29; coming to know 20–21, *21*; individual differences 15–16; making sense of the data 25–26; McAdams' integrated framework of personality 16–20; measures 23–25; methodology 21–22; multi-layered understanding, learning 27–29; participants 22–23, **22**; procedure 23; similarities 15–16
personality: McAdams' integrated framework of 5, 16–20; psychologists (personologists) 14, 15; of SWC *see* personalities of SWC: traits 17, 24, 29n1, 194
personal strivings 24, 142–143
physical health, safety net for **129**, 130
Plato 15
positive psychology 171
pre-coaching experiences: athletic career 40–42, **50**; early developmental environment 39, **50**
pre-conditions for success 59–66, **66**, 74–75; atonement for underachievement, as an athlete 61–62; early desire to help others and coach 60; identified as potential coach 60–61; insatiable need to improve 62–63; leadership qualities 59; serial insecurity 63–65, 75
preferred learning opportunities, ranking of 39
psychological flexibility 134, 153, 174, 191

"quasi-coaching" interactions 59

reasonable self-doubt 63–65, 75, 124, 133
reciprocity 83
relatedness 28, 29, 150, 154, 155, 167, 172
resilience **104**, 117–120; definition of 154–155; development of 158–161; noticing to inform action 155–157; passion for coaching 161–163; in performative environments 157–158, *158*; robust 109; time, importance of 155
righteous avengers 28
Rodrigue, F. 37
Rogers, C. 171
Roosevelt, T. 91
Ryan, R. 145; *Intrinsic Motivation and Self-Determination in Human Behavior* 28
Rynne, S. B. 37, 58

Sarkar, M. 158
Sedgwick, W. A. 82
self-actualisation 171
self-improvement 27, 117, 144, 145
semi-structured interview 24–25
serial insecurity 28, 63–65, 75, 124
serial winning coaches (SWC) 3–10; career pathways of 57–77; caring, expressions of 91–102, **92**; caring determination 81–87; definition of 6; learning journeys of 35–53; personalities of 14–29; striving and becoming 141–151; *see also individual entries*
shared leadership **92**, 99–102
similarities 15–16
simplexity 103, 106
situational leadership 83
social actor 5, 17–18, 24, 26, 27
Social Identity Theory 17
stability **92**, 94–97
standards **104**, 110–114
striving 141–151, 190; authentic care for the person 147–149; determination 149–150; living espoused values 149–150; passion 146–147; personal 142–143
structured improvisation 134, 153, 157, 174, 191
Su, R. 171, 184
surviving 141, 142; in HP environment of elite sport 153–167
SWC *see* serial winning coaches (SWC)

Tay, L. 171, 184
thriving 141, 142, 189; for achieving and sustaining success 171–172; definition of 172; from early and serendipitous exposure to high-performance environments 178–179; embodiment of 179–185; learners and life-long learning 173–177; learning from experience 178; learning from others 177; saliency of context 173
token coach education 52
Trudel, P. 37
trust 162–163; as outcome of coach caring 164–166; resolute belief in plan and processes 163–166

unconditional regard 171
unmediated learning 53n1

Vallerand, B. 161

well-being 109, 154, 157, 159, 160–163, 166
wicked problem, of HP coach development 10, 192–197; integrated learning 195–197; right people, getting 193–195
Windelband, W. 21

Printed in Great Britain
by Amazon